Strategic Family Play Therapy

SHLOMO ARIEL
The Hebrew University of Jerusalem, Israel

JOHN WILEY & SONS
Chichester · New York · Brisbane · Toronto · Singapore

Other Wiley Editorial Offices

John Wiley & Sons, Inc., 605 Third Avenue,
New York, NY 10158-0012, USA

Jacaranda Wiley Ltd, G.P.O. Box 859, Brisbane,
Queensland 4001, Australia.

John Wiley & Sons (Canada) Ltd,
22 Worcester Road, Rexdale,
Ontario M9W 1L1, Canada

John Wiley & Sons (SEA) Pte Ltd, 37 Jalan Pemimpin #05-04,
Block B, Union Industrial Building, Singapore 2057

Library of Congress Cataloging-in-Publication Data:

Ariel, Shlomo.
    Strategic family play therapy / Shlomo Ariel.
        p.   cm. — (Wiley series in psychotherapy and counselling)
    Includes bibliographical references and index.
    ISBN 0-471-92401-6 (ppc.)
    1. Play therapy.   2. Family therapy.   I. Title.   II. Series.
    [DNLM: 1. Family.   2. Play Therapy—in infancy &
    childhood.   WS
    350.2 A698s]
    RJ505.P6A75   1992
    616.89'156—dc20
    DNLM/DLC
    for Library of Congress   91–27612
                                                                    CIP

British Library Cataloguing in Publication Data:

A catalogue record for this book is available
from the British Library.

ISBN 0-471-92401-6   ISBN 0-471-93173-X (pb)

Typeset in 10/12 Garamond by Inforum Typesetting, Portsmouth
Printed and bound in Great Britain by Biddles Ltd, Guildford and King's Lynn

Contents

Part 2: Assessment through observations of family make-believe play

Series Preface

The Wiley Series in Psychotherapy and Counselling is focused on professional practice in the field of psychology, and is designed to provide scientifically sound information which can be directly used by the clinical worker, the instructor, and the student. One type of book in this series aims to provide an opportunity for authors to present exciting new approaches to counselling and psychotherapy. The present book falls into this category.

Dr Ariel provides us with a new and very promising way of practising psychotherapy with children. Starting with a solid and compelling experiential referent—the make believe and fantasy play of children—he has formulated a fascinating psychodynamic view of strategic family therapy. Using his background in linguistics and semiotics, he has found a way to create a therapy out of the play of parents and children. Because games and play provide a more or less safe way for family members to interact with each other, Dr Ariel has been able to use this medium to aid families in communicating and solving their own problems.

In addition to providing a theoretical overview of the basic concepts involved in this approach, he provides an extensive description of the assessment of make-believe play on both the micro and macro levels of analysis. At each step, well-chosen clinical examples are given to illustrate the aspects of this analysis. It would be hard to find a text, in any clinical field, which makers better use of the direct clinical observation and example. To this Dr Ariel adds equally well-documented sections on planning the therapy, carrying out the therapy, and describing the therapeutic process—including termination issues.

The book is written in a very engaging manner which is very close to the author's direct experiences as a therapist. This approach clearly illustrates how young children can be brought directly into the therapy and can share their own clear insights into how to make a painful situation much better. In addition to providing a pragmatic and insightful approach to the use of play in family therapy, he has included references to research relevant to this approach.

Certainly, as the author notes, one can never hope to become an effective therapist just on the basis of reading a book. Nevertheless, it is my opinion that this book does as much as any book can in promoting the development of psychotherapy.

FRANZ EPTING
Series Editor

Preface

Since I began noticing the existence of children, I have been intrigued and amazed by their make-believe games. Their fantasy play, with its incredible thematic richness and complexity, has not only been amusing to look at or fun to participate in. It has also seemed to pose an intellectual challenge, being so elusive, so difficult to define, describe and explain.

Having taken this challenge some fifteen years ago I came to realize that my former background in formal linguistics, semiotics, logic and human ethology had equipped me with invaluable tools for this endeavor. Play, exactly because it seemed to defy scientific description and explanation, could profit considerably from the standards of rigor and precision imposed by these disciplines. I began by attempting a formal, empirically and logically valid definition of the very concept "make-believe play". Then I set about observing children playing. Their make-believe games were recorded and analyzed with the aid of concepts and methods borrowed from semiotics and linguistics. The results of these studies were applied in the field of early childhood education. They were incorporated into manuals and courses instructing day-care workers, nursery school and kindergarten teachers in the art of observing and interpreting play and harnessing it to their educational purposes.

On a visit to a kindergarten I was introduced to a pale, shy boy named Yossef, whose mother Rachel—so I was told by the teacher—would not object to having me observe and tape him at home in the afternoon. This was the not-very-dramatic beginning of a fascinating adventure. Unexpectedly, I found myself caught in the midst of a stormy family drama. It was actually happening in the family's real life, but it was also told in their make-believe play. That is where I first witnessed the amazing therapeutic power of family make-believe play.

The kindergarten teacher did not know that Yossef's father was about to leave Rachel for another woman. Therefore, neither she nor myself could have anticipated the year of violent, heartbreaking scenes that Yossef and his six-year-old sister Adina were to be involved in. During this year I would meet Rachel and her two children once a week for a joint play session, in which I participated as an observer. Already in the first session, it became obvious to me that these play encounters were to serve not only my own purposes as a researcher, but also the participants' emotional needs. This was to become a solid piece of family play therapy, even though no therapist was present.

Never in the course of such a session would any of the participants mention the family crisis openly. Nor would they explicitly discuss their feelings or their problems. Whenever Rachel attempted to raise such an issue, the children would deny the existence of any difficulty or employ diverse evasion tactics. However, everything that was thus denied and suppressed found ample expression through the indirect medium of make-believe. Furthermore, play seemed to reflect thoughts, feelings and covert transactions which would probably never have emerged if direct communication were to be employed. Finally, a great deal of problem-solving was effected solely through the vehicle of play.

In one of the numerous story-lines played out in these sessions Yossef cast himself and his sister in the roles of a little prince and princess who were expelled from the palace by their wicked parents. For Rachel, to play the role that she was obviously asked to assume, that of the wicked queen, was an extremely stressful task. She staged a scene in which she as the queen cried and confessed that she felt bitter because the king did not want her any more. She said she was worried, because the prince and princess misinterpreted her bitterness as a sign that she did not want them.

At this point Yossef and Adina played a scene in which the little prince and princess, roaming in the wilderness, met a stray horse. Rachel was asked to "be" the horse. Then a make-believe relationship of mutual support and emotional openness was developed between children and horse.

Soon afterwards I learned that it was not little Yossef who discovered family play therapy. Leading family therapists have incorporated techniques involving play in their work. However, having read these contributions, I was left with the impression that a new continent had been discovered, but hardly explored yet. I then decided to set about exploring it. I began attempting to apply the methods of analysis and intervention I had developed previously to the play behavior of children and families seen in the clinic. This was accompanied by efforts to embed these methods in a wider theoretical context. The strange therapeutic power of play had been revealed and explored by scholars such as Sigmund Freud, Melanie Klein, Erik Erikson, Jean Piaget, Gregory Bateson, Milton Erikson and Cloe Madanes. Their insights and observations needed to be synthesized, explicated and formalized. The role of play as a mirror of covert family interaction patterns and as an agent of change had to be clarified and systematized.

The next stage was devoted mainly to efforts to integrate the results of the previous stages in the framework of a unified theoretical model. The model that was eventually constructed was based, again, on concepts and terms borrowed from semiotics, linguistics and information-processing theory.

The strategic family play therapy method presented in this book is a natural growth of all these ventures. It comprises, besides the multi-disciplinary theoretical synthesis referred to above, a wide range of relevant empirical research findings. It also incorporates my own personal experience as a practitioner and teacher of family play therapy.

What distinguishes this method is, above all, the deliberate purposeful application of well-defined structural and psychosocial properties of make-believe play in all the stages of the therapeutic process: assessment, planning, intervention and evaluation of progress. These properties have been discovered and explicated in the course of a systematic microanalysis and macroanalysis of play, conducted in the framework of the above-mentioned unified theoretical model.

The rigor of this approach by no means inhibits the therapist's creativity. On the contrary, it almost compels the therapist to be resourceful and inventive. In the eyes of the observer strategic family play therapy sessions are marked by rich, highly imaginative playful interactions among the family members and the therapist.

The book has been designed, primarily, as a handbook for professional therapists and trainees with some knowledge and practical experience in play therapy and family therapy. A learner who has studied it thoroughly will hopefully be able to design or improvise effective family play therapeutic interventions that are constructed according to the theoretical and methodological principles specified in it. However, the acquisition of skill and facility in employing this method requires a great deal of practice. Readers who are interested in practical training in strategic family play therapy are referred to Appendix 2.

Acknowledgments

Many individuals have contributed to this work, directly or indirectly, in various stages of its development. Some of the main ideas included in this book began to germinate when I conducted a research project on make-believe play and social interaction of kindergarten children in the years 1975–1977, in the Study Center for Children's Activities of the School of Education of the Kibbutz Movement in Israel. The director of the Center, Gideon Levin, and two of my colleagues, Matia Kam and Irene Sever, used to turn my attention to aspects of children's behavior that I had not noticed before, and inspired me with their creative thinking.

In 1979 I worked in the Psychology Department of Yale University, where I was in close contact with Jerome L. and Dorothy Singer. I am deeply indebted to these two not just for the opportunity to have direct access to their pioneering, highly inspiring work on play, but also for their personal support and encouragement. I must mention also Brian Sutton-Smith and Eric Klinger who, in the same year, read manuscripts of mine, made valuable comments and were helpful in many ways.

In 1980, back in Israel, I was invited by S. Tyano, then director of the Child and Adolescent Department of the Geha mental hospital, to take up a research position. He encouraged me to continue my investigations into play and its clinical applications. Soon afterwards, Cynthia Carel, director of the Child and Adolescent Outpatient Clinic in the same hospital, began to take a close interest in my work. She contributed her considerable experience in working with children and their families.

Many people have encouraged me to share my ideas with colleagues and students. I would like to thank Aliah Kedem, who initiated and organized a Child Therapy Training Program under the auspices of the Israeli Ministry of Social Welfare, in which I have been accorded a unique opportunity to train a select group of social workers to serve as both practitioners and instructors of family play therapy.

I would also like to express my gratitude to Joop Helledoorn, who not only read some manuscripts of mine and made detailed, extremely useful comments, but also invited me to conduct some workshops and lecture courses in Holland. At this juncture, I want to express my appreciation to Elleke D. Berkvens, a former participant in some of these workshops. She, together with some other workshop "veterans", has been making sustained efforts for some years now to continue studying and practising family play therapy in The Netherlands.

I would also like to thank my colleague Odeda Peled and my students and colleagues Rutti Ben Ezra, Galila Oren and Sarah Silber, who have been investing considerable efforts in attempting to master and practise strategic family play therapy. Each of them has made her own creative contributions. Many of the examples included in this book are taken from their therapeutic work.

Finally, I am deeply indebted to Elinoar Berger and Ruttie Kanner, who went through the manuscript carefully and made extremely instructive suggestions about content and style of presentation.

The Invisible Guest:
A Case History

The lady in front of me looked tense. She spoke feverishly, nervously. The subject of our conversation was her eight-year-old son, David. Since Dan, her husband, had left home David had changed unrecognizably she complained. Before that he had been an exemplary little boy. And then, overnight, he turned into a little devil. For all his being only eight, he was adept at making her life hell. He had a bagfull of vicious tricks. Once, for instance, he enticed her with an angelic smile to make him an apple cake. She toiled for a whole hour, preparing the cake for him. And then he threw the cake furiously at her and yelled: "I did not ask for an apple cake! I asked for a plum cake! Stop forcing me to eat cakes I don't like!" Once she came back home in the evening to find the blankets shredded to pieces and tufts of cotton-wool scattered all over the apartment. But what really brought her to her wits' end was his disgusting habit of smearing his excrement on the walls of his bedroom! This would make Sivan, an elegant, attractive, highly-strung thirty-year-old fashion designer, lose her habitual self-composure and self-restraint and literally run wild. But, what is more, she was stupefied by his response. When she was seized by a fit of rage, he would look at her with big, naive eyes and smile.

Dan, her husband, was a motorcycle junkie. One morning he mounted his motorcycle, drove away and did not come back. The next day they called from the local hospital and said that he was lying in the Orthopaedic Department with a broken spinal column. He had fallen off his motorcycle. Sivan rushed to the hospital. To her surprise, she discovered that she had been anticipated by another woman.

Afterwards there came a long period when David did not see his father at all. David refused to visit his father in the girlfriend's apartment. Dan insisted that he could not come to visit him at home. He was encased in a plaster cast and could not move.

I invited Sivan and David to participate in joint play therapy sessions with me. Both of them seemed to be quite eager to come.

In the first sessions Dan was not mentioned at all, not even by hint. Instead, Sivan and David enjoyed teasing one another playfully. They competed in inventing more ingenious malicious tricks. I used to have a large biscuit tin filled with placebo pills in my play therapy room. David emptied the box and asked his mother "to bake a cake" of the pills piled on the carpet. When he had finished "eating the cake", he and his mother patiently collected all the pills and put them back in the tin. As soon as they had completed this arduous task David started to swing the box violently in the air and yell: "Hail!", watching excitedly the shower of pills scattering all over the floor.

One of Sivan and David's favorite games was tying each other up with a rope. Once Sivan bound the whole of David's body and left him lying on the carpet. After a while he asked her to untie him, but she refused. He tried threats, begging and crying, but to no avail. He had to bear his punishment to the bitter end.

In the course of that period the relationship between David and Sivan improved considerably. Both of them became more relaxed. Every now and again they would spend some time together playing or having a pleasant conversation. David's provocative behavior almost disappeared.

I turned over in my mind a number of not necessarily incompatible explanations for this change. One thing, however, was quite clear. David and Sivan had found a way of turning the unpleasant side of their relationship into make-believe play. They managed to transfer their conflicts from the level of reality to the level of play. Consequently, their interpersonal reality was freed of these disturbances.

This was a very worthwhile achievement, but to my mind it only scratched the surface. One could guess that underneath the relatively calm surface a volcano was still seething; a volcano named Dan.

Initially, I tried to steer Sivan and David into producing a puppet show in which the theme of Dan's desertion and his injury would assume a symbolic disguise. However David managed to evade this issue skillfully. It was as if something in him had decided to totally blot his father out of his mind.

I had a small telescope. One day I peeped into it, directed it toward the wall and said: "One can see through this telescope all kinds of things that once existed and then disappeared".

I continued looking through the telescope with great interest and then exclaimed excitedly: "Hey I can see a planet that exploded and disappeared three million years ago!"

David looked at me attentively but did not say a word.

I addressed Sivan: "I wonder if you can see something that had once existed and disappeared."

Sivan took hold of the telescope. She took a long, concentrated look through it. Then she said: "I can see the house we used to live in when I was a little girl."

It was David's turn to use the telescope, but he refused.

The telescope game became a regular element in our meetings. In the course of time it was elaborated. One could see not only inanimate objects but also people who had disappeared and, later, people who were known to exist but who were far away. One could bring these objects or people closer or send them away by extending or contracting the telescope. One could remove the people or objects by placing the lid over the telescope's end.

For a long period only Sivan and I actually participated in this game. David was just an interested observer. Only occasionally would he peep into the telescope for a brief instant and say: "It's impossible to see anything."

Another game invented in that period was "The Invisible Guest". It was a few days before Seder, the Jewish passover night ceremony. Sivan, David and I staged a "Seder ceremony" game. In the Seder it is customary to leave the door ajar and place an empty chair and a full wine goblet for Eliah the Prophet who would hopefully enter. However, David did not want this part of the ceremony.

He forbade us to open the door or keep an empty chair by the table. After a few sessions I suggested that we place a huge doll in the empty chair, but David would not allow this either.

This chapter of our story went on for about three months. And then the show season opened. It began with David's offer to put on a show for his mother, with puppets, percussion instruments, lighting effects and proprs. This evolved into theatrical competitions, like the drama contests in ancient Greece. Each of the three of us in his or her turn presented a show. Then the other two, as a team of critics, evaluated the show.

David's first show was very instructive. He stepped on a makeshift stage constructed of stools. He put all the lights out except one spotlight. He stood there quietly for a while. Then, suddenly, he pulled the telescope out of his shirt and declared: "This is a magic telescope. It can make people appear and disappear." He looked through the telescope and then ran to the wardrobe and drew out the huge man-like puppet, saying dramatically: "You see? The telescope made this man appear." Then he said: "Now it will make him disappear." He placed the lid over the telescope's end, ran and put the puppet back in the wardrobe, saying: "You see? It made it disappear. And now you are going to see something wonderful. The telescope will make Shlomo disappear and then I'll reverse it and it will make me disappear!"

In the conference of critics following this show Sivan, assuming what she believed to be the intonation and manner of "intellectuals", said: "This was a frightening show. A little dangerous even." And then I said: "I think it was an excellent show. What I liked about it was the personification of the telescope. A very original idea. An angry telescope who does not like to be pushed around. A beautiful idea. I'm going to give this show a hundred points."

"And I'll give it fifty," said Sivan, "because it is frightening." It was her turn to put on her own show. Hers was a variation on David's. In her show the telescope could make the huge puppet appear and remain permanently.

I gave her show fifty points because it was neither realistic nor sufficiently imaginative. David refused to evaluate it.

Then came my turn. In my show the images appearing in the telescope were scorching, like the sun. I got burned. Sivan had to pretend to anoint my burns with ointment.

For this show Sivan gave me thirty. She said it was frightening and too difficult. David gave me a million points, because he liked to see me burned, but then he subtracted two millions off my mark, because my show was silly.

Within a few weeks the show contests became thematically and stylistically richer. David declared: "Today you are going to see a horror show!" He put all the lights out and hid himself inside the wardrobe. Sivan and I were waiting outside, feeling the suspense. Then he got out and stood with his back to the wall, his arms stretched sideways. A beam of light appeared when he turned the spotlight on. He had a silvered dress on. His head was covered with a silvered scarf. He spoke hoarsely: "I am the mechanized, computerized Mother of Destruction!" Then he walked toward the wardrobe and took out two dolls, representing a man and a boy, an electric torch and a drum. He spoke dramatically: "I destroy people with a laser beam," he said and began to drum, producing a thunder-like roar. He held the man-doll with one hand. He switched on the torch. A patch of yellow light appeared on the man's face. David threw the doll away violently and declared: "Destroyed!" Then he repeated this sequence of actions with the boy-doll as his victim.

The team of critics did not particularly like this show. "I don't like science fiction", I said, "but I am ready to give it thirty for the talent invested in the actual performance". Sivan just said "a disgusting show" and gave it minus million.

In her show she simply reversed the roles: the man and the boy destroyed the silvery lady.

When my turn arrived, I presented my own variation: the man, the woman and the boy attempted to destroy each other, but they failed. The torch produced just imaginary beams.

After the closing of the show season we all preferred to play freely. Sivan and David created, under my guidance, dramatic situations representing the following pattern of relationships: the character played by David displays mistrust and suspicion toward the character represented by Sivan. The latter tries to prove to the former that she deserves to be trusted.

In one of these scenes David played "a baby". He lay on the carpet, wagging his arms and hands. He was crying and screaming incessantly for a long time. This was an all too perfect rendering! Sivan tried to hug him. He pushed her away. She begged him to tell her why he was crying but he just went on crying and screaming. Sivan was at a loss. She was working herself up to a state of panic.

Then I made up my mind. I lay on the carpet next to David. I began moving my arms and legs. I cried and screamed like him but I also put what was on my mind into words. I sobbed my heart out, struggling to keep myself from bursting into real tears. David got up, sat on a chair and watched me attentively. I let Sivan know the full extent of my fear and desperation. I told her that my whole universe was in pieces. I had totally lost my confidence in the world of grown-ups. I did not know where my salvation would come from.

Sivan sat beside me on the carpet.

"What do you want me to do?" she said tearfully.

"I don't know", I said. "I want you to listen to me."

At our next meeting David had good news. He had visited his father in his father's apartment. His father's girlfriend gave them delicious cakes while they were watching the sports news report on TV.

And then he invented a new game: an adventure plane flight around the world. I had to be the pilot. David was the passenger. Sivan was excluded from the flight. She was restricted to the control tower.

The flight was full of dangers and disastrous events. Over and over again we barely escaped fatal injury or violent death. We were caught in the midst of a hurricane. We had to parachute into a jungle, where we were nearly devoured by wild animals or eaten up by cannibals. In each of these unfortunate events it was my duty to solve the problem and rescue both of us.

At that period David womld spend one afternoon a week with Dan at his place. David did not make do with this limited contact with his father. He told me about a secret plan he had: to move in with Dan. This was an unfortunate idea, because Dan had a secret plan of his own, which he had confided to me a few days earlier: to emigrate to Australia.

I encouraged Sivan to make it absolutely clear to David that he would stay with her. Her home was his home. She was the one who guarded him and took care of him. She would never leave him or let him go, under any circumstances. She did not have to resort to play to communicate this message to David. She used plain words.

This had a sobering effect on David. He gradually began the life of a normal boy of his age. He spent more and more time in the afternoons with his class-mates, playing soccer and other boys' games.

Sivan said that David and she began really talking with one another. They spoke about everything, including the most delicate, the most painful issues.

I had a clear feeling that the time was ripe to terminate therapy.

Our separation was not easy. The slices of life we had shared may have been fictitious and fanciful, but for all three of us they were more real than real.

This case has been presented to introduce the reader to the peculiar atmosphere characteristic of strategic family play therapeutic sessions. This presentation does not say much about the analysis and planning that go on behind the scene, the mechanisms that make the magic really happen. This is the chief business of the main body of the book.

Introduction

Poison in Jest

The idea of harnessing play, fantasy and make-believe in the service of solving family problems is not new. Fine examples of such uses abound in ancient and modern sources. In one of the most enchanting Biblical stories Joseph, then King Pharaoh's viceroy, conducted his touching reunion with his brothers, who years earlier had attempted to get rid of him by selling him to a caravan of nomads, in a playful manner using make-believe and trickery. He instructed his servant to hide his silver chalice in the bag of his younger brother Benjamin. Then he ordered his soldiers to seize his brothers and bring them back. He accused them of betrayal and theft. Only after he had frightened and humiliated them for a while did he tell them who he really was. Apparently he could not reveal his true identity and forgive them before he had made them pay for what they had done to him in the past. However, this wish did not necessarily have to be satisfied in reality. He could easily make do with telling his brothers what he had to tell them in a symbolic code. He used covert communication, framing the situation as some kind of private make-believe game in which his brothers were unwittingly made to participate.

In Shakespeare's play, Hamlet communicated to his mother, the queen, and King Claudius, his step-father, her husband, that he knew about their crime of murdering his father, the late king, through a group of players who reproduced the crime in a symbolic disguise. Here is a citation from the conversation that followed the presentation of the play:

KING. Have you heard the argument? Is there no offence in't?

HAMLET. No, no, they do but jest, poison in jest; no offence i'th'world.

KING. What do you call the play?

HAMLET. The mouse-trap. Marry, how? Tropically. This play is the image of a murder done in Vienna: Gonzago is the duke's name; his wife, Baptista; you shall see anon; 'tis a knavish piece of work; but what o'that? your majesty, and we that have free souls, it touches us not: let the gall'd jade wince, our withers are unwrung.

In a Kabuki play entitled *The Substitute*, by Migawari Zazen, a young lord, Yamakage Ukyo, is burdened with a wife of forceful character named Tamanoi. Planning to visit his beautiful mistress, he tells his wife that he has decided to go to a nearby temple to pray for seven days and nights. He disguises his servant with his own garments and sends him to the temple. He himself rushes off to his mistress.

His wife appears in the temple, apparently to bring some food, and quickly discovers the plot. She takes her husband's garments off the servant and puts them on, waiting for her husband to return. Soon he is seen, quite drunk and ridiculous, since he his wearing his mistress' robe. Thinking that he is speaking with his servant he describes in great detail how he has spent his time. Finally, he playfully takes his garments from his "servant" and discovers to his horror how he will have to pay for his night out.

It is not easy to decide what Yamakage and Tamanoi enjoyed more: Yamakage's night with his mistress and Tamanoi's revenge or the playful manner by which these were achieved (Richie and Watanabe, 1963).

In Mark Twain's *Tom Sawyer* Tom and his friend Joe Harper, troubled by the feeling that their families do not understand them, seek comfort by playing a complex make-believe game:

> Tom's mind was made up now. He was gloomy and desperate. He was a forsaken, friendless boy. He said nobody loved him. When they found out what they had driven him to, perhaps they would be sorry. He had tried to do right and get along, but they would not let him, since nothing would do them but to get rid of him. Let it be so. He would lead a life of crime. There was no choice.

Just at this point he met his soul's sworn comrade Joe Harper. Tom, wiping his eyes with his sleeve, began to blubber out something about a resolution to escape from hard usage and lack of sympathy at home by roaming abroad into the great world never to return.

But it transpired that this was a request which Joe had just been going to make of Tom. His mother had whipped him for drinking some cream which he had never tasted and knew nothing about. It was clear that she was tired of him and wished him to go:

> About midnight Tom arrived . . . Then a guarded voice said: "Who goes there?"
> "Tom Sawyer, The Black Avenger of the Spanish Main. Name Your Names!"
> "Huck Finn, the Red-Handed, and Joe Harper, the Terror of the Seas." Tom had furnished the titles from his favorite literature.
> (Twain, 1973)

Another example is Eugene Ionesco's play *The Chairs*, in which a very old man and his wife fill their arid lives with make-believe games, in which they beat their loneliness, fears, frustrations and desperation by creating possible worlds full of youth, power, grandeur and love.

OLD MAN. I'm very bored.

OLD WOMAN. Let's amuse ourselves by making believe.

(Ionesco, 1980).

This tiny sample of examples from the world's ancient and modern literature provides evidence for the idea that play, fantasy and make-believe have always been used as means for facilitating interactions around emotionally loaded and otherwise difficult issues in family life and solving interpersonal familial problems.

An important task facing the science of family therapy is to mobilize this folk wisdom into its ranks. The method of strategic family play therapy presented in this book represents one way of doing this.

Play as a Precision Instrument—The Trademark of Strategic Family Play Therapy

What is special about strategic family play therapy? It is the deliberate utilization of well-defined structural and psychosocial properties of play, as both diagnostic leads and therapeutic agents.

Let us look again at the adventures of the little prince and princess who were expelled from the palace by their wicked parents, described in the preface. This imaginary story constitutes a complex metaphor for the family's real drama as seen through the eyes of the players. Its plot, its main motives, the dialogue among the participants and other features symbolize overt as well as covert layers of the problematic relationships among the members of this family.

It follows that in this and other similar cases spontaneous make-believe play interactions among family members can serve as a rich source of diagnostic information. An experienced family therapist who observes such play scenes can learn a great deal about the family from what she sees and hears. The main tools by which she can analyze and interpret the observed play are her experience, her general pool of knowledge and her intuition. In many cases this would be enough, but not in every case. The symbolic meaning of the play is not always as transparent as in this example. Intuition can mislead if it is not supported by less subjective theoretical and methodological guidelines. Concepts, findings and methods that have been developed with reference to other domains are not always applicable to play. Furthermore, students and trainees who do not have a heavy load of knowledge and experience behind them cannot count on the little they carry to be sufficient.

Therefore, an explicit method for microanalysis and macroanalysis of family make-believe play interactions is proposed in this book. A family play therapist can apply this method systematically to samples of family play behavior. This would facilitate his search for the covert patterns, or hidden rules, that account for the problematic ways in which family members interrelate.

Furthermore, novices can find this method particularly useful as a training aid by which they can improve their diagnostic skills.

Likewise, a professional therapist who is sufficiently spirited and inventive stands a fair chance of proving himself to be a good family play therapist. He does not have to know much about the anatomy and physiology of play for that. However, his natural skill can be strengthened and the quality of his work improved if he does possess such knowledge. Therefore, a large proportion of this book is devoted to a rigorous analysis of the internal make-up of make-believe play and of its psychological and social functions. A strategic family play therapist who knows and understands the distinctive properties of make-believe play may be likened to a doctor who knows and understands the curative properties of the medicines he prescribes.

In the course of his encounters with the family such a knowledgeable therapist makes a series of playful moves which subtly lead the family members to perform make-believe play acts in which the structural and psychosocial properties of make-believe play are put into operation. These properties possess a "magical" therapeutic power. The very fact that the family members play in a manner that engages them emotionally breeds change. The play properties in action bring into operation slight modifications in the dysfunctional patterns chosen as the targets of intervention.

Let me present an example in which the structural play property termed "arbitrariness of signifier" was exploited as a change agent. This property is derived from the fact that in make-believe play a signifier which stands for some signified thematic content is not necessarily similar to this content. For instance, a leaf is a perfectly legitimate signifier for the content "lion" (see Piaget, 1962 and Chapters 2 and 3).

Shoshana, a divorcee, wanted to send her twelve-year-old daughter Yudit to a boarding school. Both of them claimed they could not get along with one another. They were getting on each other's nerves. I led Yudit, by a series of playful moves, to sitting on her mother's lap. Then I re-defined the lap as a make-believe "boarding school". In this way I arbitrarily turned the mother's lap into a signifier for the signified content "boarding school".

Once Yudit was sitting on her mother's lap, the two conducted a make-believe telephone conversation between "daughter in boarding school" and "mother at home". During the conversation, the two confessed that they missed one another.

This intervention was based on the diagnostic hypothesis that the mutual nagging between the mother and the daughter was their dysfunctional way of regulating the interpersonal distance between them. They were over-involved with each other, overly interdependent. Such a degree of intimacy did not suit their respective developmental needs any longer. The purpose of the intervention was to make them keenly aware of this conflict between their contradictory needs, the need for dependence (signified by physical proximity) and the need for independence (symbolized by physical distance). The trick of redefining the mother's lap as an arbitrary signifier for the signified content "boarding school" was an application of a structural property of make-believe play as a lever for achieving the desired change. By this move the mother and the daughter were made to go through two contrasting emotional experiences, representing the two opposing forces of their conflict and its absurd connotations. This playful experience was the battering-ram that toppled their dysfunctional program.

Following this intervention, the idea of sending the daughter to a boarding school was dropped, and the relationship between Yudit and Shoshaba was considerably improved (see Chapter 10).

The explicitness of the change targets and agents in strategic family play therapy makes it relatively easy to trace the process of change. Therefore the task of evaluating the progress of the therapy is quite manageable.

Why Family Play Therapy?

Considering the present abundance of different schools of family therapy, one should ask what the advantages are of the method proposed in this book. Here are some of the answers:

Accessibility to young children. In ordinary family therapy young children cannot participate in the process fully, actively and meaningfully. This is due to their cognitive and emotional limitations. These limitations can be detoured if the child's own natural medium of expression and communication, namely play, is used.

Richness and flexibility. Make-believe play constitutes a singularly rich and flexible medium of expression and communication. It speaks through words, actions, objects and materials. A piece of cloth can become a river and a piece of wood a whale. The player can be both himself (e.g. an ordinary six-year-old boy) and someone or something else (e.g. "a prince", "a horse") at one and the same time. Roles and modes of behavior can be flexibly changed at will and a limitless number of events and situations can be made up freely.

Exposure of covert patterns. Since in make-believe play the defenses are lax and stereotyped patterns of communication loosened, covert and unconscious thoughts, emotions and relationships rise to the surface. For example, in a family I worked with, the husband's mother, who lived with the family, interfered with the wife's bringing up of her children. The wife would complain to her husband, but he would always take his mother's side. In a family make-believe game with puppets, the husband directed his rage at a puppet representing "an old woman attacking a young woman", thus revealing his covert feelings.

Wealth of therapeutic means. A creative therapist who masters the language of play can invent a great variety of kinds of therapeutic moves. He may choose positions such as actor, director or audience. As an actor he can play various roles such as "the cunning wolf", or "the submissive sheep". He may use fancy dress, objects, spaces and musical instruments.

Therapeutic economy. Thanks to the fact that play in this form of therapy is employed as a precision instrument (see the previous section) strategic family play therapeutic interventions are sometimes extremely condensed and therefore highly effective. Their power is partly due to the fact that they detour defenses such as rationalization or denial, and create an immediate emotional experience. The above-mentioned reframing of the mother's lap as "a boarding school" illustrates this quite well.

The Scope of Strategic Family Play Therapy

This form of therapy is most suited to families with children for whom social make-believe play is a natural medium of expression and communication. The age range within which children have been found to be actively engaged in this sort of play is roughly 4 to 12 (see Piaget, 1962).

Strategic family play therapy has been tried successfully with children who present a wide range of problems: fears and phobias, obsessive-compulsive symptoms, depression, conduct disorders, psychophysiological disorders, hyperactivity, social maladaptation, delinquency, etc. It has also been applied with children who suffered from psychoses, mental retardation or severe neurological disorders, with a good record of achievements. However, I would not recommend using it with these populations unless special training is provided, because of the high risks involved.

This kind of therapy has proved applicable to families of various cultural and social backgrounds. Psychologists, psychiatrists and social workers who practice in Israel and in The Netherlands have acquired intensive training in strategic family play therapy and have been using it regularly in their work. It has been exercised with middle class as well as with multi-problem, socially and educationally disadvantaged families; with urban and rural families; with Christians, Moslems and Jews. Its universal appeal confirms the truism that play is a universal language.

The Theoretical and Methodological Orientation

The Sources of Strategic Family Play Therapy

Strategic family play therapy is founded on a wide-scale synthesis of concepts and methods whose origins lie in both play and family studies. These sources are specified in detail in the main body of this book. Here they will only be broadly outlined.

If the word "play" is struck out of the title "strategic family play therapy" what remains is "strategic family therapy". Indeed, the form of therapy proposed in this book claims a place in the mainstream of the family therapy tradition, which is couched in family systems theory, structuralism, cybernetics and communication theory. Within this tradition, it belongs to the narrower club of strategic therapy, whose origins lie in the work of Milton Erikson (see Haley, 1973) and Gregory Bateson (1972, 1979). It will be noted however that the term "strategy" in strategic family play therapy refers to the overall, grand plan of the whole therapeutic process rather than to specific problem-solving techniques. The latter are termed "tactics" in this book (see Chapters 9 and 10).

Putting the word "play" back in its place reveals some affinity to the work of Cloe Madanes (1982). I consider her carefully designed pretend strategies, which are based on a rigorous logical analysis of the therapeutic power of play, a major contribution. Although play has been used as a therapeutic change agent since the beginning of this century, no one before had, to the best of my knowledge, attempted to apply an explicit analysis of the inherent structural properties of play. Her work has inspired me to go on looking for new ways of harnessing the nuclear power of play.

An offshoot of the strategic use of play in family therapy has been what may be termed "magic therapy". A therapeutic session done in this style looks like a playful version of an exotic ritual. The central idea behind this, and perhaps behind all forms of strategic therapy, is that change in human systems can happen solely on the ideational level. Reality itself, if there is such a thing, may be left intact. (Cf. Papp, 1982; Seltzer, 1983; Kobak and Waters, 1984; O'Connor, 1984; O'Connor and Hoorwitz, 1984.)

Strategic family play therapy has also drawn on another (though not so different as it is sometimes claimed to be) tradition, namely symbolic-experiential family play therapy. The latter's similarity to "magic therapy" becomes obvious when one reads its characteristics, as listed by Keith and Whitaker (1981): "Scope is increased through magic and ritual; play constantly mixes the symbolic and the real; primary reality is metaphorical; there is a repeated shift from metaphor to reality and back; symbolic cues are used in an administrative reality".

So far this survey has concentrated on works which refer to play as an agent of change. However, the same sources have had much to say about play as a vehicle of therapeutic communication. Proponents of strategic therapy, as well as adherents of symbolic-experiential therapy, have invested considerable efforts in studying and developing modes of communication that are anything but straightforward. Key words describing this approach to interaction in the therapy room are "multidimensional", "many-layered", "symbolic", "metaphorical". Many scholars have emphasized the effectiveness of such modes of communication, their power to penetrate deeply, touch the inner strata, detour resistance and defensiveness and mobilize cooperation. (See Haley, 1973; Bateson, 1979; Watzlawick, 1978; Keith and Whitaker, 1981.)

The sources of strategic family play therapy are not restricted to the family therapy tradition. Its deeper roots lie in psychoanalysis, cognitive and developmental psychology and human ethology.

Sigmund Freud (1922), Melanie Klein (1960) and Eric Erikson (1940, 1965) among other leaders of the psychoanalytic movement, were keenly aware of play as a road to the unconscious; perhaps not the royal road, like dreams, but certainly one of the main roads. Each of these pioneers, in his or her own way, produced intriguing examples illustrating how children's play reflects their innermost feelings and emotions, centering around developmentally crucial themes. They also demonstrated the defensive functions of play. With the aid of play—they observed—the child regulates his emotional give-and-take with the outer world and achieves mastery over his inner world. He can be assisted in this endeavor by an attentive therapist who participates in his play activities and helps him understand their meanings.

A similar view of play was put forward by Axline (1969), although her therapeutic interventions, in the style of Rogers' non-directive therapy, were less interpretive.

The insights of psychoanalysts concerning play and its roles in the emotional world of the child have been largely confirmed and further elaborated by cognitive and developmental psychologists. Adopting predominantly information-processing and ethological perspectives, leading figures such as Piaget (1962), Singer (1973), Klinger (1971) and their followers have further investigated the roles of play as a processor and regulator of emotionally relevant information, characteristic of various stages of the child's development.

A different direction of research has been taken by social psychologists and anthropologists. These have been studying the social communicational functions of play and its nature as a mirror of the socio-cultural environment. Well-known contributors in this avenue are Brian Sutton-Smith (1984), Catherine Garvey (1972) and Sarah Smilansky (1968).

On the face of it, these psychoanalytic, cognitive and ethological studies of play have little to do with family therapy. But I have found them immediately relevant. I have never been able to really understand, however hard I tried, the view of the family as a purely abstract system, transcending its individual members (cf. Jackson, 1965). To my mind a family is a social unit consisting of individuals, each with his or her own psyche. Whatever happens in a family, happens on the interface between the individual psychological and the social communicational levels. Change in the family rules always begins with the individual, who feels capable of abandoning certain maladaptive habits and modes of thinking, feeling and behavior. Therefore, if play is to be used as a medium of therapeutic communication and as an agent of change, its psychological as well as its social functions should be thoroughly understood. Deep familiarity with the psychoanalytic, cognitive, developmental and ethological research on play and play therapy is absolutely necessary for the acquisition of such understanding (cf. Ariel, 1987; Ariel, Carel and Tyano, 1984).

The Theoretical Synthesis

Strategic family play therapy is the output of my efforts to integrate this large, heterogeneous collection of ideas and findings concerning play and family therapy into a single systematic whole. This synthesis, however, can be divided into a number of sub-systems, according to the stages of the therapeutic process.

The *diagnostic assessment* draws on an information-processing theory of family dysfunction (see Chapter 1) and is assisted by a technique of semiotic microanalysis and macroanalysis of make-believe play (see Chapters 2–8).

The *planning and execution* of the therapy benefits from the following sub-parts of the general model:

(a) A formal definition of the concept "make-believe play" (see Chapter 2).
(b) An information-processing, cybernetic analysis of make-believe play as a mechanism for regulating the level of emotional arousal (briefly "the cybernetic theory of MBP"; see Chapter 2).
(c) A semiotic analysis of make-believe play as an interpersonal communicational vehicle (briefly "the communicational theory of MBP"; see Chapter 2).

The formal definition, the cybernetic theory and the communicational theory of MBP contribute to the actual planning and execution of the therapy in two major ways:

Firstly, they provide explicit characterizations of the inherent structural and psychosocial properties of make-believe play. As mentioned above, some of these properties can be applied as change agents. That is to say, one can deduce the curative value of these structural and psychosocial properties from a close inspection of the formal definition, the cybernetic theory and the communicational theory of MBP (see Chapters 3, 13 and 14).

Secondly, the latter subparts of the general model can serve, so to speak, as a "grammar" and a "vocabulary" of make-believe play. The therapist can be aided by this grammar and vocabulary in his efforts to master and use the language of play as his major medium of therapeutic communication with the family.

The therapist should be able to trace the *progress of the therapeutic process* and exercise some control over it. This requires him to understand the mechanisms of transfer and generalization from the make-believe world created in the play therapy room into the family's everyday reality. These mechanisms are described and explained in yet another component of the theoretical synthesis. The core of this component is an integration of theoretical and empirical studies regarding the mutual influence between affect and ideation (see Chapters 2, 13 and 14). A hypothesis shared by all these studies is that emotions have a decisive influence over cognitive processes such as perception, undirected and creative thinking and decision making. The family play therapeutic interventions breed emotional experiences which, in turn, modify the family members' existing cognitive information-processing programs. The new programs are valid not just in the play room but also in the family's out-of-play reality.

A Case Illustration

Assessment

The presenting problems. Nine-year-old Ron was considered by everybody to be a failure in school. He seemed to be thick-headed, slow-witted, unable to grasp simple things such as the English alphabet and the multiplication table. He was also teased and ridiculed by his mates. While they were attacking him he would remain passive, suffering quietly.

Reading this description, you probably have imagined a rather dull young person. This is however a very wrong impression. Ron was a well built, strikingly good looking boy. Moreover, psychological tests had proved beyond doubt that his intellectual potential was very high.

Ron had a seven-year-old brother, Ben, who was viewed by everybody as an academic and social success.

I began my contact with this family by interviewing the parents. The father, Rami, a computer programmer, expressed his concern over Ron's poor performance in school. He was not so worried about his social and emotional problems. He described himself as an intelligent, rational person, a perfectionist who controlled both himself and other people. The mother, Edna, a big, strongly built woman, was anxious mainly about Ron's social and emotional difficulties. She gave the impression that she was afraid of her husband and would not dare speak her mind in his presence. But after some encouragement on my side she said hesitatingly that she disapproved of her husband's insensitive and harsh attitude toward both herself and their son Ron.

Observing the family play. Following the interview with the parents I arranged a session with the whole family. They arrived at the play therapy room, where a rich variety of playthings (toys, puppets, masks, etc.) was made available to them. They were encouraged to initiate conjoint play activities of their own choice. Many interesting things came out in the course of this session. However, here I shall refer just to one episode, which was particularly instructive with respect to understanding the covert dysfunctional patterns underlying the presenting problems:

I offered the family a selection of hand puppets representing people, animals and various creatures and fairy tale figures. Each of the family members chose one puppet.

When I saw their choices, I was astonished. The characters they selected were not just different from the visiting cards presented in the interview with the parents. They sharply contrasted with this introduction. Although I had been quite familiar with the immediate unmasking effect of the choice of toys, the complete reversal of roles in this case took me by surprise.

Rami, the father who passed for a cold, rational, domineering person, chose a puppet representing a cow. Edna, the mother, picked a lion puppet which reminded one of her big and strong physical appearance rather than of the weak and frightened facade she put on in the interview. Ron, the nine-year-old identified patient, who was described as a passive, shy under-achiever chose a puppet representing a devil. His seven-year-old brother Ben, who had been characterized as an academic and social success, picked a puppet representing a donkey.

Edna made the first move: "I am the king of this jungle," she declared.

Rami, her husband, made his cow walk toward the lion. He said in a funny tone of voice: "Do you want a pet, king? I can be your pet."

"No, thank you", said the lion, "I don't need a pet. By the way, your smell reminds me that I did not have dinner today."

At this point Ron made his devil puppet come close to his mother's lion puppet and said in a fiendish tone of voice: "Do you need a pet like me?"

Edna looked at the devil puppet, hesitating. Then she smiled mischievously and said: "Yes, why not?"

The devil joined the lion and whispered in its ear: "Let's make fun of the silly cow."

At this moment Ben made his donkey puppet stand by his father's cow puppet, and said in a braying manner, addressing his brother: "You yourself are silly."

Ron replied: "I am not, because I am the devil. Nobody can make the devil silly, not even the king himself!"

Explaining the symptoms as a function of the family's dysfunctional programs

On the basis of the verbal interview and the play observation I formulated the following tentative diagnostic hypotheses.

The interrelationships among the family members are regulated by the following dysfunctional, self-defeating plans for achieving their unattainable, apparently subconscious, goals.

Rami's deepest wish seems to be that his big, strong wife would pet him (the cow who asked the lion to take him as his pet). However, Edna (the lion) rejects him quite aggressively. She does not want to pet him. She wants a powerful, dominant man, who would make her feel feminine and help her forget that she is so big and strong. Therefore Rami has changed his approach. He attempts to get his wife's love and appreciation by pretending to be dominant and by emphasizing his intellectual strengths. Unfortunately this tactic has also failed to win his wife over to his side. She disapproves of and feels uneasy with what she takes to be his rigidity and insensitivity.

Ron is caught in a paralyzing conflict. Like a normal nine-year-old boy he wants to be close to and identify with his father. However, he perceives with his keen senses that his mother (the lion, the king of the forest) "makes his father silly". If he is too closely identified with his father she is likely to make him silly too.

One way out of this problem could be joining forces with his mother, forming a "fiendish" coalition with her. Together with his mother he could make a fool of his father ("Let's make fun of the silly cow"). In this coalition he is quite safe ("Nobody can make the devil silly, not even the king himself"). However, this tactic throws out the baby with the bath water. After all, Ron's main goal has been to be close to and identify with his father, not to be his enemy.

Another way out might be to identify not with his father's submissive, dependent side but with his pedantic and intellectual facade. This would not work either, because his mother disapproves of this side of his father too.

Ron's solution to this entanglement has been to make *himself* silly. In this way he can reach his goal of being like his father without becoming his mother's victim. He is his own victim, not his mother's. Hence his symptoms—under-achievement in school and social passivity.

Ben, the younger brother, has the same goal as Ron: to be close to and identify with his father. However, his plan has been to go all the way toward his goal. Therefore he has embraced both his father's strong (intellectual, domineering) side and his weak ("donkey's") side.

Planning

A general strategy

These tentative hypotheses concerning the presenting problems and their role in the dysfunctional family programs make it possible to design a general strategy for the therapeutic intervention. Here is one such strategy:

The required changes. Ron's presenting problems—his under-achievement in school and social passivity—have been explained above as his way of getting out of a dilemma. As he sees things, he is forced to choose between his father and his mother. If he opts for his mother, he will become his father's enemy. If he prefers his father, his mother will become his enemy. Obviously, this has to be changed. Ron should be relieved from this terrible conflict. He should be free to love, and be loved by, both his parents.

However, this is easier said than done. Ron's dilemma is not entirely misconceived. It is at least partly founded on his perceptive analysis of the reality of the relationships between his parents. His mother does seem to reject his father, both when he begs her to pet him and when he feigns strength. Ron's conflict could be solved completely if this difficulty in the relationship between his parents is resolved. This could be achieved, for instance, if Rami learned to ask for Edna's warmth and attention in a way that did not alienate her.

If the parents joined forces, Ben, the younger son, would be freed of his role in the coalition with his father against his mother and brother.

The changes that should be focused on. If the relationship between the parents is improved, the children's problems are likely to disappear. Therefore, the most economical choice seems to be to concentrate on the couple's problems. This course is, however, rather risky. The depth of Edna's inability to give love to her husband, and the intensity of his inflexibility are difficult to evaluate in advance. There is a danger that if the therapy concentrates exclusively on the couple, their problems, and the children's problems, would be aggravated—at least in the first period of the therapy. A safer course would be to attempt to free the children of their involvement in the relationship between their parents. This can be accompanied by an exploratory couple therapy.

The family play therapeutic treatment plan. The goal of releasing the children from their entanglement in the conflict between their parents can be achieved by family play therapy.

This can be accomplished by the following steps:

(a) Increasing the family members' awareness of their own dysfunctional programs:
    The therapist can subtly lead the family members to play out their dysfunctional programs in a symbolic, make-believe disguise. The play property of *basic duality* (the player plays a make-believe role and observes himself playing this role at one and the same time) will necessarily

become operative in these games. However, the therapist will not rely on the effect of this property alone. He will join the family's activity in a suitable make-believe role. Using play metaphors, he will sharpen the family members' awareness of the details of the dysfunctional programs illustrated in their playful interactions.

(b) Negotiating the possibility of releasing the children from their involvement in the conflict between the parents:

The therapist can stage such negotiations in the "as if" world of the family's make-believe play. In doing this, he activates the play property of *covert communication* (negotiating interpersonal relationships under the pretence of make-believe fiction).

(c) Letting the family experience the change:

The family is indirectly invited to go through the experience of living without the children's over-involvement in the relationship between their parents; not in real life, but in the world of make-believe. The play property of "possible worlds" (materializing unrealized possibilities in make-believe play) can be exploited for this purpose.

There are grounds for believing that this play experience is carried over, at least in part, to the family's out-of-play reality (see Chapter 13).

A tactic for a particular session

Here for illustration is the plan for one of the sessions:

This session is designated to serve the second step of the treatment plan, namely negotiating the possibility of releasing the children from their involvement in the conflict between the parents.

The particular goal of the session. To bring Edna to assure Ron that she will never deride or resent him, even if he associates with his father or identifies with him.

The main properties of play employed. Covert communication (negotiating interpersonal relationships under the pretence of make-believe fiction) and symbolic coding (the emotionally laden issues preoccupying the family members are disguised as imaginary make-believe metaphors).

Principal manners in which these properties of play will be activated in the therapy. The family will be allowed to play freely. When a suitable occasion naturally arises, the therapist will join their play in an appropriate make-believe role. He will encourage Ron to join and follow his father. If his mother rejects or criticizes his father, the therapist will attempt to persuade Ron to continue associating with his father. At the same time the therapist will somehow instruct Edna to assure Ron that she fully accepts his attachment to his father. She will not resent or deride him for identifying himself with her husband.

Therapy

Carrying out the tactic

Here, for illustration, is an excerpt from the transcript of the session whose plan has been presented above:

The family is engaged in a "space-journey" make-believe game. Edna, the mother, appointed herself the chief commander of a mission to Mars. She placed herself in the control-room of the launching base.

EDNA. Daddy and Ben, you are going to be the astronauts. You've won the privilege of being the first astronauts ever to be sent to Mars.

THERAPIST. Excuse me, commander. As the chief engineer of this project I take the liberty of intervening and suggest that this spacecraft be manned with three astronauts, not just two. It takes three to operate it properly.

EDNA. OK, Ron, you join them as the third astronaut.

The therapist brings a big cardboard box and says: This is your spacecraft. It's the best.

Rami, Ron and Ben go into the box.

EDNA *(speaking into a block representing "a microphone")*. Are you ready?

BEN. Yes!

EDNA. Ten, nine, eight, seven, six, five, four, three, two, one, take off!

THERAPIST *(making all kinds of loud noises with percussion instruments)*. She is rocketing up! Look at all that fire and smoke! That's marvelous!

RON *(going out of the box, moving as in a slow-motion picture)*. We are in outer space now. Look at me! I have no weight! I can fly like a bird!

THERAPIST *(addressing Edna)*. Commander Eden, I suggest that you tell Colonel Rambo, the astronaut in charge of the spacecraft, to get Lieutenant Ronald back into the spacecraft. He should stay close to Colonel Rambo and follow his orders. He should not do things on his own initiative.

EDNA. Yes sir, but I'm not sure he'll obey him.

THERAPIST. He'll obey him all right. All you have to do is to make it absolutely clear to him that Colonel Rambo is the supreme authority on the spacecraft.

ENDA *(into the microphone)*. Colonel Rambo, get Lieutenant Ronald back into the spacecraft!

RAMI. Yes sir, but what if he refuses to obey me?

EDNA. Use your authority.

RAMI *(curtly)*. Ron, back into the spacecraft! Do you hear me?!

EDNA. You should not be that harsh with him.

THERAPIST. In the spacecraft *he* is the supreme authority, remember?

EDNA. Yes. I forgot. Ronald, you should obey Colonel Rambo. He is the supreme authority on your spacecraft.

RON. He is the supreme jerk on your spacecraft.

THERAPIST. So if you obey him you become a jerk too?

Edna is laughing.

THERAPIST. This is not a laughing matter. What do *you* think? Do you think that obeying Colonel Rambo will turn Ronald into a jerk?

EDNA. Of course not.

THERAPIST. Tell him then.

EDNA. I don't like this word anyway.

THERAPIST. Use another word, then.

EDNA. Ronald, you should obey Commander Rambo. Who taught you to use such words anyway?

RAMI. We have some trouble here. Can we return to base?

EDNA. What kind of trouble?

RAMI. One of the engines stopped functioning.

EDNA. OK, come back, we'll fix it.

THERAPIST. I am afraid this is impossible. The spacecraft is in danger of breaking down on the way back. They'll have to solve the problem on their own, on the spot.

ENDA. Are you sure?

THERAPIST. Absolutely. I know this spacecraft like I know myself.

EDNA. You there, start fixing the engine. You two should cooperate with Colonel Rambo. Don't call him names and don't make any trouble.

THERAPIST. And if Colonel Rambo does not do a good job, are you going to blame Ronald?

EDNA. Of course not. Why blame Ronald?

THERAPIST. Ron, did you hear that?

Ron pretends to ignore him. Rami, Ron and Ben start "fixing the engine".

THERAPIST. Now they are working like a good team. How do you like them?

EDNA. I like them very much. I like it when they do things together.

PART 1

Theoretical foundations

CHAPTER 1

Family Dysfunction

Family Dysfunction—the Target of Strategic Family Play Therapeutic Interventions

The concept of *family dysfunction* is central to most schools of systemic family therapy. The first thing we do after a person has been referred to us is ask ourselves: "What is wrong with his (or her) family?" We believe that this can help us understand the difficulties for which this individual seeks help. In our minds the presenting problems of the individual are products of family dysfunction. The former can be *explained* by the latter. It follows that these problems can be *solved* by repairing the relevant dysfunctional features in the family system.

Therefore, a strategic family play therapist who wants his interventions to be effective should be able to identify those dysfunctional features in the family system which generate and maintain the presenting problems. See Andolfi, 1979; Bateson *et al.*, 1956; Minuchin, 1974; Selvini-Palazzoli *et al.*, 1973.

Current Notions Related to Family Dysfunction

The phrase "dysfunctional features" has been used above as a pre-systematic, non-scientific designation for the kind of targets to which the family play therapist should aim his playful arrows. For the therapist to be able to mark and delineate such targets, he should be equipped with a more rigorous, theory-based characterization of the class of phenomena in hand.

To the best of my knowledge, such a complete theoretical characterization is still a task for the future. However, the current family systems literature abounds with partially explicated relevant notions. The list includes concepts such as the following:

   (a) "dysfunctional (or 'faulty', 'anomalous', etc.) family rules" (cf. for

instance, Ariel, Carel and Tyano, 1984; Ariel, 1987; Jackson, 1965; Paterson, 1980);
(b) "dysfunctional (or 'faulty', 'anomalous', etc.) interaction patterns";
(c) "dysfunctional (or 'faulty', 'anomalous', etc.) interaction cycles" (cf. Andolfi, 1979; Bodin, 1981), etc.

What characterizes these notions is that they locate dysfunction in problematic habits of interpersonal communication. Some of these patterns have been analyzed, classified into distinct types and named, e.g. "double bind" (Bateson *et al.*, 1956; Watzlawick, 1968); "detouring" (Minuchin, 1974); "strange loops" (Cronen, Johnson and Lannamann, 1982); "hierarchical incongruity" (Madanes, 1982), etc. Other such patterns have not been described yet. Each therapist has to locate, isolate and characterize them in the families he works with.

Dysfunctional Family Programs

As claimed above, the current relevant notions do not yet amount to a full-fledged systematic theory of family dysfunction. Therefore I have set myself the task of developing such a theory.

The first step in constructing the theory was to attempt to synthesize and explicate the current achievements in the framework of a uniform theoretical language. I asked myself: which kind of conceptual and terminological vocabulary would capture the essence of family dysfunction best?

In the course of my efforts to find the denominator common to all the current theoretical descriptions of faulty interaction patterns in families, I came to realize that every such pattern, however termed, had the following characteristic: It is *self-defeating, due to errors in the use of the relevant information.*

This realization led me to the answer to the question posed above: *The theoretical framework most suitable to serve as a model for family dysfunction is that of information processing.*

Elaborating on the information-processing metaphor, one can liken the family to a group of goal-oriented "human computers". Each family member is "programmed" to take in information from the other family members, interpret and process it according to certain fixed routines and output information to the other family members. Information can also be stored in and retrieved from the family's pool of memories. Input can also be obtained from, and output transmitted to, family-external sources.

The stable information-processing routines, which in other conceptual frameworks have been termed, as mentioned above, "family rules", "interaction patterns", "interaction cycles", etc. will be designated "family programs" in the information-processing model. This is of course an allusion to computer programs.

Some family programs are self-defeating. They prevent family members from reaching their own goals with respect to other family members. Such programs include, to use computer scientists' familiar jargon, "bugs", that is, fundamental errors which abuse or distort the goal-relevant information in characteristic manners. These are the *dysfunctional family programs*. Such programs reduce the family's ability to attend to the welfare and happiness of its members.

Let me spell out these ideas in more detail. Here is a brief account of the main points:

The basic structure of a dysfunctional family program—goals and plans. A dysfunctional family program comprises the *goals* and the self-defeating *plans* of all the family members. The *goals* define the degree of intimacy and control each of the family members wants to achieve with respect to the other family members. The *plan* for reaching the goal consists of the *input* received by a family member from another family member, the receiver's *interpretation* of the input and the *output* the latter has decided to produce on the basis of this interpretation.

Interpretation of the input—personal (private) and interpersonal thoughts. In the second step of the plan, the family member interprets the input by attributing two kinds of thoughts to the person from whom he or she received the input. The first kind includes the other person's presumed private, asocial thoughts and feelings. The second kind includes his or her supposed thoughts with respect to other family members.

The types of errors in information processing that render the plan dysfunctional. The goal is unreachable if the plan includes errors ("bugs") which render the information processing fatally ineffective. There are two main kinds of such errors: *errors of amount* (too much or too little input or output information); the information-processing system is flooded, or, on the contrary, lacks the minimum amount of information it needs to function properly.

Errors of relevance. The plan fails to take relevant information into account, or, on the contrary, is infiltrated by confusing irrelevant information.

Now to the detailed discussion:

A Case Illustration

Nine-year-old Ezra was brought to therapy because of his violent behavior, directed mainly at his mother. I asked his mother to give me a detailed descrip-

tion of one event in which Ezra had displayed such behavior. She recounted the following episode, which had taken place in the afternoon:
    She told Ezra to sit down and do his homework. From the way she reproduced her own speech it was obvious that she had given him that instruction in a weak, whining tone of voice. He ignored her. He did not give any signs that he had heard her at all. Then she slumped into an armchair and just sat there with that tortured expression on her face. At that point he lost his temper. He started physically assaulting her, throwing things at her, until she held her temples and yelled in a crying voice: "Stop it, please stop it!"

When I had finished interviewing the parents and observing the family playing freely, I felt that I had enough information to attempt a tentative formulation of the dysfunctional program underlying Ezra's problematic behavior. I had grounds to suppose that Ezra and his mother shared the same goal: she wanted to control him and he wanted her to control him. However, his *plan*, provocation, incapacitated her, and her plan, capitulation, deprived him of appropriate parental control.

This is a quite typical state of affairs. In most of the cases treated by family therapy the family members' goals are mutually complementary, or at least not hopelessly incompatible. What makes their life hell is their abortive plans rather than any irremediably conflicting interests.

The respective *plans* of Ezra and his mother were faulty, because they included errors in the use of the relevant information. What I heard and saw in the interview and the observation led me to surmise that Ezra's conscious or unconscious decision to use provocativeness as a means for reaching his goal was based on assumptions such as:

"Mummy knows that I want her to control me."

"Mummy does not want to control me."

"If I make mummy angry, she will punish me."

These assumptions are all wrong. However, Ezra failed to use any information that would enable him to test their validity.

Likewise, his mother's plan seemed to be based on assumptions such as:

"Ezra provokes me because he does not like me."

"If I push him, he will like me even less."

These assumptions are also wrong. However, the mother failed to take into account information that could enable her to verify them.

Goals and plans. This example illustrates the basic structure of a dysfunctional family program. Each such program consists of the *goals* and the *self-defeating plans* of all the family members.

The goal of each family member involves at least one other family member. Examples of goals are:

to be closer to Daddy;
to get the children off my back;
to control my sister;
to prevent mother from dominating my sister;

It will be noted that all these goals have to do with *interpersonal distance* (intimacy) or with *interpersonal hierarchy* (dominance). This is not a coincidence. Numerous studies and case reports pertaining to family and other human systems have attested to the fact that these major human goals are the two main factors defining the structure of interrelations in a family (see for instance Andolfi, 1979; Minuchin, 1974; Olson, Russell and Sprenkle, 1983).

The information-processing and semiotic terminology proved particularly serviceable to the task of explicating the notion "self-defeating plans". This notion was defined as follows:

A family member's plan is a routine he or she has somehow devised. It is supposed to include the routes by which the family member hopes to reach his goal.

Each such routine includes the following steps:

Input. The family member attends to the information that seems to be relevant to his goal. For instance, the mother in the above example took notice of her son's provocative behavior.

Interpreting the input. Continuing the above example, the mother attributed her son's provocative behavior to his apparent dislike of her.

Output (decision on how to act). Due to this interpretation, the mother decided to sit back and refrain from taking any disciplinary measure.

It will be noticed that the mother's plan went wrong in the second step (interpreting the input). She failed to look for any confirming or disconfirming information.

The *input*, that is the external information attended to in the first step of the plan, consists solely of behavioral *raw material*. That is, it includes only observable behavioral features which can be directly grasped by one's senses—features of voice, touch or movement.

Interpreting the input—personal and interpersonal thoughts. In the second step of the plan (*interpretation of the input*) the family member attributes *meaning* to the raw material. The meaning can be of two kinds:

Personal, private thoughts and feelings. For example, a father noticed that his daughter's behavior changed. Unlike her usual self, she became very quiet and self-absorbed. He supposed that the girl was thinking about her dog that had got lost (an inner thought). He assumed that she was sad because she missed her dog (an inner feeling).

The thought and feeling that this father read into his daughter's behavioral raw material belonged to the latter's purely personal and private inner world. They were not related to the interactional communication between the two of them.

Thoughts connected with the state of interrelationships at the given moment (briefly "interpersonal thoughts". Returning to our set example, the mother interpreted Ezra's provocative behavior by saying to herself: "He provokes me because he does not like me". In this interpretation she attributed the interpersonal thought "I don't like her" to her son.

In the third step of the plan (*output—decision on how to act*) the family member decides on a course of action and acts upon this decision (produces output). This decision is influenced by his interpretation of the input. The mother in our example would decide over and over again to refrain from taking any disciplinary action against her son. This was her output (in this case a rather passive sort of response). Her decision on how to react was based on the way she interpreted her son's behavior.

Whereas in the second step of the plan the family member attributes meaning to the input, in the third step he produces meaningful behavior. The output does not consist just of behavioral raw material. It consists of the family member's private thoughts and feelings and interpersonal thoughts, as these are outwardly expressed in his external behavior.

There are a number of different kinds of interpersonal thoughts. This classification has been borrowed from the science of pragmatics, a branch of semiotics (see Austin, 1962; Bateson, 1972; Beaugrande, 1980; Gazdar, 1979; Keenan, 1971). The kinds relevant to us here are:

Presupposition. An interpersonal thought which represents an assumption that a family member holds about another family member's behavior. For example, the mother *presupposes* that her son provokes her because he does not like her.

Purpose. An interpersonal thought which specifies what a family member hopes to achieve by his output. For example, the son's *purpose* in provoking his mother is to compel her to set him limits.

Prediction. An interpersonal thought which foretells the possible results of one's output. For example, the mother *predicts* that her son will become more resentful if she punishes him.

A prediction should be distinguished from a presuppostion. The latter evaluates a family member's past or present behavior. The latter forecasts his future response to one's output.

Propositional attitude. An interpersonal thought which specifies the way in which a family member wants his output to be taken by another family member—as a joke, as a lie, as an ironic expression and so on.

For example, a father tells his son "I hate you" but his non-verbal behavior indicates that he is joking. He really wants these words to be taken by his son as an expression of love.

A Typology of Errors in Information Processing

What renders a family member's goal unreachable are "bugs", that is errors in the use of information that are built into the plan. These errors have been classified into two broad types: *errors of amount* and *errors of relevance.*

Errors of Amount

In order to reach his goal, the family member has to take in or send out just the right amount of information. If he floods himself or other family members with too much information, however relevant to his goal, or, on the contrary, avoids or holds back important information, his chances of reaching his goal are likely to be severely reduced.

The mother of a teenage daughter set herself the goal of helping her daughter to become more independent and self-reliant. Her plan for reaching this goal included pumping her daughter for information about every detail of her life out of the home (an excessive amount of input) and flooding her with useful suggestions (an excessive amount of output). Needless to say, this plan made the daughter even more dependent, less self-reliant than before.

A boy wanted his father to help him with his problems at school. However, when his father questioned him about these problems he was reluctant to enter into details (an insufficient amount of output). This prevented his father from giving him the kind of help he expected to get.

Errors of Relevance

Quite often a member's goal cannot be reached if his plan fails to take relevant information into account or, on the contrary, fails to get rid of irrelevant information.

Returning to our set example, the boy who used to provoke his mother was acting upon the *presuppositions* "Mummy knows that I want her to control me" and "Mummy does not want to control me". Both presuppositions were wrong. In fact his mother did want to control him (that was her goal), but did not know that he wanted her to. This boy's plan failed to take into account this crucial information.

In this case the failure to take relevant information into account is quite understandable. How could the boy guess his mother's unpronounced interpersonal thoughts? However, his plan failed to take into account even information that was plain and obvious. It included the prediction "If I make Mummy angry she will punish me". His own experience should have instructed him that this would never happen. However, the point is that he chose to ignore his own experience.

A husband wants more warmth and affection from his wife. She explains that she withholds her affection because she is taken aback by the aggressive way in which he imposes himself upon her and demands her love and attention. He ignores this explanation and starts accusing her of neglecting the house and the children. This latter output consists of irrelevant information, which takes him farther away from his own goal.

How to Formulate Dysfunctional Family Programs

Dysfunctional family programs may be molded into a standardized format, as follows:

Each program consists of three major parts:

(a) The goal of each family member with respect to another or other family members.
(b) The family member's plan for reaching each goal.
(c) The errors in information processing that make the plan self-defeating.

To illustrate, let me write a part of the dysfunctional program underlying the interactions between the mother and her son, which has been used as our set example above:

Mother's Goal

Control son.

Mother's Plan

INPUT—son's behavioral raw material.
    If this is considered necessary, the behavioral raw material can be described

in more detail, by specifying its characteristic spatial, motional, tactile and vocal features, as follows:

Son runs wildly toward mother, kicks a ball at her face and yells: "Goal!"
INTERPRETATION OF INPUT—

Presupposition

His *purpose* is to let me know that he does not like me.
OUTPUT—Try to ignore his provocative behavior.

Purpose

Reduce son's resentment:

Prediction

If I ignore his provocative behavior, he will become less hostile. He may even stop behaving this way, in accordance with my goal.

Errors in Information Processing

The *presupposition* is wrong. The mother has not attempted to find out what her son thinks the purpose of his own behavior is (*failure to take relevant information into account*). The *prediction* is also wrong. The mother should have learned from her own experience that inaction on her side causes her son to intensify rather than reduce his aggressive behavior. (Again, *failure to take relevant information into account*.)

Son's Goal

Be controlled by mother.

Son's Plan

INPUT—Mother's passive behavior.
Mother sits quietly, saying nothing, doing nothing, ignoring my provocations.
INTERPRETATION OF INPUT—

Presuppositions

Mother knows what my goal is. She does not want to control me.
OUTPUT—Provoke mother (e.g. by kicking a ball in her face).

Purpose

Force mother to set me limits, in accordance with my goal.

Prediction

If I make her very angry she will take disciplinary action.

Errors in Information Processing:

The *presuppositions* are wrong. If the boy attempted to find this out, he would be surprised to learn that his mother's goal was the same as his. He would also discover that she had no idea what his goal was (*failure to take relevant information into account*).

The *prediction* is also wrong. He should have learned from his own experience that his mother would never take any disciplinary action, even if he made her very angry (again, *failure to take relevant information into account*).

The above program is quite simple. Usually dysfunctional programs are more complex. Their complexity is due to the need to change the plan to meet different kinds of real or apparent obstacles on the way to the goal. Here for instance is an informal presentation of the plan of a boy whose goal is to keep his mother to himself:

If mother is busy doing something engage her by pretending to suffer pain.
If mother is interacting with younger brother, engage her by hitting brother.
If mother is interacting with Daddy, engage her by talking loudly.

Put in the standardized format proposed above, a characteristic plan will exhibit, schematically, the following general structure:

IF INPUT is Xi
THEN INTERPRET THE INPUT IN MANNER Yi
AND PRODUCE OUTPUT Zi;
IF INPUT IS Xj
THEN INTERPRET THE INPUT IN MANNER Yj
AND PRODUCE OUTPUT Zj

And so forth.

The terms "goal" and "plan" may give the misleading impression that family members are assumed to consciously and intentionally strive toward definite aims and wittingly direct their steps toward these aims. This is not so. On the contrary, in most cases family members seem to be unaware of their goals and plans. Dysfunctional programs, as formulated above, should be viewed as hypothetical theoretical constructions, created by the therapist, which purport to approximate the subconscious rules underlying the family members' behavior. In this respect, our formulations resemble a grammar of a natural language. A speaker of a language speaks naturally. He is not aware of the grammatical rules to which his utterances conform. The professional linguist attempts to explicate and formulate these rules in an appropriate theoretical language.

How Can Presenting Problems be Explained by Family Dysfunction?

As stated earlier, one of the basic tenets of systemic family therapy is that symptoms in the individual are at least partly explained by dysfunctions in his or her family system. In the theoretical framework presented above, family dysfunction has been hypothesized to reside in dysfunctional family programs or, more precisely, in information-processing errors which make the family members' plans self-defeating. Our task here is to show how symptoms presented by individual members are related to such underlying dysfunctional features.

One class of symptoms includes behavioral manifestations which form a part of the *output* generated by dysfunctional plans.

Ezra's provocative behavior with his mother in our set example above belongs to this class. It is a part of the *output* produced by his self-defeating plan for reaching his goal of forcing his mother to set him limits. His choice of provocative behavior as *output* is, as shown above, dictated by his erroneous interpersonal thoughts with respect to his mother.

Ron's symptoms, social passivity and under-achievement in school (see the illustrative case presented in the Introduction) belong to this class too.

Symptoms of this class are *direct* products of dysfunctional family programs. Another class consists of *indirect* products. Dysfunctional family programs are major generators of emotional distress. Since they are self-defeating, they are inherently frustrating. Therefore families whose major interactions are governed by dysfunctional programs produce in their members distress reactions such as tantrums, fears, depression and psychosomatic symptoms.

Ron (see above) used to suffer from secondary symptoms such as depression and listlessness. These were indirect products, side effects, of his primary symptoms.

Major dysfunctional programs seriously hamper the family's ability to deal effectively with their ordinary everyday tasks and long-range developmental missions. A third class of symtpoms consists of long-range adverse effects of such chronic malfunctioning. For example, parents' chronic inability to agree on the proper way of setting limits to their child can lead to life-long social problems in the latter.

A family play therapist should be able to identify those errors of information processing in the family's dysfunctional programs that breed such problems in the individual family members. He has to mark these errors of information processing as the ultimate targets of his play therapeutic interventions.

Identifying the errors is not enought though. In order to be able to *correct* the errors, the therapist has to understand the cognitive and emotional forces that keep them up. And then he must employ such therapeutic play tools as are potent enough to shake and topple or dissolve these forces. These matters are discussed in the following chapters.

Summary

The main concepts discussed in this chapter may be summarized as follows:

The familiar notions "dysfunctional (faulty, anomalous, self-defeating) family rules (interaction patterns, cycles, etc.)" are *explicated* by the concept "dysfunctional family programs".

A family program *consists of* each family member's *goals* of *intimacy* or *control* with respect to the other family members, and his or her *plan* for reaching these goals.

Schematically, a plan exhibits the following general structure:

IF INPUT is Xi
THEN INTERPRET THE INPUT IN MANNER Yi
AND PRODUCE OUTPUT Zi

In *interpreting* the *input* and *deciding on* the *output*, family members produce *interpersonal thoughts* such as *presuppositions, purposes, predictions* and *propositional attitudes*.

What makes family programs dysfunctional are *errors* ("bugs") in plans. There are two major kinds of such errors: *errors of amount* (too much or too little information for goal) and *errors of relevance* (no relevant information or presence of information irrelevant for goal).

Symptoms in the individual family members are either *a part of the output*, generated by dysfunctional plans or *short-term* and *long-range adverse effects of distress* produced by such plans.

CHAPTER 2

Make-believe Play

In Chapter 1 the targets of strategic family play therapy have been delimited and marked. It has been stated that play therapeutic interventions labor to cure the family of its problematic interaction patterns. In this chapter and the next we shall get acquainted with the bows and arrows aimed at these targets, namely play and its therapeutic properties.

Our attention will focus primarily on the kind of play which has been termed, variably, "make-believe play" (Ariel, 1984; Singer, 1973), "symbolic play" (Piaget, 1962) or "fantasy play" (Klinger, 1971). A trainee who wants to master strategic family play therapy must acquire a good grip of the meaning of the very concept "make-believe play". He should also become acquainted with some of those properties of this genre of human behavior that are intimately interrelated with the person's inner emotional world and outer world of social relationships. Such close familiarity is necessary if the trainee is to learn how to use the full capacity of make-believe play as a diagnostic and therapeutic tool. When family members play make-believe games together the structure and contents of their play expose covert layers of their emotional interrelations. Observing and analyzing such games is like mentally X-raying the family. Well-defined structural and psychosocial properties of make-believe play can be deliberately used as change agents. Make-believe play can also be employed as a multi-modal medium of therapeutic communication. All these sophistic-ated applications require a thorough understanding of make-believe play and its distinctive features.

A Formal Explication of the Concept "Make-believe Play"

Make-believe play is primarily a complex mental activity and only secondarily outward behavior. In other words, the player's verbal or non-verbal behavior is transformed into make-believe play if, simultaneously with the explicit be-havior the player implicitly makes the following "mental claims". (The linguis-tic neologisms "realification" and "identication" (see below) are deliberate.

Their use stresses the fact that these words are scientific terms coined for our purposes and not ordinary English words.)

Realification

Some entity which at this very moment exists only in my own mind and not in external reality is not in my own mind but in external reality. This claim is of course self-contradictory and the player is aware of this.

Example. A playing child says: "There's a lion here now." The actual behavior in this case is purely verbal. The child knows that the particular lion he has in mind is just a mental image and not something which belongs to external reality, but still he is making this claim. He *realifies* the image of the lion. The latter becomes *realified.*

The realified entity is the *signified* of the make-believe play act, that is, its thematic content. The player verbalizes this mental claim of realification (as in the above example), or selects a certain material or behavioral entity (i.e. his own or his playmates' actions) from the external environment and makes (simultaneously with the mental claim of realification) the following mental claim about it:

Identication

This real material or behavioral entity that I have selected from the external environment is not what it is. It has literally become the entity I am realifying at this very moment.

Example. The child can select a toy lion or just a piece of wood and view it as the realified lion. He can also produce body gestures and growling sounds and view himself as the realified lion. The toy lion, the piece of wood or he himself has, as it were, ceased to be what each had been and become a real lion. The toy, the piece of wood or the player have been *identicated* with the realified lion.

The identicated entity is the *signifier* of the act of make-believe play, that is, the sign which overtly expresses the signified thematic content. Thus, the toy, the piece of wood or the player himself has become the signifier for the signified content "lion".

The terms "signifier" and "signified" were introduced by de Saussure (1972). They mark the distinction between the entity that represents the content of a symbol and the symbol itself. These terms were adopted and applied to make-believe play by Piaget (1962).

The player also makes, simultaneously with the mental claims of realification and identication, the following third mental claim, a claim about the claims of realification and identication.

Playfulness

The above two claims, realification and identication, have not been made seriously, but playfully. They are nonsensical, self-contradictory claims to which I am not really committed and I am making them just for the fun of it.

It will be noted that the mental claim of identication presupposes the mental claim of realification but not vice versa. For example, the child may pretend that a lion is present in the immediate vicinity and verbalize this by saying "There's a lion here now" without identifying any object or gesture in the immediate vicinity (such as a toy lion, a piece of wood or his own gestures and voice) as the pretended "lion". But if he does identify some element in the immediate vicinity as the pretended "lion", he necessarily also pretends that the presence of this lion in the vicinity is a real event, an actual state of affairs in external reality at the time of the play.

(For more detailed discussions of this definition see Ariel, 1984; Fein, 1989.)

Psychosocial Characteristics of Make-believe Play

The definition of the concept "make-believe play" presented above specifies the necessary and sufficient conditions for certain mental-behavioral events to be correctly designated as make-believe play. However, this definition does not yet constitute an exhaustive description of all those functions and properties of make-believe play which are relevant to clinical assessment and therapy. These psychological and social functions and properties have been investigated in numerous research studies and theoretical and clinical works. (A small sample includes Amen and Renison, 1954; Curry and Arnaud, 1974; Erikson, 1965; Garvey and Kramer, 1989; Gomez and Yawkley, 1983; Fein, 1989; Klinger, 1971; Yawkley, 1986.)

Some of the ideas and findings of these studies have been integrated by the present writer in a semiotic, information-processing framework. Here is a brief summary of those parts of this theoretical integration that are relevant to strategic family play therapy, in particular to the explication of therapeutically relevant properties of play in Chapter 3.

Make-believe Play as a Regulator of Emotional Arousal

Psychologically, make-believe play, along with dreams and fantasy, may be viewed as a device for regulating the level of emotional arousal around sensitive, emotionally laden themes in the child's psyche (see Klinger, 1971; Singer, 1973).

In what sense is make-believe play such a device? Most of the themes in a child's play are emotionally significant. The child's play centers around subjects which are associated in his mind with intense fear, anger, joy, or sadness. For example, if a boy is angry at his father, who punishes him severely, he will often introduce a punitive father-figure into his make-believe games. When he introduces these emotionally laden themes into his play, his level of emotional arousal is going up. For instance, when he plays as if a toy father-figure punishes a toy child-figure, he is influenced by his own productions and becomes more angry and fearful than before. If his emotions become over-heated, he "cools himself down" by introducing less arousing, more soothing themes into his play (e.g. he makes the father-figure milder, less punitive) until he calms down. Then he is ready to step up his level of arousal again, and the emotionally charged themes come back, and so forth.

Let me illustrate this by an example: six-year-old Gabby used to introduce into his make-believe games, over and over again, the theme of "drowning". After making objects such as submarines or sailors "drown" he would exhibit visible signs of anxiety. At this point he would introduce various soothing or protective themes into his play until he calmed down and was ready to resume the "drowning" games. Once he turned the submarine that had been drowned into "a boaty submarine", a hybridization of a boat that floats on the surface and a submarine that dives. Apparently, this measure failed to alleviate his fear, so he had to take another, stronger one: he introduced a life-saving "red cross" submarine into his make-believe ocean (see Ariel, 1983).

The present discussion will center around the following questions:

It has been stated above that the player arouses himself emotionally up to an almost unbearable degree by introducing, over and over again, themes associated with unpleasant emotions, such as fear and anger, into his play. How can this phenomenon be accounted for? Why would a child cause himself discomfort by reminding himself of unpleasant themes which arouse fear or anger in him?

What are "emotionally laden themes" like? What are their properties and functions? How exactly does the regulation mechanism associated with them work?

The Prevalence of Unpleasant Themes: Beyond the Pleasure Principle

The question of why the child introduces themes associated with unpleasant emotions such as fear or anger over and over again into his play has been asked and discussed by many theoreticians and researchers since Freud's *Beyond the Pleasure Principle* (Freud, 1922). Freud himself classed this phenomenon together with post-traumatic repetition-compulsion. It has also been associated with the prevalence of themes related to emotional stress in fantasy and dreams (see Amen and Renison, 1954; Beck, 1970; Foulkes, 1978; Gilmore, 1966; Klinger, 1971; Singer, 1973). The main explanations given to this phenomenon (some backed with empirical research) have been:

Habituation

When the emotionally laden theme is retrieved from long-term memory over and over again, the conscious mind becomes habituated to it and the emotion becomes numbed, as is the case in the habituation of the perceptual mechanism to external stimuli (see Grayson, Foa and Steketee, 1982; Marshall, 1988; Shahar and Marks, 1980; Watson, Gaird and Marks, 1972).

Cognitive Restructuring

When the emotionally laden theme is retrieved from long-term memory it becomes associated with new perceptions and cognitions which "explain it away" and give it another meaning, so that it becomes less threatening. (See Foa and Kozak, 1986; Hahnloser, 1974; Ellis, Thomas and Rodruigez, 1984.)

De-conditioning

When the emotionally laden theme is retrieved, it becomes associated with pleasant stimuli, different from the stressing stimuli in the context in which it was originally taken into the psychological system (see Hahnloser, 1974).

Mastery

When the person retrieves the emotionally laden theme he controls it, becomes its master rather than victim. (See Buhler, 1930; Freud, 1937; Peller, 1959; Erikson, 1940.)

These explanations apply also to the "working through" of stressful memories in psychodynamic psychotherapy (see Fine, 1973). They have been evoked in attempts to account for the effectiveness of cognitive-behavioral therapeutic techniques such as flooding, in which the patient is overwhelmed with stress-inducing stimuli (see Marshall, Gauthier and Gordon, 1979).

Emotives

Important emotionally laden themes in people's psyche, such as anger at father being punitive, have been discussed in many studies, under various names, e.g. Freud's *complexes* (1917), Piaget's *affective schemas* (1962), Izard's *affective-cognitive structures* (1978) and Klinger's *current concerns* (Klinger, 1971; Klinger *et al.*, 1980). I use the term "emotives" and argue, with the scholars listed below, that the child's make-believe play centers round his or her emotives. Make-believe play is in this respect just one special case of a much wider range of phenomena. In fact, I believe, with a number of other scholars, that emotives are one of the major factors, if not the major factor, in regulating people's mental life and behavior.

See Freud, 1922; Klein, 1960; Erikson, 1940; Piaget, 1962; Singer, 1973 and Klinger, 1971.

A Definition of "Emotive"

"Emotive" is an inner mental state, characterized by a predisposition to respond with a particularly high level of arousal of a specific emotion such as anger, fear, joy, sadness, etc. to every external or internal stimulus which is subjectively, privately associated in one's mind with a definite theme.

To illustrate: the theme of "violence and oppression directed at weak, unprotected victims" is privately and subjectively associated in Shabtai's mind with a whole range of memories and perceptions. For example, when he recalls or sees a broken glass this immediately evokes this central theme in his mind, because the glass reminds him of a scene he witnessed of police violence against innocent victims, in which a person's eyeglasses broke. When Shabtai perceives or recalls something that evokes this central theme in him he becomes very sad and angry. He has a strong predisposition to respond with arousal of anger and sadness to every such stimulus. He has an *emotive*: "sadness and anger associated with the theme of oppression and violence against innocent victims".

The concept "emotive", as defined above, is highly relevant to the present discussion of the psychological functions and properties of make-believe play. My central hypothesis, already stated informally above, is that the themes of make-believe play center round the child's emotives. These themes are memory traces that are privately and subjectively associated in the child's mind with a definite, central, emotionally-laden theme.

Five-year-old Shalom was observed playing during a period in which his parents were going through the painful process of divorce. Here are some of the themes (signifieds) that appeared in his make-believe play at that period: a house with a broken roof; a tent in a storm; and collapsing towers in an earthquake. The occurrence of these themes in his play was accompanied by visible behavioral manifestations of unrest and anxiety. All of these signified contents seemed to be privately and subjectively associated in Shalom's mind with the central theme of "the breakdown of the home". At that period this boy had a strong predisposition to respond with an arousal of fear to every internal or external stimulus which was privately and subjectively associated in his mind with this central theme. This was his main emotive at that period, and most of the signified in his make-believe play centered around this emotive.

The signified (e.g. the house with the broken roof, the tent in the storm) may be said to *symbolize* the central theme of "the breakdown of the home". This central theme is considered the *underlying meaning* of these *symbols*. (See Piaget, 1962.)

Here are some hypotheses about emotives:

Hypothesis 1. Every person has, in each period of his or her life a small number of emotives. There are emotives which accompany a person throughout his or her life, and there are emotives which dwell inside a person for relatively short periods. There are universal emotives, that is, emotives which are present in every human being everywhere and at all times, such as fear of death. There are emotives that belong to particular groups of people (e.g. separation anxiety in babies) and there are emotives which are restricted to specific individuals in specific life-stages.

Hypothesis 2. People tend to interpret reality according to their emotives. That is to say, if a person encounters a certain stimulus, he or she associates it with at least one of his emotives. The criteria for this classification are not logical but subjective, and they are based on the person's private associations.

The above example of the broken glass is relevant here. Shabtai has an emotive "sadness and anger associated with the theme of oppression and violence against innocent victims". When he sees the broken glass he immediately relates to this emotive through a chain of associations which are private and subjective.

This hypothesis implies that not only the choice of signified content in the child's make-believe play is influenced by his emotives, but also his choice of signifiers. Let us return to Shalom, the boy whose make-believe play centered around the theme of "breakdown of the home". One day this boy was offered a wide selection of toys and playthings, but his attention turned instantly, out of all the wonderful toys on the floor, to an old plastic toy house with a broken roof. He started "fixing the roof". His attention and perception seemed to be directly affected by his central emotive. He classified the play stimuli offered to him according to his emotives and chose one that fitted his own subjective, private associations related to this emotive.

Hypothesis 3. A person grades every stimulus he or she has assigned to a particular emotive of his on a scale, specifying the intensity of the specific emotion which characterizes this emotive. Shalom graded "a collapsing tower" as very high on the scale of fear associated with his emotive, and "an unstable tent" as relatively low on this scale.

Hypothesis 4. Every person has an internal mechanism which regulates the intensity of the emotional arousal associated with his or her emotives. This mechanism regulates to some extent the operation of the various psychological processes, such as attention, perception, memory, thinking and motor action. These psychological, information-processing faculties "prefer", as it were, data which are graded higher on the scale of emotional arousal associated with one's emotives. That is, such emotionally loaded data will be more readily attended to, perceived, thought about, recalled or included in one's verbal or non-verbal output than other data. However, the feedback received from these emotionally powerful data in the course of their being processed can fan the player's emotions to such an extent that they go beyond his tolerance capacity. When this comes about, the information-processing devices "switch off". In such a case the data that are graded high on the emotional scale are kept out and milder data are let in. When the psychological system is in such a "cooled down" state, extremely emotionally loaded data are less likely to be attended to, perceived, thought about, recalled or included in overt behavior.

A woman is expecting her first baby. During her period of pregnancy one of her major emotives is "excitement, mixed with fear related to her condition and her expected baby". There are stimuli which in her own mind are graded quite high on the scale of emotional intensity associated with this emotive, e.g. a picture of a fetus. Other relevant stimuli are graded lower on this scale, e.g. pets, which remind her of babies. Imagine her leafing through a magazine which includes an article, accompanied with color photographs, about the development of the fetus inside the uterus, an article about congenital malformation in babies and an article about household pets. She would be highly likely to get interested in the first article. She would probably read it through, think about it, recall it and discuss it with her friends. She would probably take a somewhat more moderate interest in the article about pets. However, the article about congenital pathology would perhaps arouse intense anxiety in her. She would perhaps decide not to read it and try very hard to forget all about it.

These hypotheses take us back to the less formal discussion of make-believe play as a regulator of emotions above. Again, one can say that the following process applies to the child's make-believe play: his choice of signifiers and signified is regulated by his emotives and by the emotional intensity of the stimuli associated with these emotives. He will be more likely to pay attention to, perceive and perform actions with external stimuli that are privately and subjectively associated in his mind with his emotives, especially if these stimuli arouse particularly intense emotions in him. He will turn these stimuli into signifiers in his make-believe play. The previously mentioned boy was offered a wide selection of toys, but ignored all except the house with the broken roof, which he turned into a signifier in his make-believe play. This pathetic toy was associated in his own mind with the intensely feared idea of "the breakdown of the home". Likewise, a player is particularly likely to retrieve from his memory thematic content which is associated with his emotives and with high emotional intensity. This becomes the *signified* of the signifiers he has picked. The above-mentioned toy became the signifier for the signified content "collapsing roof", an image born in the boy's mind and retrieved from his long-term memory. This image is closely associated with his emotive.

The very introduction into play of emotionally straining signifiers and signified brings up the child's level of emotional arousal. If this surpasses a certain prescribed peak of tolerance, the system "cools down" or is "switched off". At this point thematic content is retrieved from memory, which is still associated with the same emotive, but is not so emotionally loaded. These become signified in the play. For example, Shalom would stop playing with the theme of "a collapsing roof" and would introduce instead the theme of "a tent shaken by wind", which in his subjective mind is less anxiety provoking. Furthermore, his attention would be turned to external stimuli that are less arousing, e.g. a piece of cloth which can represent "a tent". These will become the signifiers for this milder signified content.

The introduction of more benign, less threatening signifiers and signified into the play reduces the player's level of emotional arousal, so that soon he becomes ready to re-introduce more arousing signifiers and signified into his play.

Organizing the Signified around the Emotives

The signified content of a child's make-believe play can be classified and organized around the central themes characterizing the child's emotives and the intersecting grade of emotional intensity. For example, the themes in the play of a six-year-old boy were classified and organized as shown in Table 1.

The same classification and organization can be derived empirically by a systematic analysis of observations of the child's make-believe play, using a technique called "componential analysis". This technique is presented in detail and illustrated in Ariel, 1983.

The following predictions can be made on the basis of Table 1: the child is highly likely to introduce signified content that belongs to the thematic categories listed in a table such as this one into his make-believe play. He will prefer themes which belong to the upper row of the table. However, if his emotional

Table 1   Organization of themes around the child's emotives.

Central theme of emotive: loss of love	Sub-categories of the central theme		
	disappearance of love object	love object denies love	love object is away
Grading of emotional intensity (sadness)			
intense sadness	e.g. Mother-figure vanishes into thin air	e.g. Mother-figure refuses to feed	e.g. Father-figure lives on a distant planet
mild sadness	e.g. Mother-figure disappears but is found again	e.g. Mother-figure is forced to feed	e.g. Father-figure lives in a neighbouring house

arousal surpasses a certain peak, he will step down to signified contents that belong to the same categories, but to lower rows in the table. When he has cooled down he will go back to themes belonging to the highest row, and so on repeatedly. Empirical investigations of children's make-believe play confirm these predictions (see Ariel, 1983).

Social Communicational Properties and Functions of Make-believe Play

Make-believe play can be a solitary activity or a social activity. The make-believe play of small groups of children has been termed "sociodramatic play" (see Smilansky, 1968). This form of play is a major vehicle by which children conduct their social transactions.

To illustrate this let us have a look at the following scene, in which two five-year-old girls play a sociodramatic make-believe game in the kindergarten playground (see Ariel, 1992):

DINA. Ruth! Come here! Sit on this horse!
The "horse" is a red tube, raised above the ground on metal stands. Dina climbs up the tube, seating herself astride. She moves her straightened arms forwards and backwards, apparently denoting "riding".
DINA. Halt!
Ruth climbs up and sits on the horse in front of her.
RUTH. Move on!
She moves her straightened arms backwards and forward.

RUTH. First let's pretend the baby girl is in front and the mummy is behind, and then let's pretend you allow your baby to get lost, because, after all, you have a dog. Children, when they get lost, the dog gets them back. Come on! Let's pretend you have arrived home. You told your little girl: "Sweetie! you may get lost!" So, are you getting off?

DINA *(gets off)*. Yes. I am going home. I want you to work for me.

Dina walks some distance away from the tube.

RUTH. Mummy! Mummy! Get me this bag! I need it! Here is a blanket!

Ruth gets off the tube. She picks up a metal frame from an old table and places it on top of the tube.

RUTH. The bag.

Her intonation indicates that she is listing objects. She picks up a large piece of cloth and places it on top of the tube. She says: a blanket (pause) and food. She runs toward the center of the yard, picks up an old tea kettle. She puts various small pieces of junk inside it, until it is full. She carries it to the tube and places it on top of it. She picks up an old plastic shopping bag and fills it with little stones.

RUTH. I haven't finished yet. I am gathering food.

She places the bag with the stones on top of the tube. She climbs on the tube, starts "riding", moving her legs inwards and outwards rhythmically, calling.

RUTH. Move!

Dina gets into an old metal cot about three yards away.

DINA. Ruth! Let's pretend you are a mummy-baby. You are the queen but you are a baby girl. You are my queen-baby. All this *(sweeping the yard with her arm)* is your nursery.

RUTH. But let's pretend I didn't come to the nursery today. Move!

Dina comes close to her.

DINA. You should say "Halt!" too! *(pause)* Sweetie, here's some more food for you!

She hands Ruth a little metal net.

RUTH. Now I have arrived at the village. Fantastic! I've arrived at the village!

DINA. Let's pretend we live together in this village too.

RUTH. No, let's pretend you are at home and this is a far far away village.

On the face of it, the signified thematic content in this observation has nothing to do with the interrelations between these two girls. However, if one looks at the interpersonal messages transmitted through this semantic content one will see that the signified, thematic content was made up by the girls as part of their respective *plans* for achieving certain interpersonal *goals*. (See Chapter 1.) The choice of signified themes serves certain social-communicational functions. The girls not only express their inner world and regulate their level of emotional arousal related to their emotives through this game, but also conduct their interrelations through it.

The girls' play in this scene seems to be governed by the following rules:

Dina's Goal

To keep Ruth close to her and control her.

Dina's Plan

Step 1—Tell Ruth to stay close to me and obey me.
Step 2—If Ruth's behavior indicates that she does not agree to act according to Step 1, let her do what she wants and even help her, but attempt to modify or reframe her behavior in a way that suits my goal.

Ruth's Gaol

To keep away from Dina and her attempts to control her.

Ruth's Plan

Step 1—Accept Dina's suggestions, but in carrying them out modify them or reframe them so that they suit my goal.
Step 2—If Step 1 does not work, initiate acts that suit my goal even if they contradict Dina's goal.

Let us have a look at a number of details which seem to support this formulation of their goals and plans.

At the onset of the observation Dina gives Ruth an outright instruction to approach the horse and sit on it, apparently behind herself. She says "Halt!" to stop the imaginary horse and invites Ruth to climb on it. This seems to be in accordance with Step 1 of her supposed plan (tell Ruth to come close to me and obey me). Ruth, although Dina plays the role of "mummy" and she the role of her "baby girl", does not climb on "the horse" and sit behind Dina, as might be expected, but climbs on and sits in front of Dina, and then says "Move!" to start the horse moving. This detail in Ruth's behavior seems to be in accordance with Step 1 in her supposed plan: accept Dina's suggestions but in carrying them out modify them or reframe them so that they suit my goal of not letting Dina control me. She agrees to play the "baby" role, but behaves like "a mummy". She accepts Dina's invitation to ride the horse with her, but assumes the leader's position on horseback and controls the horse. Then she tells Dina: "Allow your baby to get lost, because, after all, you have a dog. Children, when they get lost, the dog gets them back . . . Are you getting off?" This, again, seems to be in accordance with Step 1 in Ruth's supposed plan: accept Dina's suggestions, but in carrying them out, modify them or reframe them so that they suit my goal of keeping away from Dina and her attempts to control me. She accepts Dina's role as mummy and asks for her permission to get lost. To make a concession to Dina's goal of controlling her she invents the dog. In response to this, Dina climbs off the horse, walks away a few steps and says "I am going home, I want you to work for me". On the level of signifiers Dina seems to act according to Ruth's purpose of keeping away from her. However, she attempts to keep control over Ruth by suggesting that she work for her. This accords with Step 2 in her plan. If Ruth's behavior indicates that she does not agree to act according to Step 1, let her do what she wants and even help her, but attempt to modify or reframe her behavior in a way that suits my goal. Ruth ignores this and goes on with the preparation for a long journey. When Dina realizes that Ruth is serious about it, she tries a new tactic: she gets into a cot and says: "Ruth, let's pretend you are a mummy-baby. You are the queen but you are a baby girl. You are my queen-baby. All this (*sweeping the yard with her hand*) is your nursery". In this way Dina acts again according to Step 2 in her supposed plan. She makes a concession to Ruth's attempt to get away from her and her control in two ways: by making Ruth a queen-baby, both independent and subjected to her, and by turning the whole playground into a nursery, so that even when Ruth is away she is enclosed by Dina's own boundary and thus controlled. Ruth solves this by saying: "Let's pretend I didn't come to the nursery today". Now Ruth acts according to Step 2 in her plan: if Step 1 does not work, initiate acts that suit my goal even if they contradict Dina's goal.

When Ruth arrives at a far away village, Dina makes another attempt to achieve her goal through Step 2 of her plan. She says: "Let's pretend we live together in this village too", but Ruth rejects this attempt as well by saying: "You are at home and this is a far far away village", again in accordance with Step 2 of her plan.

The similarity between this analysis and the analysis of the dysfunctional family program in Chapter 1 is striking. The informal analysis just presented can be easily reformulated in terms of *pragmatics* (interpersonal thoughts) such as *purpose, presupposition* and *prediction*) and information-processing plans. This gives some idea about how observations of conjoint family make-believe play sessions can be used as a source of relevant diagnostic information. (See Chapter 8.)

Summary

This chapter has examined the main formal and psychosocial characteristics of make-believe play that are relevant to strategic family play therapy.

The definition of make-believe play and its cognitive and semiotic correlates are displayed in outline form in Table 2.

Table 2 Formal definition of make-believe play and its cognitive and semiotic correlates.

Defining "mental claims"	Cognitive correlates	Semiotic correlates
Realification ("There's a lion here now")	Mental image retrieved from long-term memory and treated as immediately present	Signified thematic content of play
Identication (Toy lion and my gestures and voice are the lion)	Material and behavioral entities from immediate vicinity are identified with retrieved mental image	Signifiers for signified thematic content
Playfulness statement (realification and identication have not been made seriously)	Information-processing operation canceling the other two operations	A meta-statement defining the make-believe attitude

The cognitive-affective functions of make-believe play may be summarized through a particular example. The following example is an attempted simulation of the information-processing steps hypothesized as underlying six-year-old Gabby's play of "drowning submarines", given above as an example:

Observed Play

Gabby makes a block representing a submarine "drowning" in a sandbox. Afterwards he starts pulling the block out of the sand, saying: "It's a boaty submarine". He leaves the block partly sunken in the sand, and looks around for other toys. He picks a case of doctor's instruments with a red-cross design on it, pushes it into the sand and says: "There was a red-cross submarine there".

Information-processing Steps

Image retrieved from memory. Gabby retrieves the image "submarine".

Does image belong to emotive? If no, retrieve another image; if yes, go to next step. Yes. "Submarine" belongs to emotive *fear of mortal danger*.

Retrieve other images associated with this emotive. Gabby retrieves "drowning".

Make the mental claim of realification about associated retrieved images. Gabby mentally claims: "The submarine is drowning here and now".

Retrieved images have become "signifieds", that is make-believe play themes.

Turn attention to features of external environment that remind you of these realified images. Gabby turns attention to the block, which reminds him of the realified image "submarine", and to the sand in the sandbox, which reminds him of the ocean.

Act upon these features to increase their similarity to realified images. Gabby pushes the block into the sand, alluding to a drowning submarine.

Make the mental claim of identication with respect to these features and acts. Gabby mentally claims that the block, the sand and his own actions are the drowning submarine.

These features and acts have become "signifiers" for the "signifieds".

Step up level of arousal of emotion associated with signifiers and signifieds. Gabby starts being afraid of his own play of "drowning submarine".

Make the mental claim of playfulnes. Gabby knows: this is not really a drowning submarine. It is just make-believe.

Is emotional arousal tolerable? If yes, go back to first step; if no, go to next step. No, Gabby's fear is too strong.

Introduce new signifiers and signified, which are not so loaded emotionally, and combine them with present signifiers and signifieds. Gabby, to calm himself down, starts pulling the block out of the sand. The emergence of the block above the surface of the sand reminds him of a boat, but its remaining part, which is still covered with sand, continues to be associated in his mind with the image of a submarine. The signified "boat" is less threatening than the signified "submarine". Therefore he calls the block "a boaty submarine".

Is emotional arousal tolerable now? If yes, go back to first step; if no, repeat last step. Gabby's fear is still strong. He comes across the case of doctor's instruments. This object evokes the image of a protective "red-cross submarine" in his mind. He introduces this image into his play as signified, with the doctor's case as its signifier.

The social-communicational functions of make-believe play can also be summarized by an attempted simulation of the covert information-processing steps lying behind a particular sociodramatic play interaction. Let me illustrate this with respect to an excerpt of the transcript of Dina and Ruth's sociodramatic play, given above as an example:

DINA. Ruth! Let's pretend you are a mummy-baby. You are the queen, but you are a baby girl. You are my queen-baby. All this *(sweeping the yard with her arm)* is your nursery.

RUTH. But let's pretend I did not come to the nursery today. Move!

Does the signified thematic content of my playmate's play match my goals?
Dina's hypothesized answer: No. My goals are to keep Ruth close to me and
control her. Ruth's play runs against these goals. She "rides the horse" alone
and wants to "get lost".

Can I achieve my goals directly? No. Ruth will resist me.

**Introduce signifieds which are likely to suit both my playmate's supposed
goals and my own goals.** Dina offers Ruth dominant roles ("mummy",
"queen") and allows her freedom of movement ("all this is yours"). Apparently, she believes these suggestions match Ruth's goals. However, she also
offers Ruth the role of a baby, and restricts her freedom of movement within an
imaginary "nursery". These suggestions suit her own goals.

The same steps can be applied to Ruth's response.

CHAPTER 3

Therapeutic Properties of Make-believe Play

The main feature of strategic family play therapy is the deliberate use of therapeutic properties of play as change-generating mechanisms. The relevant properties can be inferred from the formal definition of make-believe play and the discussion of its psychosocial properties in Chapter 2. The present chapter is devoted to listing, defining and illustrating these properties, and discussing their various applications in the therapeutic process.

"Play"-framing

This property derives from the fact that any verbal or non-verbal behavior can, at least in principle, be framed, or defined as make-believe play and in this way "become" or "be transformed into" make-believe play. It can be framed as make-believe play by its performer. All he has to do is make, implicitly or explicitly, the mental claims of *realification*, (optionally) *identification* and *playfulness* about this behavior (see Chapter 2). A verbal or non-verbal behavior can also be framed as make-believe play by another person, e.g. a therapist. In this case it will actually become, or be transformed into, make-believe play if it is declared as such by the other person. However, the performer of the behavior has to comply with this declaration. He has to take upon himself this reframing of his own behavior and agree to make the above-mentioned mental claims about it. Then his behavior will really become an act of make-believe play.

Six-year-old Nadav and his five-year-old sister Tal were having a row, beating one another. Their father came in, and threatened to punish them if they went on. Nadav said: "We are just playing", and continued beating Tal in a playful manner.

In this case the child himself reframed his behavior as "play" (see Bateson, 1972). Assuming that he was sincere and not just attempting to mislead his father, it may be said that from the moment he told his father "We are just playing" his behavior was actually transformed into a make-believe game. A scene of real fighting that existed in his mind only and not in external reality was *realified* by his own mental claim and became a *signified*. His own behavior was *identicated* with this signified by his own mental claim and became its *signifier*, and an attitude of *playfulness* was assumed with respect to these two mental claims.

Suppose the same scene took place in the therapeutic play room. The brother and sister started fighting and the therapist said: "It's nice to see how you are pretending to be fighting". As is often the case, the children were influenced by this suggestion and actually assumed an attitude of make-believe to their own behavior, which was thereby transformed into a make-believe game. In this imaginary sequence the play-framing was done by the therapist and accepted by the players.

Some years ago I had two sisters in therapy: twelve-year-old Maya and eight-year-old Galya. The latter was crippled. She was restricted to a wheelchair. Maya claimed that she could not stand Galya. She never failed to show her hostility.

My acquaintance with Maya led me to believe that her animosity against Galya concealed her deep concern. She felt heavy, burdening responsibility toward her sister. In the terminology introduced in Chapter 1 it could be said that her aggressive attitude was a part of her *dysfunctional plan* for achieving the *goal* of disengaging herself from Galya.

In one of our sessions Maya told Galya: "I can't stand you. I really hate you". I intervened and told her: "I want you to play a make-believe game in which you say to your sister exactly the same words that you've just said".

In this case the play-framing was applied not to the original occurrence of its target verbal behavior, but to a replication of this original behavior. The play-reframing had been suggested before the actual occurrence of this replication. But the act of play-framing itself had the same effect. Maya agreed to repeat her words and reframe them as make-believe play. Her words were actually "transformed" into make-believe play.

What was going on in Maya's mind when she repeated her words as make-believe play? The following analysis can be inferred from the very definition of the concept "make-believe play" in Chapter 2.

The make-believe attitude implies that Maya was making the mental claims of *realification*, *identication* and *playfulness* with respect to the words she was uttering.

The mental claims of *realification* and *playfulness* entail: "My hatred does not exist in the real world. I am just realifying something that exists only within my own mind. I don't *really* hate her".

The mental claims of *identication* and *playfulness* imply: "The one who hates and the one who is being hated are not really me and my sister, but make-believe people. I am only identicating myself and my sister with these make-believe people".

Therefore, it may be concluded that the play-framing in this case had the effect of casting doubt in Maya's mind as to the genuineness of her hostile feelings. Her total commitment to her former attitude toward Galya was somewhat weakened. This made her more receptive to suggestions to adopt a more adequate plan for reaching her goal of extricating herself from her excessive involvement with Galya.

I should like to stress that I by no means claim that this complex mental activity is conscious or explicit. On the contrary, in all probability, most of this mental work is done instantaneously and unconsciously. A clear distinction should be drawn between the person's subjective experience and our own *analysis* of this experience.

Furthermore, the fact that this mental work is done swiftly and unconsciously adds to its therapeutic effect. If the experience accompanying the play-framing is not rational and conscious, the chances are that the desired emotional change will actually take effect. In the above example, for instance, the subconscious, instantaneous nature of the play experience prevented Maya from building up rationalizations of her resentment of Galya.

We have seen that the therapeutic effect of play-framing is derived from the very nature of make-believe play as defined in Chapter 2. In fact, this therapeutic effect is not restricted to play-framing. It is characteristic of every therapeutic use of make-believe play.

Here is a more detailed discussion of those properties of make-believe play that are implied by its definition:

Owning and Alienation

A person who engages in make-believe play, inevitably, both *owns* the content of his play and *disowns* it, in other words, is *alienated* from it. Take for instance a boy who plays as if a monster is coming toward him. Since he is making the mental claims of *realification* and *identication* he must somehow *own* the proposition that a monster is coming toward him. That is, up to a certain extent he is committed to this proposition. He relates to it, in some sense, as *his*. However, since he also makes, simultaneously, the mental claim of *playfulness* about this proposition, he also *disowns* it. He takes it as something he is by no means committed to, as something that is not his. He *alienates* himself from this proposition.

Let us return to the example of Maya who tells her sister Galya "I can't stand you, I really hate you". When this expression is reframed as make-believe play, Maya both owns it and disowns (is alienated from) it. Therefore, one can reformulate the above elaborate analysis of the therapeutic effect of the play-framing of this expression and say succinctly that what the play-framing does therapeutically is to make Maya *disown* the proposition that she hates her sister without taking it away from her. She becomes *alienated* from her former absolute conviction that her hatred of her sister is real, without fully *disowning* this conviction. Since she is not really required to fully disown it, it is easier for her to begin disowning it.

The main therapeutic use of the play properties of *owning* and *alienation* is shaking deep, emotionally invested convictions that lie behind a person's dysfunctional plans. These can be classified into *convictions about oneself* and *convictions about other people*. This classification will now be explained and illustrated.

Convictions About Oneself

Maya, who tells her crippled sister: "I can't stand you, I really hate you" can serve as an example of this category. She has a certain emotionally invested conviction about herself with respect to her sister. This conviction interferes with her capacity to process information that is relevant to her relationship with her sister. In considering the play-framing of this expression, special attention should be paid to the personal pronoun "I". One of the linguistic functions of this pronoun is to indicate the self. Therefore it is particularly relevant to the category of *convictions about oneself*. The point is that in make-believe play this pronoun refers ambiguously to two different entities: the player himself and the figure he personifies in his make-believe game. When Maya is saying "I hate you" she *owns* this statement, because she is talking about herself, but she also *disowns* it, is *alienated* from it, because she is also talking about an imaginary hater in her make-believe game. This contradiction shakes her firm conviction that she is the one who hates her sister. She begins alienating herself from this conviction, although she does not yet abandon it completely.

Convictions About Another Person

What can be said about this category is analogous to what has just been said about convictions about oneself. Imagine the reverse of the situation described above. The crippled sister Galya is convinced that her older sister, Maya, hates her. She tells her: "I know you hate me". If this expression is play-framed, that is, becomes an act of make-believe play, it can have the effect of shaking, however slightly, Galya's presupposed conviction about the genuineness of her sister's hatred of her.

When Galya plays a make-believe game in which she tells Maya "You hate me" she refers ambiguously to the sister in her mind and to her real sister. She inevitably both *owns* her conviction that her sister hates her and disowns or *is alienated from* this conviction. Therefore, she can no longer be certain that her conviction has been based on a correct judgment of reality.

The properties of *owning* and *alienation* can also have the opposite therapeutic effect, not shaking one's deep-seated convictions about self and others in which the emphasis is on change from owning to disowning, but making one accept truths about oneself or other people which were rejected or denied. Here the emphasis is on change from disowning (alienation) to owning. Putting the denied, suppressed or rejected truths about oneself or others in the frame of make-believe play can also be the first step in correcting a dysfunctional plan, in which errors of information processing such as *leaving out relevant input* or *failure to validate interpretations* interfere with the processing of information which could help one accept oneself or one's family members as they really are.

These notions can be illustrated by the following example: the mother of Ilan, a ten-year-old boy, would not let his friends visit him at home, because they left the house dirty and untidy. Ilan was angry at her, but denied his anger and justified her. However, his anger came out in a roundabout way: he would dirty and disorder the house, not on purpose, but inadvertently. For instance, he would neglect to rub the mud off his soles before entering the house. He would unintentionally break dishes.

I wanted to make Ilan *own* his anger. I tried to achieve this in a variety of ways. One of my interventions consisted of inducing Ilan by various therapeutic moves (see Chapters 11 and 12) to play the part of a boy named Poopy. His mother's name was Poopa. When Poopa did not allow Poopy to invite his friends to visit him at home, Poopy said: "I am angry at you because you didn't let me invite them, and now I'll punish you. I'll dirty and disorder the house". Then he went on throwing toys around the room.

This make-believe game allowed Ilan to *own* his anger and vindictiveness. However, thanks to this game he could also continue pretending that these were not *his* feelings. They belonged to Poopy. He could go on being *alienated* from these feelings.

In this case the mental claims of *realification* and *identication* did the job of *alienation* while the mental claim of *playfulness* did the job of *owning*. The *realification* and *identication* helped Ilan pretend that the one who was angry at his mother was not really him but Poopy, whereas the *playfulness* denied this and made him realize that the one who was angry was in fact himself.

In this example the make-believe play intervention made the child own something about *himself* he wished to disown. In the following example the make-believe play intervention made the child own something about another person that he had wished to disown.

Nine-year-old Salem used to deny the fact that his mother Sameera was a Muslim Arab. He insisted stubbornly that she was Jewish.

Salem had an irregular, troubled family history. Sameera was expelled from her village in the Galilee when she was sixteen, because she had an illicit love affair with her cousin and got pregnant. Her family married her off to fifty-year-old Avraham, formerly Ibraheem, a Muslim who had converted to Judaism. They made their home in a mixed Jewish-Arab neighborhood in Jaffa. When Avraham died of a heart attack, Sameera wanted to raise her children as muslims. Her two daughters assumed this identity willingly, but Salem wanted to solve his own identity confusion by declaring his whole family Jewish.

The therapist, Ikhlas, a trainee in a course for social workers, was herself a muslim from an Arab village in the Galilee. In one of the many sessions she had with this family she staged a make-believe game in which Sameera played the part of a muslim woman who entertains Jewish guests in her village. The guests, Sameera's children and Ikhlas, asked her questions such as: is your resting day Sabbath or Friday? Are there certain kinds of food you are not allowed to have? Then each of the participants presented folk songs and dances.

This game made Salem own something that he wanted to disown: that his mother was a muslim Arab. He agreed to accept his mother as such thanks to the alienating effect of the mental claims of realification and identication. However, the mental claim of playfulness took the seriousness away from these claims. Therefore he was able to tolerate the truth that, out of the context of make-believe, he had to deny.

Basic Duality

The fact that in make-believe play the player makes not just the mental claims of realification and identication but also the mental claim of playfulness implies that his conscious mind is divided into two parts. On the one hand he remains his own judging self, on the other he forgoes his own best judgment. He is, at one and the same time, inside the make-believe and outside it.

This is what *the basic duality of make-believe play* means. This property is particularly conspicuous and revealing when the make-believe play is verbal and includes the personal pronouns "I" or "you". Take for instance the verbal expression "I am the bad wolf", pronounced by a boy as an act of make-believe play. In fact, the reference of the personal pronoun "I" in this expression is not just doubly ambiguous but triply so. It refers to the *realified signified* (the imaginary bad wolf) and to the *identicated* speaker, who becomes the signifier of this realified signified, the "living toy" playing the part of the bad wolf. However—and this is the crucial point here—the very same pronoun "I" refers also to the speaker-player as the "director" of his own make-believe game. As the imaginary bad wolf and the actor who plays this part the boy is *inside* the make-believe play, but as the one who makes the three mental claims and stages this game he is *outside* it. He is in a position to be in control of his own play acts and observe himself doing these acts from the outside, as it were. He experiences the basic duality of make-believe play.

What are the main family play therapeutic applications of this property? They are: *increasing awareness of errors of information processing*, and *creating or revealing a dissonance between messages.*

Increasing Awareness of Dysfunctional Information Processing

The property of basic duality can be applied as a means of increasing a person's awareness of his own dysfunctional plans, in particular of the errors in information processing included in these plans. The increased awareness is likely to contribute to the family members' ability to change these dysfunctional plans by correcting these errors.

Geela wanted to help her twelve-year-old daughter Tikva be more active and independent in her social life. She used to pester Tikva with questions about every little detail of her life away from home. Tikva cooperated with her by disclosing all the information Geela requested. This pattern defeated both mother's and daughter's goals. Tikva became more passive and dependent on her mother. The errors in information processing here are *too much input and output* related to the daugher's social life away from home (see p. 31).

In one of the sessions Tikva told Geela about a boy she was interested in. Geela began to ask her probing questions. Tikva was very reluctant to answer her questions, but complied. Then I suggested they turn this very conversation into a funny puppet show.

The very fact that the dysfunctional program was turned into a make-believe game made Geela and Tikva more aware of it and think about its anomalous aspects. The property of play that created this effect was *basic duality*. The two were playing out their own behavior, but at the same time they remained their own real selves. They could observe and judge their own behavior.

The mother and daughter *realified* the mental images representing their own behavior and turned these realified images into the signified content of their make-believe play. They also *identicated* themselves with these realified images, turned themselves into the signifiers of this signified contents. However, they also knew that this realification and identication was playful, not serious. While they were doing the funny puppet show they remained their own unplaying selves. They could observe themselves and judge their own play behavior. In this way they could become more aware of the dysfunctional aspects of their own plans. When they were acting according to their dysfunctional program outside the framework of make-believe play they were just behaving. They did not pay sufficient attention to what they were doing, did not observe or judge themselves. Therefore their level of self-awareness remained low. This awareness became more acute when the dysfunctional pattern was placed in the context of make-believe play.

Using Basic Duality to Increase Awareness of Dissonance

Dysfunctional information processing is often manifested in paradoxically contradictory messages of the kind illustrated by the famous command "be spontaneous". In such cases the output includes a message, and a meta-message which contradicts the message. The message is "be spontaneous!". The meta-message is "obey me!", which cancels the possibility of the addressee being genuinely spontaneous (see Soper and L'Abate, 1977). Another example is a mother who says of her daughter "I let her dominate me". One output message is "She dominates me", the other one is "I let her do it", which implies that the mother has the power to prevent her daughter from dominating her. If she has such a power, she really dominates her daughter.

This faulty, paradoxical relationship between two output messages is an anomalous information-processing operation that can be a part of the mother's dysfunctional plan for attempting to control her daughter. I induced the mother and daughter to pretend that the mother was dominated by the daughter. This make-believe game was designed to repair this dysfunctional plan by exposing the confusing paradoxical double message. The property of make-believe play that is supposed to have this effect is basic duality. In their roles as players, actors in the make-believe game, the mother and daughter took it as a real fact that the daughter dominated the mother. However as the persons who were making the make-believe mental claims, in particular the claim of *playfulness* they were self-observers, outsiders at their own role-play. From the latter position they knew quite well that the daughter did not really dominate her mother, that the mother was the one who really dominated her daughter. The two contradictory output messages, which exist on two levels, a level of assertion and a meta level which denies this assertion, were actually placed on two levels: the in-play level and the out-of-play, self-observing and self-judging level. Furthermore, what seems to be an erroneous message, that is, that the daughter dominated her mother, was placed within the make-believe play. This framed it as a message that should not be taken too seriously. The other message, that the daughter did not dominate the mother, was placed outside the make-believe play. Therefore it could be taken more seriously. When the message saying that the daughter dominated her mother was placed within the make-believe play, the paradoxical, self-contradictory double message ceased to be problematic. It was no more problematic or confusing than the message "I am a lion" produced by a child in a make-believe game. The anomalous aspect of the information, namely the faulty, paradoxical, self-contradictory coordination of two messages, which confused both mother and daughter and defeated the purpose of establishing proper parental control and limits, was clarified by this intervention, thanks to the property of basic duality.

Using Basic Duality to Create Dissonance

My colleague Galila had in therapy two brothers: eight-year-old Tomer and ten-year-old Assa. Tomer had the habit of complaining bitterly about Assa. He said Assa used to attack him verbally or physically "for no reason whatsoever". He failed to see that Assa's attacks were systematically related to subtle provocations on his side. For example, when Assa made a mistake in his arithmetic homework, Tomer used to sneer at him. (Tomer was considered brighter than Assa.) We see here again errors of information processing such as ignoring relevant information and failure to validate.

One of Galila's interventions consisted of directing the family to play a make-believe game as follows: she played the part of a teacher who gave Tomer, the older brother, various difficult tasks. She induced Assa to sneer at Tomer when he had a hard time trying to do a task. Tomer was to react by attacking Assa verbally. Then Assa was led by Galila to play a make-believe game (a game within a game) in which he pretended that Tomer had been attacking him for no reason whatsoever. He complained to his parents about this. During this activity Galila reminded the family a number of times that they were actually playing a make-believe game.

The therapeutic effect of this use of the property of basic duality seems to lie in the creation of tension between the players' out-of-play awareness and the make-believe play they are engaged in. The latter is complex—a game embedded within a game. It includes three levels: the level in which the player is fully aware of the fact that he is just playing a make-believe game, the level in which he pretends to tease his brother subtly and the latter reacts by becoming aggressive and the level in which he pretends that he is not aware of all that. Both the fact that he really provoked his brother and the fact that he denied this have been placed within a make-believe game. Since he is the player of this game, the basic duality of his play makes him fully aware of the contradiction between what he does and his denial of what he does. This awareness must create some tension in him. This tension is likely to make him more ready to change his plan.

Arbitrariness of Signifier

The term *"signifier"* was defined in Chapter 2 as the real world entity which has been *identicated* with the *signified*, the mental image *realified* in the make-believe play. For example, in a make-believe game in which a child plays with a doll representing a baby the doll is the signifier and the realified image of the baby is the signified.

De Saussure, who first introduced the terms "signifier" and "signified" (see Chapter 2) drew another distinction: between *arbitrary* and *motivated* signification (1972). The distinction was, again, adopted by Piaget (1962) and applied to make-believe play. In motivated signification the signifier is chosen because of its similarity to the signified. For example, when a child represents a baby by a baby doll this is a motivated signification, because the signifier (baby doll) is similar to the signified (the image of a real baby). On the other hand, when a child represents a baby by a stone or a leaf, this is arbitrary signification, because there is no similarity between the signifier and the signified. In make-believe play, the signifier can, in principle, be arbitrary. There is nothing in the very nature of make-believe play that requires the signifier to be motivated, although there is nothing that prevents it from being motivated. Arbitrary signification in make-believe play is permitted.

The optional arbitrariness of make-believe play can be used as a property that brings about therapeutic change according to the therapist's goals in strategic family play therapy. That is, it can be used as a way of repairing anomalous information-processing operations that are included in the dysfunctional plans of the family members. The main uses of this property are *softening the emotional impact* of the signified (like the property of alienation) and *creating a dissonance between the signifier and the signified* (like the property of basic duality).

Softening the Emotional Impact of the Signified

The father of five-year-old Erez went abroad on a six-month study leave. Erez was convinced that his father had left for good and would never come back to him. He developed frequent fits of rage and crying in which he would demand that his mother should bring his father back home or take him to his father. His mother's explanations that his father was to come back were of no avail, all the more so because she herself found it difficult to cope without her husband. Her verbal explanations to Erez betrayed her own difficulty with this absence. Using information-processing language, we can say that Erez had a dysfunctional plan for achieving his goal of getting his father back. This plan included errors in information processing such as *misinterpretation of the input* (he could not see his father's absence as temporary), *failure to consider other possible kinds of output* and producing *too much* ineffective *output*. Of course these errors were motivated by his emotional difficulty in accepting the input, that is, his father's absence.

Ruttie, the therapist, tried verbal therapy for a while, but Erez failed to respond. Then she began to employ play therapeutic techniques. She said that the area of the room in which the toy houses and toy cars were placed was the foreign country where the father stayed for his studies. This in itself was a use of the property of the arbitrariness of the signifiers: the signified, the child's mental images of the distant, invisible, mysterious country where his father stayed, were represented by arbitrary signifiers. The distance was signified by a comfortable proximity, the invisibility by visibility, etc. This had a softening effect on the boy. His images were materialized by concrete, easily available entities. Later a doll representing the father was introduced into the game. The love and emotional contact between father and son were represented by tying the father's doll to the boy with a purple ribbon. The ribbon was again an arbitrary signifier for the image of an emotional bond. Tying the doll had the impact of alleviating the pain of longing.

Creating a Dissonance Between Signifier and Signified

The parents of ten-year-old Nisan complained that their son was aggressive and disobedient. They did much to change this: beat him, rebuke him, lock him up, but all these were to no avail. This of course was a dysfunctional plan for achieving the goal of controlling the son. The errors in information processing in this dysfunctional plan were failure to consider possible output, and failure to take into account the patterns of behavior the plan was supposed to change.

In a family play therapeutic session, I directed the family to play scenes in which the good parents did all kinds of nice things to Nisan such as feed him, caress him and give him presents, but Nisan reacted by being aggressive and disobedient. The make-believe parents were worried. They could not understand why Nisan reacted in this way.

In the course of the game I suggested that the parents used objects with aggressive content as signifiers for the nice things given to Nisan. For example, when the parents pretended to give Nisan a bagel, I handed a toy snake over to the father, suggesting non-verbally that it could serve as a signifier for the signified "bagel". Later, when they bought Nisan a make-believe walkie-talkie as a present, I suggested boxing gloves as signifiers for the walkie-talkie. These menacing signifiers were arbitrary.

In this case the property of *the abritrariness of the signifier* was used to create a feeling of tension, due to the contradiction between the signified content, which was benign and kind, and the signifiers, which suggested aggression and violence. I predicted that this would give rise to thoughts, accompanied by a feeling of uneasiness, in the parents, concerning their role in provoking their son's aggressive behavior. My hope was that the thoughts and feelings induced in this way would sharpen the parents' awareness of their own share in their son's aggressive behavior.

Covert Communication

In Chapter 2 the question was taken up of how the symbolic, semantic, sig-nified contents of make-believe play are used as vehicles for conducting social communication. The covert interpersonal communicational messages expressed by the make-believe play of two kindergarten girls was presented.

The fact that the overt signified content of the play may have covert commu-nicative functions can have strategic family play therapeutic applications. The main applications are *facilitating the expression of complex or emotionally diffi-cult interpersonal messages* and *detouring resistance*.

Facilitating the Expression of Complex or Emotionally Difficult Interpersonal Messages

Seven-year-old Shahar developed fears and demanded that both his parents accompanied him everywhere. This was a part of his dysfunctional plan for achieving the goal of having his parents exercise a more firm parental control and set limits. Both Shahar and his parents *filtered out possible output*, which could get them closer to their respective goals.

Among the reasons why Shahar would not express his wish for parental control more directly were cognitive and emotional difficulties. He was un-aware of his own needs and feelings behind his fears. Even when aware a little bit, he did not know how to express himself. He was inhibited, unable to criticize his parents for not being in control. Another part of his dysfunctional plan included the presupposition that his parents were weak and vulnerable, too weak and vulnerable to take charge. He believed he had to protect them (*leaving out relevant input*, and *failure to validate*).

In one of the family play therapeutic sessions, Shahar arranged a make-believe game, with the aid of various toys and puppets, in which his family members were sea creatures living in the ocean. He himself said: 'But the sea creatures have no king! Who is going to be their king?'' Then he gave his father a shark-doll, the biggest sea creature among the toys.

In this play Shahar made a spontaneous use of the property of *covert com-munication*. He did not complain to his father of his failure to take up the leadership of the family, or ask him to change this and take charge. He spoke about the sea and the sea creatures, but there was a covert message there, directed to his father. The covert *presupposition* was: "You don't take charge and I don't like it" and the covert *purpose* was to challenge his father to take control. It was easier for Shahar, both intellectually and emotionally, to express this message by talking about the thematic, signified content of his play than by direct verbal communication. The property of covert communication served here as a means for correcting the errors in his dysfunctional plan, especially his *leaving out relevant output*.

Detouring Resistance

The above example can be used to illustrate this application of the property of covert communication too. Since the father was not asked to take charge directly but only indirectly, he could bring himself more easily to comply and take charge, at least in the play situation, despite emotional and other difficulties he had in assuming this role.

Symbolic Coding

In Chapter 2, "symbolization" was defined in relation to the concept "emotive". It was said that the signified (e.g. the house with the broken roof, the tent in the storm, etc.) *symbolize* the central theme of an emotive (e.g. "the breakdown of the home"). This central theme may be said to be the *underlying meaning* of the *symbols*.

The property of symbolic coding is defined as the fact that in make-believe play the underlying meaning of a central emotive can be *symbolized* or *symbolically coded* by a thematic entity (signified), which is privately and subjectively associated with this underlying idea in the player's mind.

The main applications of this property in strategic family play therapy are, like covert communications, facilitating the expression and communication of complex or emotionally difficult messages and making it easier to accept such messages or react to them. The above example of Shahar, the boy who looked for a sea creature who could be the king of the ocean, represents not only covert communication but also *symbolic coding*. Shahar's emotive "fear of absence of parental authority" was symbolically coded by the mental image (signified) of the absence of a sea creature who could be the king of the ocean. Here is another example.

Ned was a well-built, good-looking, athletic eleven-year-old boy. However, his eyesight was so bad that he could not read what was written on the blackboard at school. However, he would not hear of wearing eyeglasses. All attempts to persuade him had met with total denial of the problem and stiffening of resistance. His emotive was "fear of losing his attraction and status among his peers". This fear created anomalous information-processing operations such as filtering out relevant input. He would simply reject all relevant information concerning the adverse consequences of his refusal to wear eyeglasses. He would also fail to take in all attempts to convince him that wearing eyeglasses would not really affect his attraction and social status to any significant degree.

Before I decided on a family play therapeutic strategy, I observed Ned playing spontaneously. In his natural make-believe play his problems with his eyesight and his fear of wearing glasses were symbolically coded by themes such as "an owl", "a bat", "a blindfolded prisoner" and "the absent-minded professor". His emotive of "fear of losing his attraction and status among his peers" was symbolically coded by themes such as "a street-gang leader deposed by his rivals" and "the weak monkey that was attacked by the stronger members of its group".

These spontaneously produced symbolically coded signified contents were incorporated in the family play therapeutic interventions designed to help Ned with his problem.

For example, in one of the sessions Ned played the role of "a blindfolded prisoner taken away by his captor". I, assuming the role of the captor, instructed Ned's father to be "the prisoner's friend, a member of his gang, who fights the captors and sets his friend free". Ned's father, the rescuer, took the cover off the prisoner's eyes. The prisoner and his friend were very enthusiastic that the former could see again.

Afterwards Ned, the former prisoner, became the leader of the gang. Now he was not blindfolded any more. He had excellent eyesight. This helped him lead his mates, show them the way. He told his friends how it felt to be blindfolded and what it felt like to be able to see again.

In this intervention the property of symbolic coding was used systematically to induce the desired therapeutic change. Ned was helped to communicate how he felt without and with eyeglasses; "without eyeglasses" was symbolically coded as "being blindfolded" and "with eyeglasses" as "being freed of the blindfold". (Notice also the reversal and reframing: wearing eyeglasses was symbolized by taking off the eye cover and being without eyeglasses as wearing the eyecover.) The symbol of wearing eyeglasses (being freed of the eyecover) was described as something good, which led to improvement in the social status of the boy. The father's intervention was depicted as a rescue operation, performed by a loyal comrade.

In this game Ned was willing to listen. He let himself express his feelings. He gave up his anomalous filtering out of the relevant input. These achievements were due to the facilitating effect of symbolic coding. This effect is similar to the therapeutic power of owning and alienation. The themes of the play were *owned* by Ned as symbolizing his own emotive and the real life matters associated with it. However, at the same time he could remain *alienated* from the play, pretend that the story of the blindfolded prisoner had nothing to do with himself or with his eyesight problem.

The other symbols which appeared in Ned's spontaneous make-believe play were incorporated in his therapy in a similar way. For example, in one of the sessions Ned played the part of the absent-minded professor. I instructed the other family members to play as if they were his colleagues and students. They praised him for his perceptive, penetrating eyes and for his far-sightedness. They admired his intelligence and brightness.

In another session Ned played the part of the owl. It was represented as a wise bird that could see what other animals could not. The creatures dwelling in the forest sought his advice and guidance.

In another make-believe game Ned was the weak monkey who became strong. This happened after it found a telescope, which was left in the jungle by a hunter.

Regulation of Emotions

In Chapter 2, in the section dealing with the psychological characteristics of make-believe play, it was stated that make-believe play was a device for regulating the level of emotional arousal round sensitive, emotionally laden themes (emotives). The choice of signifiers and signified is regulated by the child's emotives and by the emotional intensity of the stimuli associated with these emotives. The child is more likely to introduce signifiers and signified into his play that are associated with his emotives, especially those that arouse particularly intense emotions. It was argued that this phenomenon, which is also characteristic of dreams and fantasy, helps the child regulate the level of intensity of his emotive-associated emotions, through psychological processes such as "habituation", "cognitive restructuring", "de-conditioning" and "mastery". However, if the emotional intensity of the stimuli surpasses a certain peak the player will "switch off" and prefer to include signifiers and signified in his play that are still related to his emotives, but are associated with less intense emotions. The themes (signifiers) in the child's play can therefore be classified according to the emotive to which they belong. They can be classified further by subcategories of the central theme of this emotive (horizontal subclassification) and by the intensity of the emotion (vertical subclassification); see Table 1 on p. 46.

The child prefers to introduce themes into his play which belong to the upper row of such a table. However, if his emotional arousal surpasses a certain peak, he will step down to signified contents which belong to lower rows of the table. So in his make-believe play the child regulates his emotions in two main ways: by introducing emotive-related, highly arousing themes over and over again and by stepping down to less intense themes if a certain emotional level is surpassed.

In moving down to lower, less emotionally intense rows, the child can replace one theme by another (e.g. "a submarine", which is under water, where it is dangerous and frightening, is replaced by "a boat" which is on the surface of the water, where it is less frightening). However, the switch from a higher to a lower row or the other way round can be done by other means, such as:

Combining two themes (e.g. the submarine becomes "a boaty submarine", half a boat half a submarine, where the submarine half is under water, and the boat half is above surface).

Reversing the frightening situation (e.g. a person had drowned and died and afterwards was revived).

Introducing new, protective signifier (e.g. a "red-cross submarine" is introduced, which protects the submarine and is there to help if necessary). See Piaget, 1962.

The property of *emotional regulation*, which manifests itself in the ways listed above, can be utilized systematically in strategic family play therapy. The main therapeutic effect of this property lies in the possibility of regulating the level of emotional arousal associated with certain emotives, so that errors of information processing in one's dysfunctional plan are repaired. The assumption is that anomalies such as leaving out relevant input or output or misinterpretation of the input are often maintained by intense emotions such as fear, anger and shame, characterizing one's emotives. If the level of these emotions is reduced, the likelihood is increased for the errors in information processing to be repaired. Here are two examples:

A six-year-old boy, Edo, would not let his mother approach him in an affectionate way. He said that she was a bad mother who wanted to hurt him. His mother was offended. She became angry and aggressive. This "confirmed" her son's image of her and reinforced his dysfunctional plan.

A life history of Edo was taken. It turned out that two years before, when he was four, he had had a bad accident. He fell off a fence and broke his arm. His mother had been walking him on the fence when he fell. She was the one who carried him to hospital in her arms.

Apparently, Edo unconsciously suspected that his mother had deliberately pushed him off the fence and wanted to hurt him. He developed an emotive "fear and anger of mother's wish to hurt me". This emotive (which was reinforced by other difficulties in the mother–son relationship) lay at the basis of his dysfunctional plan with respect to his mother.

I helped Edo and his mother reconstruct the accident scene, translated into a symbolic code, in make-believe play. In the first session Edo chose to play with puppets. He made a witch puppet hit a baby puppet with a stick, after the fashion of Punch and Judy. I encouraged him to take the place of the baby doll. His mother stepped into the role of the witch. This done, I induced the witch to push the baby off the balcony.

The purpose of this, as well as other similar, interventions was to let Edo repeat the emotionally arousing theme of his emotive, symbolically coded, many times, with his mother as his co-player. This repetition was expected to have the effects of easing the intensity of Edo's fear and anger with respect to his mother. If he were freed of this burden he would be more open to see his mother as she really was and to accept her love. The anomalous information-processing operations in his dysfunctional plan which made his mother's loving messages unavailable to him would be repaired.

When Edo played this game with his mother he became very fearful. At this point I helped him "move downwards to a lower row" (see Table 1 on p. 46), that is, replace the frightening theme of "the wicked mother" by less frightening themes of the same category. Following Edo's own suggestion, "the mother-witch" became "the mother-fairy". She bandaged the boy's wounds after being thrown off the balcony.

Another idea, again, invented by Edo himself, was to turn the witch into a good wonder woman. When he fell off the balcony she, by magic, stopped his fall in midair.

Nine-year-old Yakov and his eight-year-old brother Yoel were at home when the police raided their home. They searched the apartment for heroin, handcuffed their father and took him away. In a session with Miriam, a trainee in a strategic family play therapy course for social workers, Yoel played with toy soldiers. He made them all fall and said: "I killed all the cops". Then Yakov, his brother, made a toy representing a man fall and said: "He also died". At this point Miriam decided to intervene. She made the man-toy stand up and said: "I did not die. I went with the other cops. I'll come back". The children liked this game. They wanted it to be repeated many times, with all kinds of variations.

In this scene the children, aided by Miriam, helped themselves tone down their anxiety related to the traumatic experience they had gone through. This was achieved by *repetition* and by *stepping down to a lower row*. Yakov eased his own fear and anger by "killing the cops". Then Yoel "made the man die". Miriam thought that this play act expressed his fear that his father would be killed by the police or be gone for ever. Her purpose was to help him go to a lower row. She did this by stepping into the role of the man and promising to come back.

Possible Worlds

In make-believe play unrealized possibilities can be realized. The possible worlds that may be materialized in make-believe play belong to the following categories:

A potential situation (e.g. the boy's mother becoming pregnant).
A possible but unlikely state of affairs (e.g. the boy's father being eaten up by a lion).
Impossible—unreal or improbable—situations (e.g. being in two places at the same time; a boy being transformed into a fish).

Table 3 Therapeutically relevant properties of play.

Name of property	Main characteristics	Therapeutic uses
Play-framing	Non-play behavior is framed as "play", so the player is likely to make the mental claims of *realification, identication* and *playfulness* about it.	The mental attitude of the player toward his own behavior is changed. The player's commitment to the reality and seriousness of his own behavior is reduced, so he becomes more capable of giving up errors in information processing he has been committed to, and of changing his dysfunctional plan.
Owning and alienation	Since the player makes the claims of *realification* and *identication* he *owns* the content of his play, that is, is committed to its being real. However, since he also makes the claim of *playfulness*, he is also *alienated* from this content, not committed to its being real.	Shaking one's deep convictions about oneself or others (from owning to disowning), or making one accept previously rejected truths about oneself or others (from disowning to owning).
Basic duality	Due to the claim of playfulness the player is both inside the play and outside it, a self-observer.	Increasing awareness of errors of information processing in dysfunctional plans; creating tension related to contradictions in information processing in dysfunctional programs.
Arbitrariness of signifier	There should not be any similarity between the signifier and its signified content.	Softening the emotional impact of the signified; creating tension by revealing a contradiction between signifier and signified.
Covert communication	Symbolic, signified contents of make-believe play are used as vehicles for conducting social communication.	Facilitating the expression of complex or emotionally difficult interpersonal messages; moving family members to correct errors of information processing without meeting too much resistance.

Table 3   (cont.)

Name of property	Main characteristics	Therapeutic uses
Symbolic coding	The underlying meaning of a central emotive is symbolized by a signified which is privately associated with this underlying meaning in the player's mind.	Facilitating the expression and communication of complex or emotionally difficult messages, and making it easier to accept such messages or react to them.
Regulation of emotions	Regulating the level of emotional arousal with the player's motives.	Softening the emotions that maintain information-processing errors in one's dysfunctional programs.
Possible worlds	Unrealized possibilities (potential, unlikely or impossible) can be realized in make-believe play.	Errors of information processing can be normalized in the possible worlds of make-believe play. For example, information that has been left out can be taken in in make-believe play.

The property of *possible worlds* evolves from the mental claims of realification and identication, which are unconstrained by existing reality and are not required to be true, reasonable or self-consistent.

This property can be used as a means of correcting errors in information processing included in one's dysfunctional programs, such as the following:

Leaving Out Relevant Input and Output

In play the relevant input or output can be admitted, as unrealized possibilities.

Five-year-old Shai would, every now and again, produce fits of rage and throw tantrums. His goal was to mobilize his parents to help him. He hoped in this way to make them take definite measures to save him from his fear of being left alone or abandoned. In one of the family play therapeutic sessions, he suggested that the family play the biblical story of Moses in the Ark of Bulrushes. He turned himself into baby Moses, who was left by his mother on the bank of the River Nile. However, his own make-believe story took a turn other than the biblical story. In the latter, Moses was found and brought up by King Pharaoh's daughter. Shai chose to realize another possible world, in which Moses was rescued by his parents from the rage of

Pharaoh's soldiers and taken back home to be protected and cared for by them.

In this make-believe game the property of possible worlds was spontaneously employed by the boy to let in the input and output left out. In his make-believe story the information that was missing from his symptoms and from his real daily life, namely his fear of being abandoned and his need to be rescued and taken care of by his parents, was made explicit, though symbolically disguised.

The information-processing errors *incorrect interpretation of input* and *failure to validate* can also be corrected in play by means of the property of possible worlds:

Twelve-year-old Anat was considered by her parents a failure in most significant areas of life. Her behavior constituted a constant reminder of this. She was an under-achiever in school. She was socially isolated. She had no hobbies. Instead of speaking properly she used to whine, shout or mumble.

When she was three she was diagnosed as suffering from a minimal brain dysfunction. However, a battery of tests administered to her shortly before her family was admitted to therapy revealed that her intellectual and psychomotor functioning were not in any way impaired. They were entirely within the norm. Her inadequate functioning was partly governed by her dysfunctional plan for achieving the goal of preserving her status as the problem girl who is over-protected and treated like a little child. Her parents interpreted her behavior as reflecting a genuine inherent disability and failed to validate this interpretation.

In the family play therapeutic sessions the therapist, Ruttie, used the property of possible worlds as follows:

She encouraged Anat to play various make-believe games in which she would experience success. For example, she suggested roles such as "a girl who won a prize in a dancing contest", "the best pupil in school", "a public speaker", and so forth.

Anat's parents seemed to disapprove of the whole idea of these games. They doubted her ability to play these parts properly. They told Ruttie that if she failed this would be another blow to her injured self-image.

Ruttie challenged these worries. She asked them to pretend to encourage their daughter to show her ability and put their beliefs about her to the test.

And she did pass it. In the possible worlds created in these games she produced some real achievements. For example, as a public speaker she proved herself to be quite eloquent and intelligent, to her parents' great surprise.

Summary

The therapeutically relevant properties of play discussed above and their therapeutic applications are summarized in Table 3 (pp. 70–71).

PART 2

Assessment through observations of family make-believe play

The Purpose and Nature of Assessment

Assessment as the Basis for Planning the Therapy

In the previous chapters strategic family play therapists have been likened to archers who aim their bows and arrows at the bull's-eyes of their targets. In this metaphor the bows and arrows stand for properties of play such as *owning and alienation* and *arbitrariness of the signifier* (see Chapter 3). The bull's-eye represents errors of information processing in the family's dysfunctional programs (see Chapter 1).

Obviously, an archer cannot shoot before he has identified his target and marked it clearly. Likewise, a strategic family play therapist cannot decide on a therapeutic intervention before he has pinpointed the relevant errors of information processing in the family's dysfunctional programs. In other words, he has to *assess* the family and delineate its dysfunctional features before he can plan and execute his therapeutic moves.

Current Family Assessment Methods

There exist a great variety of methods for assessing families. These methods can be classified (after Cromwell, Olson and Fournier, 1976) according to the modes of data-gathering into methods based on self-report and methods based on observations. The former includes mainly oral or written questionnaires. Individual family members are questioned about typical interactional patterns in the family, about their feelings in relation to major family life events, about difficulties in intercommunication, and so forth. Methods of the latter kind involve observations directed at the family while it is carrying out some joint activity. The activity observed may be free, e.g. dinner at home, or planned by the therapist. Planned activities were classified by Cromwell, Olson and Fournier into the following three types: problem-solving tasks, decision-making tasks and conflict resolution tasks.

Assessment Through Observations of Family Play

The following chapters are devoted to the presentation of an assessment method based on observing family members in the course of their being engaged in spontaneous, undirected play. The therapist puts at the family's disposal means such as toys, hand puppets, balls, plasticine, etc. and encourages them to initiate play activities in which both parents and children participate. He observes these activities. If he has video facilities he videotapes them. If he has not, he "videotapes" them with his eyes and records the main things he sees. During the activity and following it he analyzes and interprets the scenes that have taken place before his eyes.

My faith in this method of assessment is based on the assumption that play mirrors the family's dysfunctional programs, in particular those that are relevant to the presenting problems. Sometimes the dysfunctional programs will be reflected in the family play directly and sometimes indirectly, in a symbolic or metaphorical disguise.

Here is an example of a direct reflection: Hagai and his ten-year-old son Amiram decided to play "a boxing match". Hagai took advantage of his superior strength and gave Amiram really painful fist blows. Then he made fun of Amiram for not knowing how to defend himself.

And here is an example of an indirect reflection: Hagai and Amiram played "a marine battle" with toy ships in a sand box which served as "the sea". Hagai made Amiram's warship "drown". Then Hagai, as "the captain" of the winning ship, derided the weakness and misery of the vanquished ship.

If this assumption is right, then one can, by observing the family play and interpreting it, identify the dysfunctional programs that are relevant to the presenting problems. Hence the value of observations of family play as a method of assessment.

This central *assumption* can be supported as follows: the supposition that the dysfunctional programs which are relevant to the presenting problems are necessarily manifested in the family's spontaneous play is based on theoretical considerations and on my own clinical experience. As has been explained in Chapter 1, family members are "programmed" to act according to their dysfunctional programs. This, however, applies to every dysfunctional program, not just to those programs that are relevant to the presenting problem. But my central assumption has been that play mirrors primarily the family's dysfunctional programs relevant to presenting problems. I must show, then, that programs of the latter kind are highly likely to be manifested in family play sessions. My main argument in favor of this hypothesis is that interactions relevant to presenting problems are, as a rule, laden with intense emotions. Since emotionally laden themes are particularly likely to occur in a free, creative activity such as play (see Chapter 2), problematic interactions have a particularly high probability of occurrence in the family's free play.

Characteristically, the emotional atmosphere which surrounds "the problem child" is stormy. This can be accounted for by the hypothesis that symptoms are direct manifestations or metaphorical representations of emotional pressures related to a family crisis or to a painful transition period in its life cycle (see Minuchin, 1974). Another hypothesis which explains the emotional tension that accompanies the symptom is that symptoms are a kind of safety valve for chronic family stress (Framo, 1970; Minuchin, Baker and Rosman, 1978; Satir, 1971). The symptoms themselves, in turn, give rise to intense emotions such as worry or anger in all the family members.

The fact that play, along with dreams, daydreams and creative art, mirrors the players' emotional world, and in particular their family dramas, has long been realized by students of play and play therapy. Furthermore, the hypothesis that emotionally laden family interactions must find an outlet in family play is supported by theoretical studies and research findings highlighting the central role of affect in the regulation of attention, perception, ideation and motor action. A major finding emerging from these works is that the choice of thought contents and actions in unstructured situations, in which the mental apparatus is free of external constraints, is dictated to a great extent by the nature of affect and its intensity. (See Chapter 2 and Bativa and Khomskaya, 1984; Blaney, 1986; Bock, 1986; Bower, 1984; Frijda, Kupiers and Schure, 1989; Klinger, 1971, 1978; Mastumodo, 1986; McKenn, 1986; Perrig and Perrig-Ciello, 1985; Pillener, Rhinehart and White, 1986; Suler, 1985; Zachary, 1982; Zajonc, 1980).

The assumption that behavior patterns manifesting relevant dysfunctional programs are highly likely to occur in the family's free play has found ample support in my own and my students' practical experience. A good example showing this is the space-flight make-believe game, described in the Introduction.

The Distinctive Features and Advantages of Assessment Through Observations of Family Play

Family Play as a Kind of Projective Technique

Family play constitutes an activity which is relatively free of external controls and limitations. The family members are not asked to sit in fixed places. They are allowed to move around in the room, run, jump or roll on the carpet. They may chatter, hum or handle objects and materials. They are not given definite, prescribed tasks. They may let their imagination run loose, make up stories and dictate the course and tempo of their activity. In these respects an assessment that is based on observations of family free play resembles projective psychological tests such as Rorschach (Exner, 1986) or TAT (Murray, 1943) rather than structured tests such as MMPI (Hathaway and McKinley, 1943). In projective tests the stimuli are undefined and ambiguous, and the range of possible responses very wide. Therefore, it is commonly supposed that in projective tests the subject's responses are not dictated primarily by the stimuli submitted to him, but issue from his inner world. Thoughts and feelings that are often latent or unconscious emerge from the depths of this inner world and are projected on the stimuli. For example, in TAT the subject is shown pictures of people in various situations, whose content is open to manifold interpretations. He is asked to make up stories centering around images and situations seen in the pictures. Many subjects give these pictures private, subjective interpretations. Their stories are taken to be a mirror of the emotional themes they are consciously or unconsciously preoccupied with. The same applies to family play. The stimuli in this activity are not of the kind that dictates specific types of responses. Family members are free to create their own private make-believe world. By looking closely at this play world, the therapist can reach dark, hidden corners that are hardly accessible in other ways. Thoughts, feelings and aspects of interpersonal relationships that the family members are unaware of, or prefer to hide from themselves, are exposed and rise to the surface. This enables the therapist to get a full, multidimensional picture of the family system.

Exploring the Children's Viewpoint

Everyone who has tried to make children take an active, meaningful part in a conjoint family or group activity that is based on a verbal discussion, or on a structured task, knows how difficult and frustrating this can be. Children, especially young ones, become bored. Their attention wanders. And then they become as disruptive as only children know how to be and they get on everyone's nerves. But if they are allowed to play they become as involved and excited as only children can become. In family play sessions, children are *really* present. They involve themselves in the activity, heart and soul. They feel what is going on in the room is truly theirs, because *play* is something that *belongs* to children.

Looking closely into children's contribution to family play can endow the assessment with dimensions that cannot be reached otherwise. In particular, such a close scrutiny makes it possible to gain knowledge of the children's own peculiar conception of the family and the interrelationships within it. Here is an example:

Michael and Aviva considered themselves to be a happy couple. Michael treated Ran, Aviva's five-year-old son, as his own. Ran called Michael "Daddy", although his real daddy was someone else.

Ran's unmarried biological father never fully admitted his fatherhood. His relationship with his son had been extremely unstable, and when Michael entered the picture he seemed to have vanished into thin air.

Michael and Aviva brought Ran to my clinic not because of any problem at home, but because of his behavior problems in kindergarten.

In the assessment session, Michael, Aviva and Ran made up the following, among others, make-believe scene, represented by hand-puppets: Michael chose the part of "Columbus". Then Aviva, after some hesitation, decided to be "Queen Isabella". Ran wanted to be "the prince, her son, who lives in the palace with her". Columbus, on his way to America, happened to come upon the palace and stayed there for a few days as a guest. Afterwards he left, to continue his mission. When he asked Queen Isabella what the name of her lovely prince was she said "Christopher".

When Columbus had left, Prince Christopher invited a man called Papa to stay with him in the palace. Papa was represented by a devil-puppet. Christopher said that if Columbus came back Papa would kill him.

Having watched this scene, I formed in my mind the following interpretation:

In the make-believe world Michael stepped out of the part of the faithful, dutiful husband and step-father and became Columbus, the daring explorer. He did not settle down in the palace with the queen and her son, but only stayed with them for a few days as a guest and then moved along to go his own way. Aviva named her son "Christopher", Columbus' first name. Apparently, this symbolized her wish that Columbus would not leave but stay in the palace permanently. Ran brought his natural father back home, thinly disguised as Papa, the devil who was going to kill Christopher if he came back.

All that had no trace in the family's conscious picture of themselves, as they described it in the initial verbal interview. The make-believe play exposed covert patterns and feelings that lay underneath the neat and happy surface.

Heterogeneity of Modes of Expression

Family play constitutes a singularly rich source of diagnostic information about the family, thanks to the fact that it makes use of a wide range of means of expression and communication, such as speech, sounds, movement, various objects and materials, etc. This wealth enables the family members to give vent, directly or symbolically, to a heterogeneous selection of themes and messages. A child can express his wish to feel dominant instead of domineered by assigning his father the make-believe role of a horse and himself the role of the rider. A woman expresses different or even contradictory aspects of her relations with her husband in a concise, concentrated manner by casting herself in the role of a farm woman who works hard out in the field, and her husband in the role of a scarecrow, stuck in the field to frighten the birds away. A girl expresses her wish that her parents spend more time at home with her, but also her anger at the fact that they never do it on their own initiative, by tying them down with a rope, pretending to take them prisoners.

The next chapters are devoted to a detailed presentation of specific techniques of observation and analysis.

CHAPTER 5

Preparations for the Assessment

Arranging the Play room

Family play, observed by the therapist, takes place in a special family play therapy room. Preferably, this should be a medium-sized room. If the room is too small, one cannot move about freely, so the natural development of the activity is likely to be arrested. On the other hand, a very large room stimulates the children to run about; the activity tends to disintegrate and diffuse round a wide area and it is not easy to keep track of its course.

The therapist wants family members to feel free to sit or even to lie down and roll on the floor if they feel like it. They are likely to feel more comfortable doing this if the floor is at least partly covered with a carpet. Some low chairs or cushions suitable for both children and adults should be available. A variety of lightning facilities (a central lamp for bright illumination, a lamp providing dimmed light, colored lights and so forth) in different parts of the room can be used to change the atmosphere in the session. Furniture should be minimal, to keep the room free of obstacles and enable the participants to move freely around the room. Too much furniture cluttering the room can cause excessive stimulation. It is also preferable for the room to be painted in neutral colors.

It is advisable to keep the various toys and other play things in special storage containers, out of the children's reach, so that the therapist can supervise the choice of the objects and materials made available to the family in each session, in accordance with his own diagnostic and therapeutic considerations.

If the therapist has a wide range of toys and play objects and materials at his disposal, he will be able, in each session, to flexibly select a suitable subset and let the family enjoy it. Table 4 contains a classified list of play means found serviceable.

Before the family gathers in the play room, the therapist chooses suitable play objects from his inventory and places them in various visible locations round the room. The choice of play means is not coincidental, but dictated by various considerations such as the following.

Table 4   Play means for family play therapy room.

Type	Kinds	Main age group (years)
Puppets and dolls	Soft squeaky animal puppets;	1–2
	little plastic dolls representing animals or people;	2–6
	dolls representing people or animals, with movable parts;	2–6
	dolls that can be dressed and undressed, representing people;	3–6
	hand-puppets representing a family, "nice" animals and ugly ones or legendary figures.	4–. . .
Toys representing various aspects of the environment	Baby things;	1–6
	miniature furniture; household objects and kitchen utensils;	2–6
	doctor and nurse instruments;	3–8
	motor vehicles;	3–9
	weapons, army and police;	4–11
	money, commerce;	6–10
	country life;	4–10
	industry.	5–10
Masks and fancy dresses	Masks of people, animals and legendary figures;	5–. . .
	blankets and various rugs;	1–11
	various types of fancy dress, representing different types of people and historical periods.	4–. . .
Constructions and containers	Sandbox;	1–7
	doll's-house;	2–7
	puppet show theater;	4–. . .
	boxes and containers of various sizes.	1–. . .
Assembly and construction	Building blocks, various sizes;	3–7
	puzzle game; Lego.	3–12
Drawing and painting	Finger paints, body paints and make-up;	2–. . .
	blackboard and chalks;	4–. . .
	water colors, pastel crayons.	3–. . .
Tools and materials	Tools for cutting shapes and sewing;	5–. . .
	carpentry tools;	9–. . .
	play dough, plasticine;	2–9
	paper and fabric with glue;	4–. . .
	wood and plastic.	9–. . .
Electronic media	Cameras, a tape recorder, a video recorder.	10–. . .
"Junk"	Various pieces of household and industrial refuse.	2–7

Table 4 (cont.)

Type	Kinds	Main age group (years)
Sports and movement	Balloons, soft balls; targets and safe darts; jumpropes; boxing gloves.	2–. . . 6–. . . 6–. . . 9–. . .
Musical and percussion instruments	Drums, bells and rattles; xylophone, recorders, harmonicas	2–. . . 6–. . .
Table games	A selection of standard table games for various ages.	
Children's books	Picture books of people, animals or familiar objects, made out of durable material; picture books with simple texts, naming familiar objects, people and animals; picture books with simple stories, dealing with familiar events and situations; picture books with fairy tales; jingles and nursery rhymes.	1–2 1–3 2–4 4–10 1–6

The Diagnostic Information Available

The family rarely arrives at the play room as an unknown entity. Usually, when the therapist meets the family for an observational assessment for the first time he has already conducted some telephone or face-to-face interviews with the parents and familiarized himself with the presenting problems and with many background details. The choice of the play means takes this information into consideration. Here are some examples:

Shoola, the mother of ten-year-old Gadi, called my clinic and told me how helpless she felt with Gadi. He was violent. She and her husband had a hard time attempting to set him limits. I wanted this pattern to be manifested in the family play session so that I could study it in detail. Therefore I decided to include in the collection of play means made available to the family objects that on the one hand encourage energetic, even aggressive, activity but on the other hand require acting in the framework of clear rules: play balls, boxing gloves and toys representing police weapons.

My colleague Galila had in therapy a nine-year-old girl, Beena. Her presenting problem was somatic complaints with no physical basis. Galila learned from an initial oral interview with Beena's parents that the family members were very reserved. They would speak only about neutral subjects and were not accustomed to expose their feelings. Beena's symptoms seemed to be directly related to this familial habit. Galila was interested in looking more closely into this pattern. Therefore she decided to supply the family with play means which encourage projection of emotionally laden themes in make-believe play, such as hand-puppets, masks and fancy dress.

The Ages of the Family Members and Their Interests

To arouse interest in the family members and stimulate them to a diagnostically significant activity, the therapist should attempt to adapt the choice of play means to their ages and inclinations. He can learn also about these from a prior interview with the parents. People like to do things they are good at and are familiar with. If they like dressing up they can be given fancy-dress, masks and make-up. If they enjoy making music they should be provided with musical and percussion instruments and if they prefer painting they will be offered paper and paints. Each person should be allowed to express himself or herself and communicate in his or her own characteristic style.

But what should be done if the therapist has no prior information about the family? If this is the case he can distribute many play-things of various kinds round the room, watch the activity and see which toys and other objects are selected spontaneously and what kinds of games are initiated. Later he can remove the play-things which have been ignored or found irrelevant.

Getting the Family to Play

One of the queries very often raised by novices is: how can parents be made to agree to play like little children? How can one persuade an adult to overcome the shyness and inhibitions which make it difficult for him to act in a childish manner? Moreover, how can one convince a parent that something so serious as therapy can be carried out by means of something so frivolous as play? My experience has shown that the difficulty is not so great as it may seem. My students and myself have hardly ever encountered a case in which family members, children or adults, refused and persisted in their refusal to take an active part in the family play. Many times we have been amazed to see how an adult who at first impressed us as being stiff, pedantic, strict and lacking any sense of humor was transformed after a few minutes into a child rolling on the carpet, mewing like a cat or quacking like a goose.

The willingness to play applies equally well to adults or children coming from non-Western cultures and from disadvantaged social strata. It seems that the power of play is greater than the power of personal or social inhibitions.

The therapist is advised to prepare the parents in advance for the fact that the assessment and the therapy are going to be conducted mainly through play, and get their consent, at least in principle. Parents might accept the idea of play a little more readily if it is suggested to them that this is the most suitable method where children are concerned. Play is children's natural medium of expression. In a talking therapy they get bored and find it difficult to keep track of the conversation or take an active part in it.

Before the family gathers in the room for the first time, the therapist, as explained above, prepares the room and the play means for their arrival. When they come into the room he welcomes·them with some words referring to the nature of the room and states his expectations. After such introduction the therapist sits aside and waits. In most cases, the initial reaction of all the family members is shyness and hesitation. The therapist does not have to intervene at this stage. After a few minutes the children are likely to start exploring the room and its content. They will turn their parents' attention to certain objects, asking questions such as "What's this?" "What does one do with this?", requesting help (e.g. "Daddy, help me put these boxing gloves on") or inviting a parent to participate (e.g. "Mummy, let's play with this doll's-house"). In most cases, this will be the beginning of a spontaneous game involving the children and at least one of the parents. If this does not happen, the therapist can help the children and their parents to start playing, in various manners such as:

Modeling

The therapist joins the children and plays together with them. In this way he sets an example for the parents, hoping that they follow his model and join the game.

Here is an illustration: when the family got into the room, the parents sat frozen in the corner. Ten-year-old Danny started to explore the toys scattered on the carpet. He found a pair of toy handcuffs and began playing with them on his own. When I realized that neither Danny nor any other family member was going to use the handcuffs as a means for making contact with one another and developing a meaningful play activity I approached Danny and asked him: "Do you know what these are?" Danny said: "Yes. They chain prisoners with them, like they show on TV". I said: "Shall I chain you or you chain me?" "I'll chain you", Danny replied. I showed him how to lock and unlock the handcuffs with a little key. Then I let him chain me and walk me around the room. At a certain point in the stroll I said: "Now you are being the cop and I am your prisoner." At this moment Danny's father started to show signs of interest in the game. He got up and was following the game with some curiosity. Then I said: "OK, now you are going to set me free". I handed the little key over to Danny, who released me. Now the father addressed Danny, saying: "How about you chaining me now?" This move made any further intervention on my side redundant, because a lively game of make-believe between father and son developed from that point on.

Inviting the Parents to Join

If the parents fail to spontaneously join the play activity shared by therapist and children, the therapist can, in his role as a peer in play, invite them to participate. He can do this by directly asking the parents to join in, or by less direct communication, such as handing a suitable toy over to the parent or assigning the parent a make-believe part in the play. For example, in the handcuffs game described above I might have addressed the father directly and said something like: "Daddy, please join us". Or, I might have assigned him a part in the play, saying: "Daddy is a prisoner on the run" or I could have simply taken hold of his hand and chained his wrist with a handcuff, smiling sweetly.

Using the Children as Ushers

If the therapist has used up all the tricks in his bag for making the parents move, there are always the children to do this job for him. Occasions are bound to arise in the course of the children's play, in which they need a parent in their game, as a helper, as a partner, or as an actor. This is the point where the therapist can use the child as a "bait" to entice the parent into the game.

In a family play therapy session a boy named Gal played an amusing and inventive game, in which he was "a record player". He stretched his arms and turned around singing a song. Then he repeated the same song and afterwards became slightly upset and complained that there were no more interesting records to play. I said: "But you are just a record player! How can a record player know which records to play? You need a disc jockey. Would you like your daddy to be your disc jockey?"

In another family play therapeutic experience, a girl called Tammy reconstructed a visit to the local museum with her parents the day before. She asked her parents to join her game as "the daddy and mummy", but they were too shy to start acting. Then I pointed at the parents and said to Tammy: "Look at these statues! Aren't they beautiful?"

Asking the Parents to Direct the Show

The therapist can address the parents' sense of responsibility with respect to their children and ask them to take charge of their children's game. Once they are involved as initiators or organizers they can be drawn into the role of active participants in one of the ways described above.

Nine-year-old Monny and his eight-year-old sister Bar were examining masks and fancy dress. Monny picked a rabbit's mask and was trying to fit it on his sister's face, but could not fix it. Ruttie, the therapist, addressed the parents:

"They want to do a show with masks and fancy-dress, but do not seem to manage with the masks. Would you help them?" The parents agreed. Bar was a rabbit and Monny a wolf. Ruttie said: "And what are Mummy and Daddy going to be?" The father said: "I'll be the hunter", and Bar said: "Mummy will be Mother Rabbit". The father, enthusiastic, suggested the following story: "The little rabbit went for a walk in the jungle. The bad wolf was lying in wait for him. But the wolf did not know that the hunter was already out to chase him. Meanwhile Mother Rabbit got very worried".

The ideas proposed in this chapter are applicable of course to all the stages of the therapy, not just to the initial assessment.

CHAPTER 6

Recording and Transcribing the Observations

The Usefulness of the Recording and Transcription Techniques

We are now about to go into the heart of the matter of family assessment based on observing free play.

The following pages include a presentation of techniques for recording and transcribing observations of behavior in general, and family play behavior in particular. The term "recording" refers to the videotaping of the observed family play, or, if videotaping facilities are unavailable, to the writing of a description of the observed activity. The term "transcription" refers here to a detailed analytic representation and organization of the videotaped or hand-recorded activity, using a specialized technical language. Appropriate analogies are: recording music by audiotaping and transcribing it by writing it in musical notation; recording a terrain by taking aerial photographs of it and transcribing it by drawing a topographical map.

These techniques serve the following purposes:

Improving Observation Skills

Novices in family therapy who are asked to observe family play activity, experience, characteristically, a strange feeling of being lost, unable to make head or tail of the whirlpool of fast-moving, ever-changing scenes. This difficulty should by no means be considered a proof of lack of skill or ability. It is natural in view of the characteristic richness and complexity of the activity observed. The training of strategic family play therapists includes practice in transcribing, microanalyzing and macroanalyzing videotaped samples of family make-believe play, using the techniques presented below. This method has proved to be highly effective. Novices who have undergone such training have demonstrated a considerably improved ability to apprehend and describe accurately the family make-believe play activities they have observed or participated in.

Systematizing the Assessment

Transcribing and microanalyzing recorded stretches of family make-believe play is an extremely laborious and time-consuming task. It is practicable and manageable as part and parcel of routine family play therapy assessment only if applied to a very small, though representative, sample of the recorded activity. Despite this restriction, it is highly recommended that the habit of including a piece of work of this sort in the assessment be formed. This can improve upon an impressionistic analysis in a number of important respects:

Revealing the family members' private codes

Very often major clues, crucial for the observer to be able to interpret the family's play behavior and infer its dysfunctional programs, are barely perceptible. Being a part of the family's own private code, they manifest themselves in subtle distinctions that can be noticed and understood only by the family members themselves. When the therapist records, transcribes and microanalyzes a sample of the family's play behavior his chances of noticing and deciphering such distinctions are raised considerably. This is illustrated in the following example:

Shimon, a six-year-old boy, was raised by his widowed mother in his grandparents' home.

Shimon considered himself "the man of the house". No one had the right to tell him what to do or not to do. Should any trouble befall his mother he would be the one to rescue her and put everything right. His mother felt quite helpless *vis-a-vis* this attitude. Her helplessness, in turn, reinforced Shimon's illusory omnipotence.

I invited Shimon to play with his mother in the play therapy room. Throughout the session he was very busy playing with the toys, but did not utter a word. His favorite toy was an eagle. He moved its wings vigorously and made it pounce on his mother, over and over again. His mother reacted in two different ways: several times she pushed the eagle away and said impatiently: "Shimon, stop it. I don't like this game". But at other times she caressed the toy eagle and said: "You are a soft little bird". There seemed to be no apparent reason for this inconsistency in her responses.

This session was videotaped. The moments of contact between Simon and his mother were transcribed and microanalyzed by my student Sarah. This close inspection revealed the following: the mother's tender, affectionate response was not coincidental. It came regularly after Simon had introduced almost imperceptible changes in the way he handled the toy eagle. In those moments he lowered the eagle a little, moved its wings more slowly and bent its left wing.

Sarah and I asked ourselves what these slight differences meant. We came, independently, to the same conclusion: the latter gestures appeared to signify a tired out, weakened eagle whose left wing was perhaps wounded or broken. They seemed to signal to Shimon's mother: "I am exhausted. I can't continue pretending to be so powerful. Help me". His mother was able to read this signal, understand it, perhaps subconsciously, and respond as Shimon expected her to respond. She shared a private code with Shimon, so subtle that it could not be perceived offhand by an external observer. It could be deciphered only with the aid of a painstaking application of our transcription and microanalysis techniques.

Avoiding bias

An impressionistic description and analysis of observed family play tends to be biased. It is influenced by the observer's limitations, subjective tendencies and predispositions. The above-mentioned transcription and analytic techniques secure more objective, more balanced representations. Their user is more likely to report what he actually heard or saw, rather than what he *thinks* he heard or saw. He stands a better chance of forming a reliable and valid account of the behavior observed.

A Method for Hand-recording Observations

If the therapist has no videotaping facilities he is left with no choice but to hand-record what he sees or hears. Those who have attempted to record an accurate description of a complex activity while it is actually going on know how difficult this task is. A myriad of things happen at the same time and quickly slip away. It is not easy to take them in. It is not easy to focus on any single one of them and it is even more difficult to record them. It is hard to find suitable words for describing what is being seen and heard, since natural, everyday language is not suited for an accurate objective description of ob-served behavior. Most of the expressions representing human behavior in ordinary language are rather vague and ambiguous. Their meaning depends on the specific context and on the observer's viewpoint. In such expressions objec-tive criteria are mixed with subjective, emotional or judgmental criteria. Take for instance the word "hold", as it is defined in *Crabb's English Synonyms* (1916): "'hold' is a term of a very general import. To *hold* is a term unqualified by any circumstance; we may hold a thing in any direction, hold it up or down, in a straight or oblique direction . . ." Or take Crabb's definition of "smear": "To 'smear' in the literal sense is applied to such substances as may be rubbed like grease over a body; if said of grease itself, it may be proper; as coachmen *smear* the coach-wheels with tar or grease; but if said of anything else, it is an improper action, and tends to disfigure, as children *smear* their hands with ink, or *smear* their clothes with dirt".

Considering all these difficulties, hand-recording seems like "a mission impossible". However, various techniques have been developed for overcoming such obstacles. The following method has been found useful for reducing the difficulty of looking, listening and writing at the same time. The observer concentrates on watching and listening for a short time, no more than three minutes. During this time span he turns himself, as it were, into a videotape recorder. He lets his eyes and ears do their own independent job as fully and accurately as possible, with little interference from non-sensory sources. Then he disengages himself from the observed activity for a few minutes and concentrates just on writing, attempting to retrieve and reconstruct as many details of what he heard and saw as possible. He does not have to formulate his descriptions in full well-formed sentences. He can make up a shorthand system of his own and for this particular purpose, using various kinds of clues and mnemonic devices which will help him recall and fill in the missing details later on. In each line or paragraph of this first draft the verbal and non-verbal behavior of each of the family members will be described in the following sequences: spatial behavior (relative location, distance and direction), verbal and vocal behavior (words said, speech and other sounds pronounced and the manners in which they were uttered), motional behavior (postures, movements and facial expressions) and manipulative behavior (the ways in which people, objects and materials are touched and handled). Here is an example:

The following family make-believe play activity was observed by a group of Dutch trainees in strategic family play therapy in Amsterdam.

Els, playing the role of a ten-year-old girl, got hold of two pieces of blue plastic string and laid them on the carpet, so that two long, parallel winding lines were formed. Then she put a doll representing a little girl inside a toy boat and moved the boat slowly on the carpet between and along the two plastic strings. At this point it became obvious to me that the two plastic strings represented a river. While the "little girl" was sailing on the river in her boat, the girl's father and mother (played by Pim and Tineke) were absorbed in their own play, which went as follows: they both put on hand puppets. Mother's was "a bloodhound" and father's "Mickey Mouse". The hound was chasing Mickey Mouse, barking fiercely, whereas the latter was running away toward the river, shrieking. At this moment the boat carrying the little girl started moving toward Mickey Mouse, until it reached the river bank. The girl invited Mickey Mouse to climb on her boat with a hand gesture. But the hound pounced upon the boat and drove it into the river with loud barks.

This episode was hand-recorded by the observers, using the above-mentioned technique. Here is the telegraphic description recorded by one of the trainees:

Segment 1

Els: Room center, kneeling, back to parents. 2 blue strings right hand, put parallel, about 10″ wide.
Pim: About 1 yard away from girl, perpendicular to girl, kneeling. Mickey on right hand.

Segment 2

Els: Bent over 2 plastic. Girl doll into toy boat with left hand. Moves boat slowly on carpet along 2 plastic, between.
Tineke: Arm with hound toward father. Sharp thrusts of hand. Barking.
Pim: Turns toward daughter. Hand with Mickey moving fast toward daughter. "Please don't bite me!" with squeaky pleading voice.

Segment 3

Els: Front toward father. Move boat fast toward father until touches string (river bank?). Makes doll's arm stretch toward Mickey. Bends doll's arm three times upwards.
Pim: Looks at Mickey and doll. Makes Mickey go closer to doll.
Tineke: Arm with hound fast toward doll. Pushes doll with boat with strong thrusts, barking.

Immediately after the observation, the observer re-reads what he wrote, adds details from memory and reformulates the laconic expressions in a fuller, more readable style.

If this is feasible, the recording should be done not by the therapist himself, but by a trained observer or a co-therapist behind a one-way mirror.

Again, it is impossible and unnecessary to record everything. One should sample interactions that seem intuitively to be revealing. Special attention should be given to recurring patterns and to unexpected sequences that take the observer by surprise.

The Initial Stage Chart

For the reader of a hand-recorded protocol to be able to get a more or less clear picture of what actually happened in the playroom, the written description should refer to some initial state, which includes the relative positions of the participants and the relevant objects in the room at the onset of the observation. Thus, for instance, if the reader of a protocol encounters a sentence such as "The boy crawled two yards forward", he cannot possibly visualize where the boy came from and where he proceeded, unless the location and orientation of the boy before he crawled has been mentioned in the protocol.

How can the boy's former location and spatial orientation be specified? They can be specified, for instance, by describing the movements that eventually brought the boy to his present location and orientation (e.g. crawling one yard leftwards). They can also be specified by portraying his original position, at the onset of the activity.

The *initial stage* of an activity can be represented graphically by a chart such as Figure 1, which is based on a single picture taken out of a videotaped observation or on direct observation. In such a chart the initial stage is depicted schematically. It is represented as if viewed from above. To arrive at such a drawing, the following two mental operations should be performed: (1) the three-dimensional view seen horizontally (see Figure 2) has to be transformed into a vertical view, like an aerial photograph. (Imagine yourself lying on the roof and looking at the people and objects in the room through a hole in the ceiling); (2) the observation should be placed within an imaginary square.

Operation (1) is not easy to perform, since it requires visual skills not possessed by everyone in an equal degree, such as estimating the distances between and the orientation of people and objects seen horizontally and imagining how they would look from above. Despite these difficulties the decription from above should not be forgone. Only such a view renders it possible to see clearly the locations, relative distances and orientations of people and objects in the activity area. Even if the view from above is not accurate but based on rough approximation, it is preferable to a direct representation of a horizontal view, which conveys very little relevant information.

Operation (1) can be omitted if a mirror is hung over the activity area diagonally, slanted at 45 degrees. The activity will be reflected in the mirror as if it is looked at from above.

Crossing co-ordinate lines are drawn on the initial stage chart, as displayed in Figure 1. The points where these lines meet the perimeter line of the square are numbered clockwise from zero upwards, starting with the new central point on the bottom line. These co-ordinates and their ordinal numbers render it possible to specify the approximate directions of the objects and people in the activity area. For example, the front of the father's body in Figure 1 is turned to direction 6. The mother's elbows, which are placed on the table, are directed to 0.

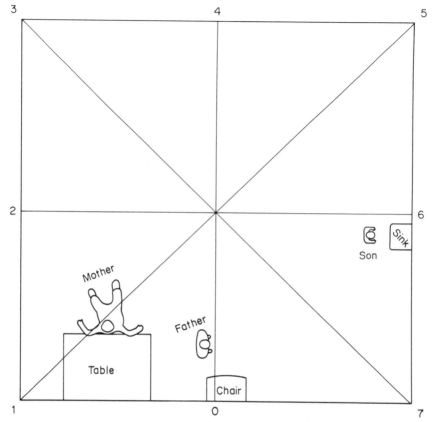

Figure 1   Initial stage chart, vertical view

The sink is directed to 2, and so forth. If the direction of an object, a body or a part of the body is not parallel to any of the co-ordinate lines, the + and – marks may be used. For example, the mother's left knee is turned toward 3+.

If the location or direction of a body changes, the change can be described in relation to its location or direction in the initial state, as these have been specified in the initial stage chart.

For example, with the initial stage chart in Figure 1 as a description of the initial state in the room, one can write: "Son turns around through his left shoulder and walks three yards toward 4–, then he crawls toward 1 until his forehead touches his mother's knee". Looking at Figure 1, the reader of this statement can very easily visualize the movements of the boy crossing the room.

Figure 2   Initial stage chart, horizontal view

The General Format of a Transcription Page

The video-recorded or hand-recorded observation is transcribed on pages of standardized format as displayed schematically in Table 5. The vertical dimension is divided into columns, each of which is labeled by an ordinal numeral, from left to right. The numbers represent time units of a standard duration (e.g. 30 seconds, 60 seconds, etc.). The standard duration of the time units is determined by the transcriber according to his purposes and the technical devices he has at his disposal. The smaller a standard unit is, the greater the refinement and accuracy of the transcription.

On the horizontal dimension the verbal and non-verbal behavior of each of the participants in the play activity is transcribed. Four rows are allocated to each participant. One row is devoted to a general impressionistic description of the participant's behavior at each time unit, formulated in ordinary language. In the other three rows the same behavior is described more accurately and rigorously. One row is devoted to the participant's vocal and linguistic behavior. Ideally it is transcribed both in ordinary English and in a phonetic transcription. Another row (which is subdivided into a suitable number of lines) is devoted to the participant's spatial (proxemic) and motional (kinesic) behavior. Ideally, these aspects are transcribed by Eshkol and Wachman's Movement Notation (see 1958) and Ekman's facial notation (see 1978). The

Table 5   The general format of the transcription page.

Time units	1	2	3	4	5	. . .
Behavior of each participant						
General description						
Vocal-linguistic						
Motional (kinesic) and spatial (proxemic)						
Touching (manipulative)						

fourth row (which is also subdivided into lines) is for transcribing the participant's touching (manipulative) behavior, that is, the contacts between his or her
body (mainly his or her hands) and other human or non-human objects in the
room. Ideally, this is transcribed by Touchnotation, a notational system developed by the present writer to transcribe behavior involving contacts.

These technical notational systems are too elaborate to be introduced here.
The reader is urged to take courses in which they are taught or at least to learn
them from books. Here are some references:

Phonetic transcriptions: International Phonetics Alphabet (IPA) 1964, Singh
and Singh, 1976.
Movement Notation: Eshkol, 1980.
Ekman's Facial Action Coding System: Ekman, 1978.
Ariel's Touchnotation: Ariel, 1985.

Transcribing Vocal-linguistic Behavior

One of the participants in a family play activity says something, e.g. "I am a
baby monster and I am now being born". The first step in attempting to
transcribe this utterance is to specify its duration, using the columns in the
transcription page, which, as mentioned above, are labeled with ordinal numer-
als representing standard time units. Suppose the observation was transcribed
from a videotape and the standard size of a time unit was determined to be one

second. The time it took the boy to produce this utterance was measured with a stopwatch, and was found to be five seconds, starting in the tenth second and ending in the fifteenth second. Therefore, this sentence should be transcribed in the row devoted to the boy's vocal-linguistic behavior, within the columns labeled 10–15 as shown in Table 6: ample space should be left within the same row for a phonetic transcription of the same sentence. It is not necessary though to write every sound produced by each participant in the family play in a phonetic alphabet. Only special phenomena whose meaning is not readily understood should be transcribed phonetically, e.g. unexpected lisping and other baby talk characteristics in an older child, stuttering, unusually drawn out vowels, atypical intonation patterns, etc. The phonetic transcription directs one's attention to and sharpens one's perception of phenomena that might turn out to be relevant to the interpretation of the family play behavior.

Table 6   Transcription of vocal-linguistic behavior.

Time units		1	2	3	...	10	11	12	13	14	15	16	17
Boy	Vocal-linguistic					I am a baby monster and I am now being born							

Transcribing Spatial and Kinesic Behavior

It will be observed that body motional and spatial behavior goes on not only when the person observed speaks out but also when he is silent. Therefore, the transcription of the proxemic and kinesic behavior of a given participant does not usually cover the same time units as the transcription of his or her vocal behavior. Suppose one wants to transcribe the proxemic (spatial) and kinesic (motional) behavior of the boy who said "I am a baby monster and I am now being born" (see above). This boy moved in the room space and changed his facial expressions not just in the five seconds in which he uttered this sentence, but also in other time units. Therefore, the transcription of his spatial and kinesic behavior will occupy not just the columns numbered 10–15 but other columns as well.

In Table 7 I provide an informal description, in ordinary everyday English, of this behavior. The vocal behavior of the boy is also included, for comparison.

The expression 0+ refers to the initial stage chart. One can see clearly how the spatial-motional behavior is related to the vocal behavior time-wise. The boy walked toward the center of the room before he pronounced his sentence. Then, when he said it, he was lying on his back, wiggling his arms and bent legs, opening and closing his mouth and raising his protruding head, apparently playing the role of the baby monster. Completing the utterance of this

Table 7   Transcription of spatial-motional behavior.

Time units		1	2	3	4	5	6	7	8	9	10	11	12	13	14	15	16	17
	Vocal-linguistic										I am a baby monster and I am now being born							
Boy	Spatial-motional			Walking two steps toward 0+, fast							In room center, lying on back. Wiggles arms and bent legs. Opens and closes mouth. Head raised, protruding. Turns to lying on stomach.							

sentence, he turned over to lying on his belly. This latter move symbolizes perhaps the idea of "being born".

A more detailed and precise representation of the spatial-motional behavior will require the use of Eshkol-Wachman's Movement Notation and Ekman's Facial Action Coding System.

The decision of what to transcribe should again be dictated mainly by whether the meaning or communicative functions of the movement in question are obvious or not.

Transcribing Touching Behavior

One row (with as many sub-rows, or lines, as needed) will be devoted to transcribing the touching (manipulative) behavior of each of the participants in the activity. The touching behavior, like the vocal and spatial-motional behavior, will be described in ordinary everyday language in the appropriate columns in the transcription page, but special phenomena, in particular contacts with objects, materials or people whose meaning is not readily interpretable should be rendered in Touchnotation.

Table 8 contains an informal, everyday language description of the touching behavior of our boy.

The behavior of the other family members participating in the family play session can be organized and transcribed in the same manner. Table 9 shows a schematic representation of the resulting score.

Table 8 Transcription of spatial-motional behavior.

Time units		1	2	3	4	5	6	7	8	9	10	11	12	13	14	15	16	17
Boy	Vocal-linguistic										I am a baby monster and I am now being born							
	Spatial-motional		Walking two steps toward 0+, fast								In room center, lying on back Wiggles arms and bent legs. Opens and closes mouth. Head raised, protruding. Turns to lying on stomach.							
	Touching		Holds baby bottle in right hand.				Drops bottle.				Scratches carpet with finger nail.							

Table 9 The general format of a transcription score.

	Time units	1	2	3	4	5	6	7	8	9	10	11	12	13	14	15 ...
Boy	Vocal-linguistic															
	Spatial-motional															
	Touching															
Father	Vocal-linguistic															
	Spatial Motional															
	Touching															
Mother	Vocal-linguistic															
	Spatial-Motional															
	Touching															

Such a score equips its reader with a clear, detailed picture of the play behavior of all the family members. Like the score of a trio, it tells one what kind of music was played by each participant at any given moment, and which harmonious structures were created by the whole ensemble.

CHAPTER 7

Microscopic Analysis of Transcribed Observations

From Microscopic to Macroscopic Analysis

As was pointed out in Chapter 6, transcribing the family play observations involves meticulous analysis and much interpretation. However, transcribing is just the first stage of the deciphering procedure. Let us now move to the next stage, in which one attempts to uncover and describe the meaning, communicative functions and structure of the observed play behavior. In these stages one proceeds from the particular to the general, that is to say, from a *microscopic* examination, in which the behavior is broken down into small units, and each unit is looked into separately, to a *macroscopic* overview, which uncovers and formulates broad generalizations applying to interrelations among these units.

The transcription constitutes an initial microscopic description and interpretation of the behavior on the *raw-material level*. On this level the manifest, physical, partly observable behavior is described. As was specified in Chapter 6, behavior on this level may be sorted into vocal-linguistic, motional, spatial and tactile. However, the raw-material level serves mainly as a medium for expressing meaning. The meaning which is manifested on the raw-material level is analyzed and described on two other levels: the *semantic* level, where the *private thoughts and feelings* expressed by the raw material are analyzed and described, and the *pragmatic* (communicational) level, in which the *interpersonal thoughts* expressed by the same raw material are specified (see Chapter 1). For example, in the context of a family play session, a boy bared his teeth at his mother. On the raw material level this is regarded as a facial expression with specific characteristics that can be described accurately by Ekman's Facial Action Coding System. On the semantic level this facial expression stands for the make-believe thematic content (private thought) "a panther baring its teeth", and also for the emotive meaning (private feeling) "anger". On the communicational level this can be interpreted as an interpersonal thought, a message to the boy's mother to stop paying so much attention to his father.

The *structure* of the family's play behavior is the set of interrelations among the raw materials, their thematic and emotive meanings and their communicational, interpersonal meanings. The *macroscopic* view looks for structure. The structure is explicated as a system of *rules*. The latter are sorts of formulae, stating as succinctly as possible what kinds of actual or potential interrelations among the various raw-material, semantic and communicational units can exist, and which such interrelations cannot possibly exist under any circumstances.

Here are three examples, to illustrate the concept "rule":

(1) David always uses toys made of soft materials to express aggressive contents in his play (e.g. a shark made of wool).

This rule is a kind of concise formula describing a fixed relation between a class of raw-material units (soft toys) and a class of semantic units (aggressive themes).

(2) When Hava wants her mother to leave her alone she pretends to be asleep.

This rule describes a relation between a communicational message ("leave me alone"), semantic content ("being asleep") and certain raw-material features (going through the motions of sleeping).

(3) When Shaul picks a toy representing a lethal weapon his mother leaves the room on some pretext.

This rule represents a fixed relation between raw material and semantic entities introduced by Shaul (a toy weapon and the real weapon it represents) and raw-material and communicational entities generated by the mother (her *presupposition* (see Chapter 1) that the boy's choice of a toy constitutes an act of aggression against herself, and her spatial and motional acts of leaving the room).

This procedure of induction and generalization from a microscopic to a macroscopic analysis is quite different from what people usually do when they observe other people's behavior and attempt to make sense of it. What they actually do is the following. They sample a few details. Then, on the basis of these details, they draw broad generalizations. Later, when additional details come in, they modify these generalizations to make them fit the new information. One sees a five-year-old boy dressing up and admiring himself in front of the mirror, imitating his six-year-old sister. One concludes that this boy is attached to his sister and identifies with her. This generalization will be varied if and when a different situation is encountered, e.g. one in which the boy plays "war" with other boys, with his sister as "the enemy". This is not the same as the linear step-by-step progress from a microscopic to a macroscopic analysis proposed here. Admittedly, the latter is less natural, more constrained, than the former. However, the microscopic–macroscopic procedure is more systematic and not so prone to over-generalizations and other errors of judgment. It is particularly useful to use this procedure in the stage of training, in which the practitioner has not yet acquired the skill and facility required for analyzing and interpreting the family's play behavior.

The Steps of Microscopic Analysis

The procedure of microscopic analysis is described schematically in Table 10.

Table 10   Procedure of microscopic analysis.

Steps	Level of semiotic analysis	Analytic operations
First	Raw material	Dividing the transcribed activity into units
Second	Semantic	Attempting to determine the thematic and emotive contents of each unit in the given context
Third	Pragmatic	Describing combinations of activity units that have a communicational meaning. Describing the interpersonal thoughts expressed by each combination

Let me now specify each of these steps in detail:

Step 1: Activity Units

The first step in the microscopic analysis is dividing the transcribed activity into units. Activity units are the building blocks by which the activity of each family member is constructed.

An *activity unit* is a group of raw-material features (vocal-linguistic, spatial, motional and tactual) which has a distinct semantic or communicational meaning. None of its subgroups is meaningful.

Let me illustrate this notion by a simple example: a military salute. This act does not ordinarily have a distinct thematic or emotive meaning, but it does have distinct communicative functions, such as transmitting the message that you acknowledge the other person's superior rank. These functions are possessed by the whole aggregate of motional and spatial features constituting the salute, not by any subgroup of these features. For instance, touching one's temple with the tips of the right hand fingers and standing at attention position without holding the elbow at the appropriate angle would not be considered a salute.

Suppose that in a child's play walking on all fours and barking has the meaning "dog", whereas walking on all fours and mewing has the meaning "cat". None of these combinations of movement and sound is, by the above definition, an activity unit, since each of them can be divided into smaller meaningful elements, namely walking on all fours, barking and mewing. Imagine however a girl making funny movements with her back touching the wall. The meaning of this combination of motional and spatial features in the context in hand is "the man on TV". In this case the spatial position (back to the wall, touching the wall) and the movements constitute together a single activity unit, since each of them in itself has no independent meaning.

In Step 1 the transcribed activity is examined and divided into activity units. The performer of this task may use both the above definition and his own common sense and intuition.

Step 2: Semantic Interpretation of Activity Units

The difference between a semantic interpretation (assigning thematic and emotive meanings to activity units) and interpretation of communicational meaning is that in the former the focus is on the private meaning that the activity unit has for its producer, and not on what the producer wants to impart to other people through this unit. In other words, the semantic interpretation refers to personal, asocial aspects of meaning and the pragmatic interpretation to interpersonal, social aspects. Let us go back for a minute to the activity unit consisting of the girl making funny movements with her back touching the wall. On the semantic level this unit has a thematic meaning, "the man on TV". Apparently it also has an emotive meaning. It seems to express the girl's excitement or restlessness. These are private, personal meanings, reflecting a slice of the girl's inner world of fantasy and feeling. However, the same activity unit can also serve as a medium for sending a message to other people. The message can be, for instance: "You spend too much time watching TV at the expense of paying attention to me, so now I am the man on TV and you will have to pay attention to me". This would be the communicational meaning.

The semantic meaning of an activity unit cannot be determined by any mechanical procedure. It should be inferred from the raw-material features of the activity unit itself and from the specific context in which the unit in question occurs. Often the producer of the activity unit himself or herself will explicate its semantic meaning. He will say for instance: "I am the man on TV". In some cases it would be appropriate to ask the player what he or she meant. In other cases the interpreter would have to rely on an educated guess.

Step 3: Finding Combinations That Have a Communicational Meaning

Often, a communicational meaning (interpersonal thought; see Chapter 1) will be attached not to a single activity unit, but to a combination of activity units that roughly corresponds to a sentence in a verbal language. For example, a child will produce two activity units—one whose semantic meaning is "lion" and another whose semantic meaning is "roaring". However, only the combination "the lion is roaring" will have communicative functions, such as a threat, directed to his sister, that she should keep away from his mother. Therefore, before one attempts to assign communicative functions to activity units, one should sort out those combinations of activity units that carry these communicative functions.

Step 4: Revealing the Interpersonal Thoughts

This is a crucial step. None of the components of the micmoscopic analysis captures the essence of the system of interpersonal relationships in the family better than the analysis of the family members' interpersonal thoughts.

The main types of interpersonal thoughts, namely *presupposition, purpose* and *prediction*, have been discussed and illustrated in Chapter 1.

What has been said above about the process by which semantic meaning is revealed and determined applies just as well to the discovery and formulation of interpersonal, communicative meaning.

The Reliability and Validity of the Interpretations

It was stated above that the semantic meaning of activity units cannot be determined mechanically but must be inferred from the context. The same applies to the communicational meaning (interpersonal thoughts). Let us recall that the interpretation of semantic or communicational meaning is in a sense an attempt to read people's minds. Therefore there is always an element of surmise and speculation in such interpretations. The same activity units can be interpreted in a number of different ways. It is not always easy to decide which of them is preferable. This raises the problem of the reliability and validity of the microscopic analysis.

The very fact that what is at issue is an attempt to reveal private thoughts and feelings makes the question of reliability and validity at this juncture problematic. The adequacy or inadequacy of competing interpretations offered for the same combinations of activity units can be tested, in the long run, by seeing which of the interpretations proposed add up to a consistent, complete and coherent picture.

In a family play session, eight-year-old Neemy and her seven-year-old sister Eira were playing in the sand box. They were "sailing in a love boat". Their five-year-old brother Assaf threw a rope into the sand box and pretended to "climb up the love boat". This scene was videotaped and analyzed by a group of students in a family play therapy course for social workers. Most of the students agreed that the *purpose* of Assaf's act was simply to join his sisters and feel that he is a part of their group. However, one of the students insisted that although this seemed to be the obvious interpretation, Assaf's act had in fact a different purpose: to be accepted by his father. She based this hypothesis on the following considerations: the "love boat" in the sisters' game had a destination: the king's castle on the shore. The king was, of course, their father. She also noticed that the two sisters and their father formed a kind of play triad, and whenever their brother tried to join in he was subtly rejected by the father. Further observations considerably reinforced this latter interpretation as against the majority's interpretation. It was noticed, for instance, that Assaf refused to participate in the sisters' games, although they invited him to join in, when the father was not included. In these cases he preferred to try and make a direct contact with his father.

This example suggests that the microscopic analysis is not in fact as atomistic as it seems to be. It is a dynamic procedure, in which the context is taken into account and in which interpretations are added or discarded as further relevant information streams in. The considerations on which the ultimate decisions as to the choice of the best interpretations rest are global and quite complex. The kind of thinking on which these considerations are based can on principle be explicated and formalized, but this task is beyond the scope of this work (see Ariel, 1992).

The Role of the Microscopic Analysis in the Assessment

Basically, the microscopic analysis is not an end in itself, but a means to an end. It serves as a prelude to the macroscopic analysis. The entities which strategic family play therapy attempts to change, namely, the family's *dysfunctional programs*, are defined by a macroscopic analysis, not by a microscopic one. However, this does not mean that the microscopic analysis has no independent diagnostic value. Quite the contrary; the actual process of assessment and therapeutic intervention takes place entirely on the microscopic level. The therapist comes to the session equipped with broad macroscopic generalizations about the family's dysfunctional programs. However, he still has to perceive and attempt to understand the minute details of the verbal and non-verbal behavior of the family members at any given moment, before he can decide on an appropriate intervention. The microscopic analysis is an ongoing process that continues incessantly during the whole of each session.

An Example of a Microscopic Analysis

The procedure of microscopic analysis proposed above will now be illustrated by the following description, based on a videotaped family play therapeutic session conducted in my clinic. First this episode will be described in an informal style, so that the reader may have the feel of it. Then a small selection of activity units, transcribed in ordinary English, will be presented and interpreted.

Some Background

The family includes Gad, a forty-year-old man, his thirty-year-old wife Neta and their five-year-old adopted boy, Yoram. For both parents this is their second marriage. Yoram was adopted by Neta when she was still married to her first husband. Gad, who divorced his wife to marry Neta, left three children with his first wife. He has found it difficult to accept Yoram and treat him like his own son. Neta, too, had difficulties in realizing her acquired motherhood. Gad's difficulty in this respect added to her own. Yoram's behavior was no help. He was aggressive, babyish and uncooperative.

An Informal Description

Yoram kneels by Gad, who sits on an armchair. Neta sits on a chair a few yards away from Gad and Yoram. The therapist, Sari, kneels in another corner of the room, facing the family. Various toys are scattered on the carpet.

Yoram holds a squeaking toy shark in his right hand. Gad wears a hand-puppet representing a fish on his right hand. Neta also wears a hand-puppet representing a fish.

Yoram gets up. He makes his shark attack his father's fish with sharp thrusts, squeaking violently. His father evades the attacks. He winces. He says in a quiet, though somewhat anxious voice: Oh, no, no, no! You are not going to get me!

Yoram makes his shark bite Gad's arm.
GAD *(shocked)*. You bit my arm!
YORAM. I did not.
GAD. You did!
YORAM. That's impossible. It's not a real one.
Yoram quits Gad and approaches Neta, making his shark attack her fish in the same manner. She smiles and evades him, saying pleadingly. Please shark, don't eat me up! I don't want you to eat me up!

Yoram makes his shark bite her arm.

Neta pulls her arm away with a sharp movement. Her face becomes serious and wears an amazed expression. She says in a somewhat childish tone. What a frightening shark!

YORAM. I ate you up. Now I want to eat more fish.

NETA. What an enormous belly he has! There's room there for so many fish!

Yoram picks another hand-puppet representing a fish from the carpet and throws it at Neta.

SARI. Maybe you can become friends with the shark. If you become his friends he is not going to attack you.

NETA *(to Gad)*. Perhaps we can speak nicely with him, and then he will not eat us up.

SARI. A hug can be helpful too.

Yoram stands between his parents. He moves the shark in the air with arching movements, apparently pretending that it is swimming in the water.

GAD. If you don't eat us up, I'll give you other fish to eat, OK?

YORAM. No, he is not hungry any more *(squeaking)*.

NETA *(smiling gratefully)*. So you will not eat us up.

YORAM. Let's pretend it's an ordinary fish, a different one.

(His tone is now mild and childish. His movements limp).

NETA *(surprised)*. Is it not a shark any more? What are you?

YORAM. A fish.

NETA *(in disbelief)*. You don't want to eat us up any more?

YORAM. No, because a fish does not eat up. A fish swims.

GAD. Can we swim with him?

YORAM. No, only he swims.

NETA. Come to me, shark.

YORAM *(yelling in a whining voice)*. He is not a shark!

Neta attempts to caress the toy shark in his hand.

NETA. You are a cute shark. Do you want to be my friend? You are a special shark. All the other sharks in the sea eat up people and fish, but you are a special shark.

Yoram makes his shark squeak violently. He evades his mother's caresses. He sits on the carpet.

GAD. Are you not a shark? May I join you?

YORAM. He is not outside. He is at home. He went to bring over another fish.

NETA. We are all right. We are still alive. Where does the shark live? Where does he live? Where does he live? *(She asks this question nervously)*.

YORAM. Let them come too.

Yoram walks slowly away from his parents with the shark held in front of him in both hands. His parents get up and follow him slowly.

NETA *(nervously, anxiously)*. Yoram, Yoram, where are you going with that shark?

Analysis of activity units

Figure 3 shows an initial stage chart. The activity units are represented as segments of an ordinary English transcription. The standard size of each unit is 30 seconds. The time units of each activity unit are numbered separately, from 1 on. The expression AU will serve as an abbreviation for activity unit and the expression CAU for combination of activity units.

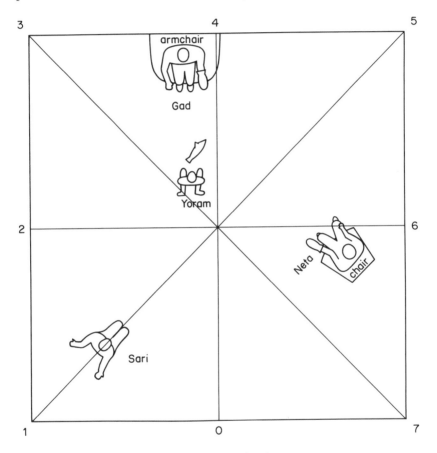

Figure 3   Initial stage chart for Yoram and his family

Here is a citation from the informal description:
"Yoram gets up. He makes his shark attack Gad's fish with sharp thrusts, squeaking violently".
This segment is a combination of activity units, which can be transcribed as shown on Table 11.

Table 11   Transcription of first segment of Yoram's behavior.

CAU1										
	1	2	3	4	5	6	7	8	9	10
Vocal-linguistic		sharp squeak			sharp squeak			sharp squeak		
Spatial-motional		Stands about the intersection of 4+ and 5+ (see initial stage chart), facing 4+, where father sits. Pursues father's evading movements.								
	Stretches arms forward with a sharp thrust toward father's fish		Bends arms at elbows		Repeat thrust		Repeat bend		Repeat thrust	
Tactile		Presses toy shark firmly to chest with both hands. High muscular tension and pressure.								

This combination of activity units includes the following activity units:

AU1: Toy shark.
Semantic interpretation: thematic meaning—a shark.

AU2: Vocal-linguistic: sharp squeak.
Spatial-motional: thrust.
Touching: firm hold, tension and pressure.
Semantic interpretation: thematic meaning—shark attacking.
Emotive meaning—aggression, anger.

AU3: Repetition of squeaks and thrusts.
Semantic interpretation: repeated attempts to catch victim.

AU4: Facing toy fish and directing thrusts toward it. Coordinating the thrusts with the latter's evading movements.
Semantic interpretation: fish attacked by shark.

Communicational interpretation of CAU1

Presuppositions: Father does not like me, thinks I am bad. He is also afraid of me.

Purposes: Punish father for his rejection. Make him feel my anger.

Now to the next combination of activity units. Here is another citation from the informal description:

"Gad evades the attacks. He winces. He says in a quiet, though somewhat anxious voice: 'Oh, no, no, no, you are not going to get me!'"

This citation is now transcribed in Table 12.

Table 12   Transcription of first segment of Gad's behavior.

CAU2										
	1	2	3	4	5	6	7	8	9	10
Vocal-linguistic						Oh, no, no, no (fast), you are not going to get me! (quiet, slightly trembling)				
Spatial-motional	Flinch. Pulls hand with fish puppet back. Sits. Faces Yoram					Flinch. Pulls hand with fish puppet up				

This combination of activity units includes the following activity units:

AU5: Fish puppet: Semantic interpretation: a fish.

AU6: Vocal: fast, slightly trembling voice. Motional spatial: flinches, pulls hand back or up. Faces Yoram.
Semantic interpretation: thematic meaning—fish afraid of attacking shark.
Emotive meaning—mild fear.

AU7: Oh, no, no, no (fast), you are not going to get me!
Semantic interpretation: thematic meaning—fish challenges attacking shark.
Emotive meaning—mild anger.

Communicational interpretation of CAU2

Presuppositions: Yoram's *attitude* is not just make-believe. His aggression is real, and directed at me personally.

Purpose: Challenge Yoram. Show him that he is not as powerful as he thinks.

Let us now look at another combination of activity units, which is included in the following citation from the informal description:

Yoram: "That's impossible. It's not a real one".

Table 13   Transcription of second segment of Yoram's behavior.

CAU3										
	1	2	3	4	5	6	7	8	9	10
Vocal-linguistic		That's impossible. It's not a real one! (loud, whining)								
Motional-spatial		Faces father, front turned toward 4+. Body limp								
			Holds shark by tail. Arm hanging, limp. Pressure of holding increases.								

The transcription is shown in Table 13. CAU3 includes the following activity units:

AU8: Body limp. Arm hanging, limp.
Semantic interpretation: emotive meaning—lowering of aggression. Some frustration.

AU9: Vocal-linguistic: That's impossible. It's not a real one! (loud, whining).
Touching: Pressure of holding increases.
Semantic interpretation: thematic meaning—denial of biting. Denial of reality of shark.
Emotive meaning—anger, frustration.

Communicational interpretation of CAU3:

Attitude: Literal.

Presupposition: Father is angry because I attacked him.

Prediction: Father can counterattack; punish me.

Purpose: Deny own former aggression, to appease father and prevent his counterattack.

The last activity unit to be analyzed is included in the following citation: "Neta: (nervous) Where does the shark live? Where does he live? Where does he live?"

The transcription is shown in Table 14.

Table 14   Transcription of first segment of Neta's behavior.

AU10										
	1	2	3	4	5	6	7	8	9	10
Vocal-linguistic			Where does the shark live? Where does he live? Where does he live? (fast, sharply, loud.)							
Motional-spatial	Standing facing Yoram.		Walks toward Yoram, palms upwards, forearm bent toward Yoram.							

Semantic interpretation: thematic meaning—uncertainty concerning the shark's (Yoram's) home. (The immediate context is Yoram's previous utterance: "He is not outside. He is at home. He went to bring over another fish". The wider context is apparently the fact that Yoram is an adopted child in a second marriage family).

Emotive meaning: anxiety, almost panic related to the thematic meaning.

Communicational interpretation

Presupposition: Yoram does not want to share a home with me. He prefers sharing his home with someone else ("another fish").

Purpose: finding out whether the presupposition is correct.

Admittedly, such analysis is an arduous, painstaking job. Having read the above example, you wonder, perhaps, what can really be gained by doing such a jigsaw puzzle with bits and pieces of perfectly good English sentences. Note, however, that the informal narrative description was brought in above for no other purpose than facilitating the task of reading. Originally the microanalysis was not a re-organization and interpretation of any written text. It was transcribed directly from a videotaped documentation of the family's play

interactions. Such technical transcription and semi-formal analysis and interpretation are much more informative than any informal, narrative representation. The former conveys diagnostically relevant information of the
following, among other, kinds:

Timing. Take for instance CAU2. It shows clearly that various vocal, spatial
and motional raw-material features co-occur, that is, are produced
simultaneously, in Gad's reaction to Yoram's attack: the trembling voice, the
tempo of speech, the expression: "Oh, no no no, you are not going to get me!",
the flinching and the evading, upward pulling of the hand with the fish puppet.
The fact that this coordination of raw-material features has been displayed so
clearly facilitates the interpretation of Gad's behavior on the semantic and
pragmatic levels. The simultaneous occurrence of all these features reveals
Gad's fearful and evasive attitude with respect to Yoram.

Incongruity. In CAU3 incongruity is displayed between the limpness of
Yoram's body and arm and the increasing pressure he applies on the shark's tail
he is holding. This co-occurrence, again, facilitates the interpretation of the
behavioral raw material on the semantic and pragmatic levels. The incongruity
leads one to suppose that Yoram is angry and frustrated (this is expressed by
the increased hand pressure); but that he, at the same time, denies the reality of
his aggression (this is manifested, among other ways, by the limpness).

Differentiation of units. The division of the manifest behavior (raw material)
into activity units and the attempt to interpret each unit separately helps identify many illuminating bits of information. Take again the above example. What
appeared, prior to the microscopic analysis, to be a single undifferentiated
whole, has turned out to be a combination of raw-material units that convey
different, even contradictory, kinds of information: AU8 (body limp; arm
hanging, limp) seems to express "lowering of aggression" and "some frustration", whereas AU9 (increased pressure) appears to mark anger.

It will be observed that although only a tiny sample of activity units has been
microscopically analyzed, this analysis has already thrown some light on some
central aspects of the system of interrelationships within the family. It revealed
for instance that Yoram's relationship with his father includes attribution of
aggression and fear of retaliation. It also exposes his mother's belief that he
rejects her.

CHAPTER 8

Macroscopic Analysis: Unmasking the Dysfunctional Family Programs

The microscopic analysis yields a series of semantically and communicationally interpreted activity units. To complete the assessment, however, one has to expose and describe the dysfunctional family programs (see Chapter 1). The discrete units obtained by the microscopic analysis do not tell us much about such programs. The latter reside in global interrelations among classes of such units, not in separate units. Such interrelations are exposed and described by the macroscopic analysis.

A Procedure for Revealing and Formulating the Dysfunctional Programs

Before I set about explaining and demonstrating how this can be done, I would like to emphasize that a fully mechanical procedure for discovering the family programs cannot possibly be developed. What can be proposed is a set of heuristic procedures for facilitating the process of generalization and reasoning that eventually leads to the formulation of programs. Macroscopic analysis is basically not mechanical but creative.

It is advisable to propose more than one solution, that is, more than one program, covering a given portion of the microscopic analysis. Later on the competing programs proposed can be compared. The one that covers the data in a more interesting way—more revealing, more parsimonious and more complete—will be preferred.

The programs are exposed by looking closely at the sequence of microscopically analyzed activity units of each of the participants. Special attention is given to the *interpersonal thoughts* expressed by these units, notably the *purposes* and the *presuppositions*. This close examination is carried out with an eye to general features shared by sets of units, and to changes, turning points, in the stream of consecutive units. The context in which these changes or turning points are embedded should always be taken into account.

Let me illustrate these principles with respect to the microscopic analysis of the play of Yoram and his adoptive parents in Chapter 7.

The first step in the analysis consists of listing the main combinations of activity units of each participant. The *purposes* and *presuppositions* expressed by each such combination are specified.

Let me illustrate this step by interpreting a sample of Yoram's activity units:

(1) Yoram gets up. He makes his toy shark attack Gad's fish with sharp thrusts, squeaking violently.
Presuppositions: Father does not like me. He thinks I am bad. He is afraid of me.
Purposes: to punish father for his rejection; make him feel my anger, test the limits of his tolerance of my "badness".

(2) Make his shark bite father's arm.
Presuppositions: Father challenges me. (He said: "You are not going to get me!"). He won't let me make him pay for his rejection.
Purposes: Make Father feel my anger and punish him, despite his attempts to evade; test his tolerance.

(3) Yoram: That's impossible, it's not a real one.
Presuppositions: Father is angry because I attacked him (made my toy shark bite his arm).
Prediction: Father can counter-attack, punish me.
Purposes: Deny my own former aggression to appease father and prevent his counter-attack.

Already at this early stage it is advisable to raise questions belonging in principle to more advanced stages of the analysis. The first question is: What do the various communicative functions of the different activity units have in common? If one looks at the first two combinations of activity units produced by Yoram above, it seems that they share the *presuppositions* that father thinks Yoram is bad, rejects him and is afraid of him. They also share the *purpose* of punishing father for his rejection and making him feel Yoram's anger.

Had our attempt to expose Yoram's *program* and write it down been based just on these two combinations of units, we would have said that Yoram's *goal* is identical with the above-mentioned *purpose*. We would also have said that his *plan* is based on the above-mentioned presuppositions. We would have added that his output consisted of attacking his father, in accordance with his goal. However, a quick look at the third set of activity units analyzed above shows that the picture is not as simple as that. In this set Yoram's purpose changed. He no longer wanted to provoke his father, to punish him and make him feel his anger. On the contrary, now his purposes were to deny his own former aggression, to appease his father and prevent his counterattack. Since the purposes have changed we can no longer say that the purposes of the first two combinations of activity units were identical with Yoram's ultimate *goal*. Had his ultimate goal been just to punish his father and make him feel his anger, he would not have denied his aggression nor have attempted to appease his father when his goal was about to be achieved. It seems then that Yoram's ultimate goal is different, not identical with any of the *purposes* listed above.

Furthermore, the third combination of activity units manifests a change of tactics. It is a *turning point* in the sequence of activity units, in which Yoram reverses his previous course of action to meet new circumstances. Formerly he attacked. Now he denies the fact that he attacked. Such turning points, in which a new tactic is adopted to meet certain conditions, give us a clue as to the structure of one's plan. The person whose behavior is analyzed interprets the input in a certain way and produces a certain kind of output in one set of circumstances. He interprets the input in another way and produces a different kind of output in another set of circumstances.

So one can draw some general methodological principles already from this little piece of analysis: in attempting to generalize over several combinations of activity units one should pay special attention to turning points, where a person's presuppositions and purposes change or even seem to be incompatible with his previous purposes and presuppositions. Then one should look at the context for the correlates of this shift.

Another relevant question is: what happens when a person's purpose has been achieved? If his purpose is identical with his ultimate goal he can be expected to be satisfied. If he is not satisfied he probably has a different goal in mind.

When all Yoram's activity units have been subjected to this procedure, his goal and the basic structure of his plan begin to be clarified. Here is an informal presentation of these:

Yoram's goal. To be accepted by his adoptive parents as their beloved son.

Yoram's plan

(1) If I can judge from father's or mother's behavior that he or she regards me as bad and dangerous, then I pretend to threaten him or her with aggression. The main purpose of these threats is to push their fear and negative image of me to their limits and in this way test whether my goal can be reached or not.

(2) If my goal has not been reached by Step (1) (that is, the parent in question continues to be afraid of me and view me as bad) then I step up

my aggression and realize the threat, always in make-believe, with the same purposes as in (1).

(3) If my goal has not been reached by Step (2), and the parent in question intensifies his or her reactions (that is, becomes even more frightened and angry), then my reaction depends on who the parent in question is. If it is my father, I predict that he will counterattack, therefore, to prevent this counterattack, which is inconsistent with my goal, I should stop my aggressive behavior, deny its aggressive intent, leave my father, join my mother and go back to Step (1). If the parent in question is my mother, I predict that she will not counterattack. Therefore I should go back to Step (1).

(4) If Step (3) has led to results that are in accordance with my goal, that in, my parents no longer regard me as bad and dangerous and indicate their wish to make peace with me and be my friends, then I stop playing the aggressor's role. However, I refuse to let them join me and be in my company. This refusal is based on my presupposition that they still do not believe I am not really bad. It is also based on my prediction that they can resume their former rejecting attitude at any moment.

If they attempt to ascribe the role of the aggressor to me, I reject this attribution.

The main purpose of this step is to test the strength of their belief that I am not really bad and their determination to win me over as their beloved son, in accordance with my goal.

How was this formulation of Yoram's goal and plan reached? The crucial step was looking into turning points. In these crossroads the input received by Yoram from his parents, or rather his own interpretation of the input, changed. The output he had produced, including his purposes, changed accordingly. In the observation analyzed there were three such main turning points: at first Yoram interpreted the input he received from his parents as expressing their fear and rejection of him. His aggressive output had the purpose of punishing them for their rejection and testing the limits of their tolerance of his aggression. In the second phase the parents' output and Yoram's interpretation of it changed. He understood that they wanted to be nice and friendly with him. He became convinced that they realized that he could be less aggressive if they accepted and loved him. Accordingly, he changed his output and purposes. He stopped being aggressive, denied his former aggression, disengaged himself from both parents and kept them at a distance. His presumed purposes were now to assume a standby position, giving his parents a chance to prove that they really want to love and accept him. In the third phase the parents' output and Yoram's interpretation of it changed again. The parents, in particular the mother, indicated that they understood (at least for the time being) that Yoram was not bad any longer. They expressed their concern that he did not want them to be good to him. They made efforts to join him. Accordingly, he changed his output. He indicated to his parents that he would let them join him and accept their love. However, he still played a passive role, expecting them to make the first move.

It seems then that Yoram's purposes and his various kinds of output are in a *complementary distribution* with respect to each other. That is, different kinds of output and different purposes occur in different contexts. To be more exact, they occur in contexts where the input, and Yoram's interpretation of the input, vary. This complementary distribution provides the skeletal structure of Yoram's *plan*. However, it was also hypothesized that the plan serves a single ultimate *goal*. The various *purposes* are subordinated to this goal. How can one determine the *goal*? In searching for the *goal*, considerations of the following kinds come into the picture:

Psychobiological Considerations

As was mentioned in Chapter 1, theoretical and empirical studies of families have indicated that goals of family members are related to interpersonal intimacy or interpersonal control. Furthermore, psychobiological studies and common human experience have emphasized the child's dependence on his parents' love, acceptance and protection (see Goldfarb, 1945). Therefore, it is more reasonable to assume that a child's ultimate goals are to be dominated by his parents and enjoy their love and acceptance than to assume that his ultimate goals are to punish his parents, test them or keep them away.

Structural Considerations

The complementary distribution of Yoram's *purposes* implies that his purposes are not independent but interdependent in the following two senses. First, the different purposes are organized around two common parameters: aggression (being aggressive versus being non-aggressive or even denying own aggression) and *sharing personal space* (participating in the parents' space, letting the parents into own personal space versus keeping the parents at a distance). The two parameters are interrelated: when Yoram is aggressive he invades his parent's personal space. When he is non-aggressive he keeps them at a distance or invites them into his own personal space.

Secondly, the various kinds of purposes are in a sense arranged on an ordinal scale. They are embedded within one another. The occurrence of one purpose rather than another depends on the question of whether the latter has been achieved. For instance, Yoram's second set of purposes (assuming a standby position, in which his parents are given a chance to prove that they really love and accept him) was adopted by him only after his first set of purposes (wanting to show his parents his anger at their rejection and test the limits of their patience) had been achieved. Likewise, his third and last set of purposes (signalling to his parents that he was willing to accept their company and their love) was assumed by him only after his second set of purposes had been achieved.

These considerations show that the last set of purposes is closer to Yoram's ultimate goal. The first two classes of purposes appear to be means to an end rather than ends in themselves. The purposes which have to do with Yoram's aggression seem to be subordinated to the question of whether he shares his personal space with his parents, which apparently is the overriding dimension.

One can derive from this example general methodological principles and a set of procedural steps for exposing and formulating one's goals and plans from a microscropic analysis of one's play behavior:

(1) Find common features shared by sequences of communicative functions (especially purposes and presuppositions).
(2) Describe the complementary distribution, that is, what sorts of input (including purposes) one does produce when the input (including its interpretation) is such and such. This is the skeletal structure of one's plan.
(3) What underlying parameters do the various types of purposes belong to? What kinds of dependency relations hold among these parameters?
(4) Which purposes serve as means to other purposes? That is, which purposes are assumed only if certain other purposes have already been achieved. The goal is the purpose that does not serve as a means to an end, and which belongs to the overriding parameter. This parameter has to do either with intimacy (interpersonal distance) or with dominance (interpersonal control).

Looking at Yoram's goal and plan, specified above (which constitute a part of his family program), one can see that they have been arrived at by a procedure such as the one described above.

Identifying the Errors in Information Processing

So far we have seen how programs can be exposed and formulated by applying a macroscopic analysis to the results of the microscopic analysis. However, we have not seen how the dysfunctional aspects of dysfunctional programs can be located and described. In fact what should be identified are the errors of information processing which make the program dysfunctional. The main types of errors, as listed in Chapter 1, are *errors of amount* (processing too much or too little information) and *errors of relevance* (processing irrelevant information or failure to process relevant information).

Locating and describing such errors involves looking at a family member's plan and trying to figure out how information is processed by this plan. Take for instance Yoram's plan as described above. The first clause in the plan includes the following:

> (1) If I can judge from father's or mother's behavior that he or she regards me as bad and dangerous, then I should pretend to threaten him or her with aggression. The main purpose of these threats of aggression is to push their fear and negative image of me to their limits and in this way test whether my goal can be reached or not.

Quite clearly, the output produced by this clause includes an error of relevance: failure to process the relevant information that by pretending to threaten his parents with aggression he reinforces his bad image in their eyes.

Looking at the whole of Yoram's plan, not just its first clause, it seems that he takes in the relevant input from his parents and assigns the correct interpretations to it, although he does not validate his interpretations. What is dysfunctional in his plan is the fact that he fails to consider possible outputs. He does not think of taking active and positive actions which could help him achieve his goal of gaining his parents' love and acceptance. This error is based on another error, failure to take into account the influence of his own aggressive output on the input he gets from his parents, in which they see him as bad and dangerous, or as a lone wolf.

I would like to stress again that people are not necessarily aware of the errors of information processing they make.

A Formal Analysis of the Presenting Problems

There are a number of reasons why the presenting problems should be formally explicated before an attempt to explain them through the family dysfunctional programs is made. One reason is that the people who give the therapist a verbal description of the child's presenting problems ("symptoms"), usually the parents or some other caretakers (teachers, nurses or the like), tend to describe them in vague, subjective, non-observational terms. The father would say: "He is a good boy, but sometimes I don't know what gets into him. He acts as if he was really crazy". The mother would say "He does everything to annoy me". The older sister would say "He pretends to be a problematic child, but in fact he is not", or the like. These descriptions leave the therapist with no clear picture of what is there to explain. Another reason why the presenting problems, or symptoms, should be formally explicated is that they are messages, input and output in the family information-processing system, like any other kinds of messages. If one really wants to understand them one should decipher and describe them like any other message, otherwise their meaning would remain obscure and the question of what is explained would arise again.

The information required for constructing a formal explication of the presenting problems can be acquired from the care-taking adults (usually the parents) through a verbal interview. Additional information can often be obtained from observations of the child's behavior in family play sessions. Basically, the formal explication of the presenting problem consists of providing a detailed description and interpretation of the characteristic problematic behavior and its typical contexts. These can be done in the semiotic theoretical language employed throughout this work. The "symptom" is first described on the raw-material level. Its vocal-linguistic, spatial-motional and tactile characteristics are specified. Then it is interpreted on the semantic level (emotive and thematic meanings) and on the communicational, pragmatic level (interpersonal thoughts: purposes, presuppositions, etc.). The description of the context includes the characteristic time and place in which it occurs, the characteristic stimuli of the environment and the typical responses to it. The stimuli and the responses can also be described on the three levels of analysis—raw material, semantic and communicational. The questions in the interview should aim at acquiring the necessary information for constructing such a description and interpretation. Here is an excerpt from such an interview. The identified patient is Adir, a seven-year-old boy.

MOTHER. I don't know. When his father is not home I can't control him.
THERAPIST. You can't control him only when his father is not home?
(This question is relevant to a more exact specification of the context of the problematic behavior.)
MOTHER. When his father is home he is an angel. His father does not even have to do anything. His very presence is enough.
FATHER. Yes, that's right.
THERAPIST. Can you recall a specific event, something that happened today or yesterday, in which Adir got out of control?
MOTHER *(trying to recall)*. Yes. Yesterday I was sitting with my sister.
THERAPIST. Where?
MOTHER. In our living room. We were talking about her daughter. Adir was sitting there.
THERAPIST. Where? I was not there so I cannot see the picture.
MOTHER. He was sitting in an armchair, watching TV. We were sitting at the dining table. Now when I come to think of it, she was telling me how marvellous her daughter was, what an excellent pupil she was, and I was assenting to what she said, being enthusiastic just like her, saying things like 'That's great!' and the like, and he probably got jealous.
THERAPIST. Probably. What did he do then?

MOTHER. He suddenly came over to me and sat on my lap, hugging my neck. Sometimes he behaves in an extremely childish way.

THERAPIST. How did you react?

MOTHER. I said: Get off my lap! Can't you see I'm talking with Ora? You should stop acting like a baby! Then he comes off my lap and punches me right in the belly, quite hard. I started to chase him around the room, screaming: "Wait till daddy comes home!" and he ran away, giggling, until I got out of breath. Then he went back to his TV—I think he spends too much time watching TV—and I got back to talking with Ora.

FATHER. I have never witnessed such a scene. I find it hard to believe that such things really happen.

The therapist asked the mother to describe other scenes in which she could not control her son. After a number of such scenes were described in sufficient detail the pattern became clear and well articulated. It could then be described as follows:

A Formal Explication of Presenting Problem

Context

Time and place: in the afternoon, in the living room.
Stimuli: father's absence from home; the presence of a guest to whom his mother gives all her attention. The mother sits with the guest at the dining table, facing the guest. The mother talks with the guest about the guest's children, how nice and clever they are. The mother expresses her enthusiasm with exclamations.

Child's Behavioral Description

First combination of activity units:

Raw material: Spatial-motional—Sits on an armchair, watching TV, facing away from his mother and her guest.

Semantic: Emotive meaning—Watchful and alert. Attempts to control his anger.

Communicational: Presupposition—I am now being excluded from my mother's interaction with her guest.

Prediction: My mother is soon likely to start praising the guest's children.

Purpose: Let mother interact with her guest until she overdoes it.

Second combination of activity units

Raw material: Spatial-motional-tactile—Sits on his mother's lap, hugging her violently, disturbing her view of her guest.

Semantic: Emotive meaning—Anger.

Communicational: Presupposition—My mother is more impressed by other children than by me. She does not love me or appreciate me enough to express this.

Purposes: To stop mother's disturbing interaction with her guest and take from her by force what she does not give willingly.

Third combination of activity units

Raw material: Spatial-motional-tactile—Hitting or punching mother in the belly.

Semantic: Thematic—The belly is the place where other children come from. Emotive—Great anger.

Communicational: Presuppositions—Mother not only refused to stop the disturbing interaction with her guest and give me love and attention, she even told me off and insulted me in front of her guest by calling me "baby". This proves and reinforces my belief that she does not love and appreciate me.

Purposes: To punish mother and show her my anger, and also symbolically to explain to her what I am angry about, by hitting her where other children come from.

Fourth combination of activity units

Raw material: Spatial-motional—Running away around the room.
Vocal—Giggling.

Semantic: Joy following victory.

Communicational: Presupposition—My mother can't get me.

Predictions: She can't retaliate for what I did to her, because she can't catch me, and when my father comes back home he will not do anything to me, because I'll behave like an angel.

Purposes: To avoid retaliation and make my mother continue feeling punished and humiliated.

Context

Mother's responses:
   To first combination of activity units: ignores Adir and continues talking with her guest, not facing her son.

To second combination of activity units: gets angry, pushes her son away, telling him to get off her lap and accusing him of behaving in a childish manner and disturbing her interaction with her guest.

To third combination of activity units: running after the boy, attempting to catch him, crying that his father will come home and punish him.

To fourth combination of activity units: getting out of breath, giving up and coming back to sit with her guest and talk with her.

A formal explication of this sort provides a detailed description of the presenting problem and clarifies its meaning and communicative functions. Now that this explication has been proposed one can begin to understand, for instance, why Adir sat on his mother's lap and hugged her so "childishly" and why he punched her right in the belly. Maybe not every detail in the above analysis throws a new light on the case, but one should recall that this example has been brought here just to illustrate the technique of formal explication. In actual practice one should go with the analysis only as far as practically required.

Explaining the Presenting Problems on the Basis of the Dysfunctional Programs

The last step in the process of assessment is attempting to *explain* the presenting problems, as these have been explicated formally.

The question of how the presenting problems can be explained by family dysfunction has been discussed in Chapter 1. There, symptoms have been classified into three types according to the manner in which they are related to the family's dysfunctional programs. The first type comprises behavioral manifestations which form a part of the output generated by dysfunctional plans. The second type includes stress reactions indirectly caused by dysfunctional programs. The third type consists of long-range adverse effects of chronic malfunctioning resulting from incapacitating dysfunctional programs.

The formal explication of the presenting problems helps to decide which of these three types the symptoms in hand belong to. It also renders it easier to trace the errors of information processing which account for the symptoms. For example, the formal explication presented above supports the supposition that Adir's problematic behavior was a part of the output generated by a dysfunctional program regulating his relationships with his mother. Furthermore, this explication was revealing from the point of view of the question: what kinds of errors of information processing were included in this dysfunctional program.

Yoram was described by his adoptive parents, Gad and Neta, as "aggressive, babyish and uncooperative" (see Chapter 7, p. 107). A formal explication of

these presenting problems helped establish the connections between these behavioral manifestations and the errors of information processing in Yoram's
dysfunctional plan (see p. 120). These symptoms were his way of testing the
limits of his parent's tolerance.

Summary

The main steps in the process of strategic family play therapeutic assessment are
summarized in Table 15.

Table 15   Strategic family play therapeutic assessment—main steps.

Data-gathering instruments	Data sources	Methods of analysis	Results of analysis
Presenting-problems interview	Parents or other care-taking adults.	Semiotic analysis on raw-material, semantic and pragmatic levels.	Formal, explicit analysis of presenting problems.
Observation of family free play, recorded and transcribed	The family.	Microscopic semiotic analysis on raw-material, semantic and pragmatic levels.	
		Macroscopic analysis of microscopically analyzed data.	Formulation of dysfunctional family programs, including errors of information processing.
		Relating formally analyzed presenting problems to dysfunctional programs.	Explanation of presenting problems.

PART 3

Planning the whole therapy and individual sessions

CHAPTER 9

Planning a Strategy for the Whole Therapy

What is a Strategy?

Before one starts to do the actual therapy, it is advisable to design a general strategy for the whole therapy.

The concept "strategy", as it is used in this text, refers to a general *approach* to solving the therapeutic problem, that is, to "repairing" the errors of information processing which breed the presenting problems, so that the latter are likely to be solved, or disappear spontaneously.

The Connection Between the Assessment and the Planning of the Strategy

When the therapist sets about planning his strategy he must take into account the information provided in the assessment. The main goal of the strategy is to solve the presenting problems by correcting the errors of information processing in the family's dysfunctional programs. These errors and the manner in which they influence the presenting problems are specified in the assessment. Other sorts of information should be taken into account as well, such as the family members' areas of interest and media of expression, their motivation in general and for the therapy in particular, their resistance to therapy and its sources. These will be discussed in detail below.

The Concept "Strategy" in this Work and in Other Schools of Strategic Family Therapy

I have not found a formal definition of the concept "therapeutic strategy" in the family therapy literature. However, judging from the way this concept has been used in practice in most of the works I have come across, it has been employed in a sense that is more akin to what is termed "a therapeutic tactic" in this work (see Chapter 10). That is, the concept "strategy" usually refers not to the general, grand plan of the whole therapeutic process, but to the specific plan for a specific therapeutic intervention, designed to achieve a specific subgoal of the series of goals which the whole therapy sets out to achieve (see, for instance, de Shazer, 1982; Haley, 1963; Madanes, 1982).

The Components of a Strategy

A strategy includes the objectives of the whole therapy, the mechanisms by which the therapist will attempt to achieve these objectives, and the manners in which these mechanisms will be put into practice. These three main parts of the strategy can be broken down further into components, to be specified presently. The therapist can construct the strategy step by step, according to these components. In each step different kinds of information, drawn from the assessment, will be utilized.

It is advisable to construct at least two alternative strategies, compare them and choose the better one, or synthesize them. The question of how a strategy is assessed in comparison with an alternative, competing strategy, is taken up below.

The Components Referring to the Objectives of the Whole Therapy

(a) Which of the dysfunctional programs described in the assessment are to be changed?
(b) Which errors of information processing in these dysfunctional programs should the intervention be particularly directed at?
(c) What kinds of changes in these errors will the intervention attempt to achieve?
(d) What is the rationale for each of the decisions made in (a)–(c)?

The Components Referring to Priorities among these Goals and Subgoals

(e) Which of the above-mentioned targets of change will be given the first and highest priority? Which of them will be tackled first and which later? In other words, what will the sequential order of the goals and subgoals be?
(f) What is the rationale for the decisions taken in (e)?

The main relevant considerations are:
Priority should be given to change-targets that are likely to sow the seeds for further desirable changes, which will occur spontaneously. Such a decision can help in making the therapy more economical.

It is better to focus upon change-targets that are not liable to raise unbending, insurmountable resistance on the part of the family.

It is preferable to concentrate on change-targets whose attainment is unlikely to have undesirable side effects.

The Components Referring to the Mechanisms by Which the Therapist Will Attempt to Achieve these Objectives

(g) What kinds of mutations will the therapist attempt to effect in each stage of the therapy?

"Mutations" should be distinguished from "goals" or "change-targets". In this book, the term "mutation" refers to therapeutic manoeuvres which hopefully lead, step by step, to the attainment of a particular goal, or change-target.

For example, a therapist may attempt to reach the goal of helping a boy accept his new stepfather by leading the family through the following mutations: (1) Letting the boy give vent to his rejection of his stepfather in a symbolic disguise, in a series of family make-believe games. (2) Negotiating a contract regulating his relationship with his stepfather, again in a symbolic, make-believe play disguise. (3) Exposing the contract that has been achieved; that is, discussing it frankly and openly, not in make-believe.

(h) What are the main therapeutically relevant properties of play (see Chapters 2 and 3) that will be applied in the therapist's attempts to bring about these mutations?

The main properties applied in these mutations are *symbolic coding* and *covert communication*.

(i) How will these properties be actually activated in the therapeutic process?

(j) What other, non-play, mechanisms of change, will be applied and how will they be actually activated?

(k) What is the rationale for each of the decisions made in (g)–(i)?

The Components Referring to the Manners by Which these Mechanisms will be put into Practice

(l) How will the therapist use himself and the means available to him to facilitate the activation of these properties?

(m) What kinds of difficulties in carrying out this strategy (technical difficulties, resistance, limitations in the family members, etc.) are expected, and how does the therapist plan to detour or overcome them?

(n) What is the rationale for each of the decisions made in (l) and (m)?

To illustrate, let me propose a strategy for Yoram and his family (see Chapters 7 and 8).

An Example: A Strategy for Yoram and his Family

The Main Objectives

A close inspection of the dysfunctional program presented in Chapter 8 and in particular the errors of information processing, leads one to fix upon the following main therapeutic objectives:

Making Gad, Yoram's father, Neta, his mother, and Yoram himself realize that their goals are mutually complementary: both the parents and Yoram want to be loved and accepted by the other side.

Helping the family members become aware of those errors of information processing which make their plans self-defeating. More specifically, Yoram should learn how his aggression and avoidance influence his father and mother's attitude toward him: his father interprets these as a challenge to his parental authority and his mother as rejection of her motherhood. The parents should learn that their responses reinforce Yoram's suspicion.

Leading the family members to alternative, more gratifying, avenues toward their goals: their common craving for love and acceptance is best served if they trust each other and give each other unconditional warmth.

Where should the "center of gravity" of the therapy be placed? The main therapeutic efforts can, at least in the beginning stages of the therapy, be aimed first and foremost at the mother. This is based on the following considerations: of all the three family members, the mother is the least likely to offer unbending resistance to the therapeutic efforts. The father's difficulty in accepting Yoram is not due just to the boy's difficult behavior. He still harbors his own guilt for having left his former wife and three children and must cope with it. Furthermore, he has not *chosen* Yoram. He got him as a part of a package deal when he married his adoptive mother. The latter, on the other hand, has chosen Yoram. Her difficulty with him is due just to her misinterpretation of his problematical behavior. As for Yoram himself, he believes that he has been going to great lengths to show his parents that he wants their love. In all probability he would consider it too dangerous for him and therefore refuse to completely forgo his aggression or avoidance of them.

When the mother begins to trust Yoram and genuinely accept him and give him her love, he is likely to abandon his plan with respect to her and give in. This however can adversely influence the father, who would feel left out. At that stage he may even resort to subtly sabotaging Yoram and his mother's achievement. This can be counterbalanced, perhaps, by encouraging the mother to support the father and treat him more warmly. Furthermore, if Yoram is assured of his mother's acceptance, he is likely to become, with some help from the therapist, more ready to listen to his father. This would close the circle of the triadic interrelationships.

Mechanisms and Manners

First mutation

Exposing the dysfunctional program in make-believe play.
Main therapeutically relevant properties of play employed: *symbolic coding, basic duality*.
The main tasks of the therapist will be focusing and interpreting the dysfunctional program.

Second mutation

Softening up the mother's fear of being rejected by Yoram.
Main therapeutically relevant properties of play: *symbolic coding, regulation of emotions*.
In the first mutation it will be pointed out to the mother that Yoram does not really reject her. However, it is quite likely that she will find it emotionally difficult to accept this. The purpose of this mutation will be to help her play out and build up defenses against her fear of being rejected. The therapist's main role will be to serve as her director.

Third mutation

Supporting the father.
Main therapeutically relevant properties of play: *covert communication, possible worlds*.
If the former mutations lead to a greater intimacy between Yoram and his mother, the father is likely to feel left out (see above). The purpose of this mutation is to give him support by encouraging the mother to give him warmth and Yoram to listen to him.
The therapist will serve as a make-believe go-between.

Assessment of Strategies

As suggested above, it is advisable to construct at least two alternative strategies, compare them and choose the better one or synthesize them. This often happens spontaneously, for instance when the therapy is designed by team work in which different people suggest different strategies. However, even if only one strategy is proposed, it is better to evaluate it, in order to forestall difficulties and errors that can arise when the strategy is implemented.

The criterion by which strategies can be evaluated is: *degree of agreement between strategy and assessment.*

The questions here are:

Does the strategy take into account all the important elements of the assessment (the formal definition of the presenting problems, the dysfunctional programs and the errors of information-processing operations included in them and other relevant information, such as the family members' motivations, sources of resistance, style of expression and communication, etc.)?

Is it related to these elements in a meaningful, non-superficial way?

Effectiveness: How likely is the strategy to succeed? Will it really achieve the expected results? Is it feasible?

Economy: Is the strategy sufficiently economical in terms of the investment of time, money, efforts and burden?

CHAPTER 10

Strategic Family Play Therapeutic Tactics

Strategies, Tactics and Moves

The concepts "strategy" and "tactic" are parallel. In most cases the strategy is too complex and all-embracing for one to be able to carry it out at one go. Therefore it has to be divided into sub-strategies. The term "tactics" refers to such sub-strategies. A tactic may be said to be a miniature strategy which constitutes a part of the overall strategy and covers not the whole therapy but one specific phase in it.

The global entity called "a tactic" is analyzed into components that are roughly analogous to the components of a strategy. Like a strategy, a tactic is planned in advance according to these components. The tactic is put into operation more or less as planned, though flexibly (see Chapter 11) through a series of moves, that is, concrete actions performed by the therapist in the course of the session.

The Components of a Tactic

When a therapist designs a tactic he, as mentioned above, constructs it step by step, with each of its basic components taking a specific form. Here is a list of the basic components:

The Main Objectives

(a) The dysfunctional program the therapist wants to change by means of the therapeutic intervention in order to solve the presenting problems (see Chapter 1).
(b) The errors of information processing in this dysfunctional program the therapist wants to focus on (see Chapter 1).
(c) The changes the therapist hopes to effect by means of the intervention.

(d) The rationale of the decisions taken in (a)–(c).

The relevant considerations are the same as in the designing of a strategy, namely:

Priority should be given to change-targets that spontaneously lead to other desirable changes.

Change-targets that are likely to be met with unbending resistance or have undesirable side effects should be avoided.

Mechanisms of Change

(e) The main mutations (see Chapter 9).
(f) The therapeutically relevant properties of play employed.
(g) How are these properties going to be actually put into operation?
(h) The rationale behind (e)–(g).

The Execution of the Tactic

(i) Which of the family members is going to be actively involved in the intervention?
(j) How is the therapist going to use himself and the means at his disposal to bring about the desired changes? This refers to the general description of the methods of intervention rather than to the specific moves by which they will be carried out.
(k) What facilitating factors can the therapist expect to find that may help him carry out the tactic? What obstacles can he expect to meet? How does he plan to overcome the obstacles?

In Chapter 9 it was recommended that the relative merits of a strategy be assessed by proposing at least two alternative competing strategies and comparing them, employing criteria such as degree of agreement with the assessment, effectiveness and economy. This recommendation applies equally well to tactics.

Some Examples

To illustrate the process of constructing tactics according to these components and putting them into practice, let me now present a few cases, taken from my own or my students' therapeutic work.

Case 1: The Scriptwriter

The scene takes place in Jack Reilly's office. Jack is an FBI agent. He sits in his armchair behind his desk. His feet are propped up on his desk. Other people are present in the office: Senator Crosby, a stout man in his mid-forties, his pretty wife Jane and their twenty-year-old son Robert. They are in the midst of a stormy discussion concerning some shady financial business deal in which they are all involved.

ROBERT. I'm going to wash my hands of this whole affair.
JACK *(through his teeth and the cigar that is stuck between them).* You are involved whether you like it or not.
A sharp knock at the door is heard. Everybody freezes, scared.
LOUD VOICE *(calling from outside).* Open in the name of the law!
JACK *(removes his feet from the desk).* We've been caught red-handed. We're lost.
ROBERT. I am going to hide in the cupboard. *(He gets into the cupboard and shuts the door behind him).*
JANE *(taking hold of Senator Crosby's hand).* Let's hide!
(She pulls him toward the cupboard, whispering). Robert, open the door, let us in.
ROBERT *(holding the door fast, to keep it closed).* Take your hands off! There's room for just one person here!
JANE. You are abandoning your own father and mother!
ROBERT. That's an accurate description!
JACK. He's found a good way not to be involved, eh?
COP *(with a drawn gun is breaking into the room).* Hands up!

This scene was not taken out of a crime-and-the-law TV series, although the general air and style are no doubt borrowed from this genre. It is a part of a family play therapy session. "Jack Reilly's office" was in fact my own office. "His desk" was my desk. His "cigar" was my pen. The characters were: Senator Crosby: Yakov Gold, an electronics engineer; Jane: his wife, Dinah; Robert: their twelve-year-old son, Shaul. Jack Reilly, and, later, the cop: I, the therapist. The plot and characters were the invention of Shaul, who also improvised and directed the various play activities, but the parents and myself made our own contributions occasionally.

Here are some background details:

Shaul was brought to therapy by his mother, because during that year he would lock himself up in his room and refuse to come out. In the safety of his room he used to spend the time writing—quite obsessively—"TV series" in tiny, dense, barely readable characters, which, with few exceptions, were really just an illegible, meaningless scrawl. When he was asked why he was writing in this manner his answer was: "to save paper".

In the initial intake interview only the mother arrived, although both parents had been invited. She unfolded the following picture in front of me:

Her husband Yakov was spending money obsessively on soccer lottery and on useless articles given as gifts to her. In this manner he would compensate himself both for what he had taken to be his wife's rejection of his love, and for the fact that he lost his status as a soccer star, which he had enjoyed in his youth. His irresponsible wasting of money got him entangled in heavy debts. There were also some rumors that he had embezzled some sporting club money and this affair was hushed up. The family was forced to sell its apartment and move to rented apartments. From time to time they were visited by creditors and execution officers. Dinah was making desperate efforts to cover the debts. These efforts put her under great physical and mental strain, but also strengthened her position *vis-a-vis* her husband. She tended to accuse and criticize him scathingly, and he would react by being on the defensive and making all kinds of excuses. This was the atmosphere in which Shaul grew up.

It is easy to see that the play episode cited above, as well as many other episodes in the joint family play, is a symbolic representation of the family situation described above. Shaul's "hiding in the cupboard when the police raided Jack's office" and his refusal to let his parents in recall his locking himself up in his room, apparently to escape his own involvement in the family drama.

I invited parents and son to talk together, but it was absolutely impossible to bring Yakov and Shaul to admit that there existed any problem or difficulty in the family. The father painted an idyllic, rosy picture of the family relationships, and his son remained stubbornly silent. In view of this state of affairs I attempted to reach a comprehensive diagnostic evaluation, using the methods described in previous chapters. On the basis of this evaluation I designed an overall strategy for a family play therapy.

The following tactic was conducted within the framework of this strategy in accordance with the components specified above. The play episode given above is, as will be shown below, governed by this tactic.

A Tactic for the Gold Family

The dysfunctional program I decided to focus on can be formulated informally as follows:

The father and son, each in his own way, resist any attempt made by a party inside the family (e.g. the mother) or outside it (e.g. the therapist) to fully admit that there are problems in the family, to specify and formulate these problems and to look for solutions. The father denies his financial entanglements or attempts to justify them with all manner of excuses. He refuses to admit that there is a real conflict between himself and his wife. His son withdraws, remains silent and behaves as if he is not involved.

Let me reformulate this program in the language of goals and plans introduced in Chapter 7:

Father's Goal

To keep his wife; to prevent a rift between her and himself.

Father's plan

Presuppositions

(1) My wife and son are not fully informed about the extent and gravity of my financial entanglements. They do not fully realize how guilty I really am.

(2) My insistence that there is no conflict between myself and my wife stresses the positive side of our relationship and prevents it from deteriorating.

Predictions

(1) Should my son and wife realize the full extent and gravity of my misdeeds and the depth of my guilt, my wife will become extremely upset and angry. Consequently, she will dangerously widen the rift between us and may even decide to leave me. This contradicts my goal.

(2) Therefore, I should do everything to resist any attempt to make me fully admit my guilt or acknowledge the existence of the conflict between myself and my wife.

Output

Should some agent inside or outside the family produce evidence of my guilt or of the existence of the conflict with my wife, I had better produce meta-expressions which devalue my guilt or the conflict and explain them away.

Son's Goal

To keep his parents together; to prevent the widening of the rift between them.

Son's Plan

Presuppositions

If I cooperate with the therapist or with my mother and am willing to admit that there is a conflict between my father and my mother and that my father is guilty of various offences, I support my mother against my father. Therefore I contribute to widening the rift between them. This contradicts my goal. On the other hand if I follow my father's lead and deny the facts I support my father against my mother and, again, contribute to aggravating the conflict. This also contradicts my goal.

Output

Therefore I should remain silent and pretend that I know nothing and am not involved.

The errors of information processing on which the intervention will be focused, and the changes the therapist hopes to effect in them:

The father's plan is based on his failure to realize that his wife, his son and the therapist do know about his misdeeds and are in fact aware of his guilt. It disregards the fact that the conflict with his wife exists, despite the fact that it is not openly discussed. It also ignores the constructive, well-meaning intentions of his wife and his therapist when they wish to bring these "secrets" into the open. (Failure to take relevant input into account.)

Moreover, the father's plan does not include any procedure for finding out whether his course of action really does the job. (Failure to take relevant output into account, failure to validate.)

Also, his plan fails to realize that the rift between his wife and himself is due to the fact that he does not let discussion become open. It ignores the fact that this has nothing to do with the depth and gravity of the conflict.

The son's plan is based on his prediction that disclosing what he knows about his father and his relationship with his mother will widen the rift between his parents. This prediction has not been put to the test. (Failure to validate and ignoring possible output.)

These errors of information processing must be corrected. The father should be helped to realize the illusory nature of his attempts to deny or justify his financial entanglements and shut his eyes to his wife's anger. He must be made to realize that these are open secrets. He should be encouraged to admit the existence of these problems, learn to express his feelings and discuss them openly with his family and with the therapist. Eventually, he is likely to learn that exposing these problems not only does not aggravate them as he feared, but even helps solve them.

Likewise, the son should be helped to cooperate with his mother and the therapist by admitting that he is aware of what is going on and inwardly he is deeply involved. This can lead him to realize that his cooperation not only does not make things worse but, on the contrary, contributes to making them better.

Rationale

These errors of information processing bar any attempt to solve the problems with or without external help. No solution can be found if the very existence of the difficulties is denied and any attempt to name them, discuss them and look for solutions is banned. Once the reality of the situation is acknowledged and owned, the erroneous presuppositions and predictions included in the father's and son's plans can be exposed, put to the test and repaired. The father and the son are likely to discover that their goals are better served by giving up these presuppositions and predictions than by keeping them. The open debate that is expected to ensue can lead to an improvement in the family atmosphere and in the son's presenting problems. These problems seem to be an almost direct manifestation of his plan. Let us look at this more closely:

The Son's Presenting Problems

Locking himself up in his own room and writing obsessively: these actions seem to have the purpose of creating an impenetrable barrier between himself and his parents' problems.

Writing "TV series" in an illegible handwriting: apparently these stories are symbolic representations of the family drama. However, their illegibility serves, again, the purpose of not letting anyone suspect that he knows what is going on and is personally involved. He said he was writing in this way "to save paper". This expression seems to symbolize and at the same time disguise his own deep involvement in the problem of his father's irresponsible wasting of money. It betrays his identification with his mother's efforts to economize and reduce the damage caused by his father's vice.

What are the therapeutically relevant properties of play that will be instrumental in bringing about these changes?

The main properties put into operation will be regulation of emotions, symbolic coding, and owning and alienation.

The property of *regulation of emotions* was defined in Chapter 3 as the fact that play expresses emotionally laden themes (emotives). Content is chosen by the players to be included in their make-believe play because these contents represent situations, thoughts and fantasies which are, for the players, permeated with intense emotions. In the free, exciting atmosphere of play the controls and defenses of the players loosen, therefore their emotions emerge to the surface and the contents associated with them break open. (See Chapter 2.)

Accordingly, it is reasonable to suppose that if Shaul and his family are encouraged to play make-believe games, emotionally laden contents associated with their denied familial problems are bound to unintentionally penetrate these games, bypassing the censoring screen.

This prediction proved correct. In the play therapeutic sessions conducted with this family, themes representing the above-mentioned problematic family situations and relationships repeatedly broke through the censoring screen. It should be emphasized that I did not do anything to solicit or elicit such themes beyond merely suggesting that the family played make-believe games on topics of their own choise. This is clearly illustrated in the play episode cited above. In it, the family members spontaneously brought up thinly disguised versions of themes such as the father's corruption, the son's anger at his parents and his wish to disengage himself from their problems. These very themes were left out of the initial verbal interview.

The property of *symbolic coding* was defined in Chapter 3 as the fact that the contents of play can be coded symbolically. For example, one's father can be symbolized in play by another figure, which is associated in the player's mind with the image of his or her own father, e.g. "senator", "king", "elephant". This property of play reduces the difficulty of expressing denied or repressed thoughts and feelings, since it renders it possible for these experiences to be expressed without being fully exposed. The symbolic disguise enables the players to uncover their own inner world without feeling naked.

Therefore, it may be expected that if members of the Gold family play make-believe games in the therapy room, the problems whose expression is blocked by the above errors of information processing will surface in a symbolic disguise.

This is what actually happened in the play scene described here. Issues which had been systematically evaded in the previous abortive verbal interview were introduced into it freely and spontaneously, though in a symbolic code. The senator's office of the game stood for the family's home. Shaul's room became a cupboard, his father became a senator and so forth.

The property of *owning and alienation* was defined in Chapter 3 as the fact that in play the player both owns the contents of the play and alienates it from himself. For example, if a child pretends to hit his father, he simultaneously owns his aggression and is alienated from it. He owns it because he actually plays it out. He alienates it from himself because in his mind the one who is hitting his father is not himself but "the make-believe boy in the game". He knows that "it is not for real, it is only a game".

These properties can also be expected to make it easier for the members of the Gold family to forgo the activation of the above-mentioned dysfunctional program. Thanks to the fact that what they are supposed to do is framed as make-believe play, they can allow themselves to lift the ban on revealing sensitive familial issues. The property of *alienation* will make it possible for them to pretend that their problems are not really theirs, that the presence of these problems in the room is not real. However, due to the property of owning, it will be impossible for them to completely ignore these problems.

In the above play episode, all the members of the Gold family quite definitely owned the father's misdeeds. They also owned Shaul's reluctant involvement and the other matters the family refused even to discuss in the verbal interview. They could own these because they could also alienate these matters from themselves and pretend that they belonged to different people, such as Senator Crosby, his wife Jane and their son Robert. They could pretend that it was all just a part of one big make-believe game.

As explained above, it is expected that the play properties work by themselves, automatically as it were, by the very fact that the family members play make-believe games. The therapist's main task, then, is to encourage the family members to play make-believe games, freely and spontaneously, on any theme that comes into their minds.

How is the therapist going to use himself and the means at his disposal to bring about the desired changes?

As stated above, the main task dictated by this tactic is to bring the family members to playing make-believe games. Therefore, the therapist's efforts should be directed primarily at creating a playful atmosphere. He can achieve this by putting himself at the family's service as an actor and a provider of play means.

The therapist can also reinforce the automatic working of the play therapeutic properties described above. This can be done by means such as bringing up relevant contents that have not been brought up by the family, reflecting and emphasizing important points. In the above play episode the therapist actively participated in the roles of Jack Reilly and the cop. He represented external danger (the police). He also reflected Shaul's responses and interpreted them ("You are involved whether you like it or not", "He's found a good way not to be involved, eh?")

Two difficulties can be expected: that the family will refuse to play make-believe games; that the dysfunctional program will prove resistant to the therapeutically relevant properties of play specified above. That is to say, the family's resistance to letting out any information related to their problems may be so strong that the facilitating factors embodied in play would not be effective in allaying it. One possible way of overcoming this difficulty is to let the family play for time and to wait until they bring up the evaded issues spontaneously. It may be supposed that if the family members are allowed to engage themselves in free activities these contents will sooner or later infiltrate these activities.

It should be stressed again that every tactic, including the one just presented, is a plan for *one* among *many* strategy-governed interventions.

Case 2: The Boy Who Begged to Differ

Now we are going to meet again Yoram and his adoptive parents Gad and Neta (see Chapters 7, 8 and 9). Family play therapy with this family was undertaken by my student Sari. She found and formulated another dysfunctional program regulating interactions in this triad. The latter dysfunctional program was different from the one presented in Chapter 8, but it reflected the same fear on each side, parents and Yoram, of being rejected by the other side. Here is an informal presentation of this program:

Out of worry that Yoram would remain an outsider, a foreign body in the still frail new family organism, Gad and Neta were demanding that Yoram conform to their own habits and life-style. He was expected, for instance, to eat the same food for supper, avoid using words that they considered unacceptable, stop making what they considered uncouth body and face gestures, etc. In reaction to these demands, Yoram would put the family to the test by deliberately behaving in an irritating manner.

At a certain stage of the therapy this program gave rise to numerous head-on clashes between Yoram and his parents at home.

Sari's detailed formulation of this program went as follows:

Yoram's Goal

To be accepted and liked by his parents and become a full member of the family.

Yoram's Plan

Presuppositions

My parents view me as a stranger, a foreign body in the family. Therefore they do not treat me well. They put pressure on me and make all sorts of demands.

Prediction

If I continue acting in a different, non-conforming way, they will understand that I am angry and dissatisfied. Then they are likely to change their attitude and make special efforts to accept me.

Output

Behave in a way that deviates from their standards and contradicts their expectations.

The Parents' Goal

To have Yoram as a full member of the new family, an equal partner, not an outsider.

Their Plan

Presuppositions

Someone who does not behave like the rest of the family cannot really be an integrated member of the family. Yoram does not behave so. Therefore he does not really belong to the family yet.

Output

Put pressure on Yoram to conform and behave like his parents. Tell him off if he does not.

In the framework of his overall strategy, Sari planned the following tactic for changing, at least partly, this dysfunctional program:

A Tactic for Yoram's Family

The errors of information processing and the changes required:

The parents fail to take Yoram's goal of becoming an equal member of the family into account. They also ignore Yoram's plan. They do not understand how their own plan reinforces Yoram's deviant behavior.

Yoram does not realize that his parents have the same goal as him. He does not comprehend their plan and does not realize how his own plan influences their plan.

The main efforts in the family play therapeutic intervention will be directed at the following:

(a) The parents' presupposition that someone who does not behave as the other family members do cannot really be an integrated member of the family.

(b) Yoram's provocative behavior and the negative feedback he gets.

The parents will be helped to see their presupposition is erroneous. A family member can behave in a non-conforming manner and still be a full participant in the family life.

The two parties will be shown how they reciprocate in provoking the very behavior they complain about.

Rationale

Yoram and his parents have the same goal. Furthermore, the therapist's acquaintance with the family has led her to believe that their dysfunctional program is motivated by erroneous conceptions and misunderstanding rather than by deeper motives issuing from the personalities of the family members. Her experience with this family convinced her that as soon as they realized their errors of judgment, they would be both willing and able to discard the erroneous conception and the related behavior, and adopt different, more useful rules of conduct.

The therapeutically relevant properties of play and their application

The property of play that is going to help the family realize that there is no contradiction between being different and becoming a full member of the family: *possible worlds*. This property derives its power from the fact that in make-believe play unrealized possibilities can be realized (see Chapter 3). The therapist will attempt to create play situations, in which the idea that there is no contradiction between individualistic mannerisms and cooperation or harmony is illustrated in a concrete manner.

The main property of play that is going to show the two parties how they provoke the very behavior they complain about is *basic duality*, which derives its power from the mental claim of *playfulness*. (See Chapters 2 and 3.) Due to this claim the player is both inside the play and outside it, an observer of self. One of the major applications of this property in family play therapy is increasing the family members' awareness of errors of information processing in their dysfunctional plans. (See Chapter 3.)

The family members will engage in a make-believe game of their own choice. The therapist will intervene, attempting to lead the participants to behave in a manner which is analogous to the way Yoram and his parents provoke each other in the real world.

How is the therapist going to use herself and the means available to her?

Generally speaking, the therapist will let the family members develop their own free play activities, using a variety of means such as toys, musical instruments and creative materials. She will subsequently join them as an active participant.

The property of *possible worlds* can be activated as follows: each time a family member attempts to censor an independent individual expression and organize the family into a uniform, homogeneous activity, the therapist will "rebel" and initiate a different activity of her own. Having drawn the family's attention toward herself in this manner she will use her authority—in an easygoing, playful manner—and arrange a play activity in which each person does his or her different thing, and yet mutual reciprocality and general harmony evolves. She will also reinforce—again in a light, playful manner—this familial achievement.

Rationale

This manner of approach is based on blocking the usual course of the family activity and structuring it differently by the therapist. The therapist plays a central active role in directing the activity, commenting on it and modeling various manners of conduct. The decision to intervene in this directive manner has been influenced by the above-mentioned hypothesis, that the dysfunctional program does not reflect deep psychological motives, and also by the family's being open and cooperative. The therapist assumes that in this family her directive style of intervention is not going to touch sensitive nerves. On the contrary, it will be met with gratefulness and understanding.

The activation of the property of *basic duality* for demonstrating to the family members how they provoke each other will be done as follows: the family will be engaged in a free make-believe play. Since the interactions governed by the dysfunctional program described above are imbued with intense emotions, these interactions are highly likely to surface in this play, in all probability in a symbolic disguise. If such an interaction emerges, the therapist will assume a role in the game which will enable her both to direct the family members to behave in a certain way and to comment about their own behavior. In this role she will instruct them to provoke one another in a manner which reflects the way it is actually done in the family. She will comment upon these provocations, emphasizing how they encourage the very behavior they seem to be criticizing and expect to prevent.

Expected obstacles and ways to overcome them: the parents are likely to resist the therapist's attempts to encourage Yoram to go his own way. The therapist can try to overcome this resistance in the following ways:

As mentioned above, she will assume the role of "the rebel", and in this way free Yoram of this role.

Since all the family members will be encouraged to do their own independent, distinctive thing, Yoram's odd behavior is likely to become less conspicuous.

So much for the tactic. Sari, in a number of sessions, put it into operation in diverse play situations, by means of a variety of moves. To illustrate these moves, let me describe the following episodes from one of the sessions:

Episode 1: The Foundling

All manner of toys were scattered on the carpet. Yoram picked up a fluffy toy dog. He sat in the corner, hugging the dog, sucking his finger.

Sari, addressing the parents, said excitedly: "Look, he found a stray dog! Why don't you take it home? I am a vet. Daddy! Mummy! Do you allow Yoram to bring this stray dog home?" The parents indicated their assent.

Sari said to Yoram: "Let's bring it home".

Yoram did not budge. He remained sitting silently, hugging the dog and sucking his finger. Sari, addressing the parents, said: "It does not know how to walk yet. You should teach it how to walk. You should teach it all kinds of things".

Gad told Yoram: "Do you want me to teach it how to walk?" Yoram nodded. Gad, hesitantly, took the dog and made it walk on the floor, saying: "You should move your legs this way. Watch it, you can fall".

Sari said: "That's wonderful. He can walk a little already. What other things are we going to teach it?" She addressed Neta: "Do you have any suggestions?" Do *you* have any suggestions?"

"We can teach it to fetch a bone when we throw it", said Neta.

"We can teach it to bring the morning newspaper", said Gad.

"We can teach it to shake a hand", said Neta.

Sari encouraged Gad and Neta to go on teaching the toy dog all these skills. Yoram held the dog and made it go through the motions.

Then Sari said: "Let's teach it to talk, so that we can speak with him".

Neta told the dog: "Say hullo!"

Gad said: "Say: I like the sound of money".

Yoram remained silent.

Sari said, worriedly: "It is silent. It can't talk like us. I think we should help it. Perhaps we should force it to talk".

Gad: "How can we force it?"

Sari: "I am not sure. Order him? Yell at him? Beat him up? Punish him? I'll show you". Sari approached the toy dog, slapped it across the face and said: "You should speak in the same way we do, you hear me?!" Then she made the toy dog charge at her fiercely and bite her hand. "Ouch!" She cried and said indignantly: "This dog bit my hand! This dog has no respect! Someone should put it in its place!"

She addressed the parents: "Perhaps you can control it and make it learn our human language". While she was saying this she handed the toy dog over to Yoram, who looked quite miserable.

Neta, obediently, addressed the dog and said: "Please, say something. She (referring to Sari) wants you to say something".

Sari said: "Do what you are told to do. Neta wants you to say something".

Yoram and the dog remained silent. Yoram looked at Neta, very tense.

Sari: "It does not want to speak your language. It is a bad dog. You should train him, using strict methods".

Neta: "But he will bark at me and bite me!"

Sari: "Then you should bark at it and bite it back! Perhaps this will help".

Analysis

The main purpose of this intervention was to make the family realize that they provoked in one another the very behavior they were complaining about. The therapist set into motion the property of *basic duality* in having them both play out their typical interaction pattern and reflect on it. She utilized Yoram's obvious identification with the toy dog as a lever for developing the story of the stray dog adopted by the family, obviously a direct allusion to Yoram's status in the family. Then the therapist made various moves whose purpose was to instruct Yoram and the others to behave in a way that reflected their dysfunctional program and the errors of information-processing operations included in it. In this way they could both play out this program and reflect on what they were doing to each other.

Episode 2: The Happy Orchestra

Yoram was very fond of music and rhythm. Sari brought a box with all sorts of musical and percussion instruments. Each member of the family chose one instrument. Gad suggested that all of them should play and sing a well-known children's song, and they all agreed to do so.

Sari made the following move: she picked a recorder, and while everybody was singing and playing, she started to play a completely different tune. The parents stared at her, partly bewildered and partly amused, and then she said: "I don't want to disturb you, but I feel like playing something else". Gad said: "That's all right, but are you willing to wait till we finish this song?"

"OK", said Sari, "but then I suggest that we do something else. Instead of all of us singing and playing the same song, each of us will sing or play something of his own". The family agreed to this suggestion. Each one in his or her turn played or sang another song. Each of the songs was a well known favorite.

After this round of individual presentations ended, Sari made another move and said: "Now I suggest that we make up songs. Instead of singing a song that already exists, each will invent a tune of his or her own".

They all, each in his or her own turn, made up their own song. Then Sari reached her third, principal move and said: "Now I suggest something else. We'll form an orchestra. All of us will play together. But we shall not play the same melody. Each of us will make up his or her own private melody, but we shall try very hard to make our melodies harmonize, so that the music produced by the whole orchestra comes out beautiful and pleasant."

The family accepted this suggestion, and started improvising, forming an ensemble, which sounded quite tolerable.

Finally, Sari said: "We were good. Everybody played his own special tune, but also took the others into account, and we all made a fine piece of music together."

Analysis

The main property of play that was activated was *possible worlds*. The dream of harmonious reconciliation of differences came true in the symbolic make-believe world of play. In her hope that the activation of this property would influence the family in the desired direction Sari counted mainly on the power of the pleasant emotional experience the family went through in this play, with Yoram as a full, equal participant.

Anticipating some resistance to her moves on the side of the family, Sari freed Yoram of the role of the rebel who disturbs the family's peace and took it temporarily upon herself. She also applied the principle of harmony of differences not just to Yoram but to all the family members.

Episode 3: The Journey

Sari brought glove-puppets for a puppet show. Neta suggested that everyone should choose a puppet and they all make a show. Each of the parents took a puppet, but Yoram picked a toy car and started moving it to and fro on the floor. Neta told him: "Yoram, leave that car alone! We are making a puppet show! Choose a puppet for yourself!"

Yoram ignored her and continued moving the toy car.

Neta said angrily: "OK, we are not going to let you participate in our show. We'll make a show with puppets and you'll stay outside and not be a part of us!"

At this point Sari made the following move: she took a man's puppet and said to Yoram: "I am the director of this show." She put the puppet inside Yoram's toy car and said: "The director says to the driver of this show: Drive fast! It's late! Take me to the show because I'm late!" Then she went on to take additional steps. She told Neta: "You are the playwright. What's the main theme of this show?" Neta said: "A journey". Sari said: "Fine! The director says that in this journey Yoram is the driver".

Afterwards, when the family members were walking together on their imaginary excursion, Sari said: "This is a wonderful journey. Each one has a role. One is a driver, one prepares food, one is the guide. We all do what we like best and what suits us best, and yet we enjoy ourselves together very much".

Analysis

This intervention has the same purpose as the one represented in the former episode. The main property of play activated in the latter episode is, again, *possible worlds*.

What Sari achieved by her moves was assigning Yoram a significant role in the joint family play activity, the role of the driver.

Case 3: The Referee

Ten-year-old Boaz was brought to my clinic by his parents Avner and Ora Green, who were worried by his disruptive, uncontrollable behavior at school. The structure of the interrelations between Boaz and his parents had been revealed quite clearly in the intake interview. Ora began to sigh and complain how much she suffered from the situation. Avner said to her angrily: "You are not talking to the point". Ora threw at him: "Stop shutting me up!" and Avner told her "Who are you to tell me what to do?" At this point Boaz intervened and said: "Daddy, this time *you* started it". Avner went for him furiously: "You are not going to tell me whether I started it or not. You are not a parrot and you don't have to repeat everything your mother says!" And then moving from Ora to Avner: "Come off him, will you?"

Later on this scene repeated itself in a different variation, but that time Boaz came out in defence of his father against his mother. It was easy to see that the relationship between the three was governed, among other things, by the following dysfunctional program: the father and mother would argue angrily about one issue or another. Boaz would intervene in their row in the role of "a referee". He would try to determine which of the two was right and who was wrong. The parent found "guilty" by Boaz would start attacking Boaz for being cheeky, with the encouragement of the other parent. The parent found "not guilty" by Boaz would stand up to defend Boaz. Then they would forget the original issue and start fighting about Boaz. Clearly, what we have here is a perfect instance of the dysfunctional pattern termed *detouring* by Minuchin (1974).

Put in the language of goals and plans, this program can be formulated as follows:

Parents' Goal

To avoid a direct open conflict between them.

Parents' Plan

Presupposition

Boaz is directly involved in our conflicts. Whenever we quarrel, he is willing to support one of us against the other.

Output

If Boaz takes sides, we stop quarreling about the original issue and start quarreling about him.

Boaz's Goal

To prevent his parents from fighting about important differences between them.

Boaz's Plan

Presupposition

My parents are unable to solve the differences between them.

Output

Whenever they fight, I support one of them and draw fire toward myself.

The errors of information processing and the changes the therapist has to effect in them are:

In their plan, the parents do not take into account Boaz's plan. Apparently, they are not aware of his lack of faith in their power to solve their own problems. They do not seem to be concerned about his willingness to become a victim in order to help them. They do not see the damage their plan can cause him.

Boaz's plan fails to validate his prediction that by serving as a referee between his parents he can stop their fighting and help them solve their problems.

The changes required: Avner, Ora and Boaz should become aware of their dysfunctional program and the damage it causes to the family. Boaz should be freed from his role in the triangle.

All the change-targets listed above, except the last one, have to do with making information available to the family, which has been formerly ignored by them. The properties of play that can be activated for this purpose are symbolic coding, covert communication, emotional regulation and basic duality.

The change-target of freeing Boaz from his role in the triangle can be approached with the aid of the play property of *possible worlds*. In the present context, this property can be put into practice in order to help the family experience the potential state of affairs in which their son is detriangulated (cf. Minuchin, 1974), that is, taken out of the dysfunctional triangle.

Rationale

The general experience with the dysfunctional pattern that has been termed "triangulation" or "detouring" (see Minuchin, 1974) as well as my own experience with this specific family, has instructed me that the goal of persuading the family members to give up the habit of dealing with the marital difficulties through a child is not at all easy to reach. The emotional investment in the dysfunctional program and the secondary gains from it are quite massive. Therefore attempts to expose the errors of information-processing operations and to persuade the family to give them up directly and verbally are bound to fail. The family is more likely to accept the intervention and invest energy in attempting to change if the emotions associated with the dysfunctional program are tempered as a result of the use of the property of *regulation of emotions*. The family will be willing to face their errors in information processing if these errors are exposed by indirect means, with the aid of the properties of *symbolic coding*, *covert communications* and *basic duality*.

How will these properties be actually put into practice in the intervention?

The therapist will let the family members play their own spontaneous make-believe games. Assigning himself in various suitable make-believe roles, he will attempt to modify certain make-believe situations in such a way that they serve as symbolically coded, metaphorical translations of the dysfunctional program described above. In this make-believe version of the dysfunctional programs the interactions among the family members will be distorted and caricatured, as if seen through a curved mirror. This will render it possible for the properties of symbolic coding, basic duality and regulation of emotions to be activated.

The therapist will attempt to induce the family members to spell out the thoughts underlying their interactions in the symbolic language of make-believe play (covert communications). He himself, in his make-believe role, will attempt to expose these thoughts in a playful manner.

When the dysfunctional program has been exposed, the therapist will attempt to lead the family to play a make-believe situation in which Boaz is extricated from the triangulation (possible worlds).

The therapist will make available to the family toys and play objects with aggressive connotations, such as boxing gloves or weapons. He will let the family members develop their own free play activities. However, when a suitable opportunity arises (e.g. when the parents pick up the boxing gloves) he will join the game as an actor-director and try to involve the family members in a game which reconstructs their typical dysfunctional behaviors in an exaggerated manner.

Rationale

The members of this family love playing and also look for opportunities to let out aggression. The presence of stimuli with aggressive connotations is likely to provoke them to initiate aggressive games. If the therapist joins in such a game and assumes a playful attitude, hopefully the family members will cooperate and be willing to let him submit their own game to his direction.

Expected obstacles and ways to overcome them are:

The parents may very well be taken aback by the brutality of the game and by the grotesque reflection of their own faces in the curved mirror. The therapist will help them overcome these uneasy feelings by reminding them that it is "only play". He will also use his authority, in a light, playful manner, and gently press them to perform their tasks.

Here is an episode, taken out of a session in which I attempted to put this tactic into practice:

Episode: The Boxing Match

Avner, Boaz's father, picks up a pair of boxing gloves off the carpet and examines them. He points at another pair, which are placed on the carpet, and asks Ora, his wife, with an amused smile: "Do you want them?"

I am holding a short stick, representing "a microphone", and am announcing into it ceremonially: "Ladies and gentlemen, you are now about to watch *the* boxing match of the century, between the world heavy-weight champion (I am laying my hand on Avner's shoulder, indicating that Avner should put the boxing gloves on) and the budding star, the US champion!"

Ora, eagerly, is putting her own pair of boxing gloves on. She rushes at her husband and showers him with fist blows. He retreats.

I (addressing Boaz): "Referee! Pay attention! Has any of the fighters committed an offence?"

Boaz: "Mummy did."

I: "You mean Ed, the US champion. Hey, Ed, how do you like this referee? He says you have been playing unfair."

Ora: "He is the one who is being unfair. I was strictly sticking to the rules."

I: "Hit him then".

Ora looks at me, quite confused.

Ora: "Hit the referee?"

I: "Yes. That's the way Ed is".

Ora gives Boaz some mock fist blows. Then she goes back to Avner, who becomes more and more aggressive.

I: "Referee, who is committing an offence now?"

Boaz: "Daddy".

I: "You mean Abe. Hey, Abe, the referee says you have been playing unfair".

Avner (smiling): "Should I hit him?"

I: "Of course!"

When this had been going on for a while, I put a top hat on and rushed toward the fighters, waving my arms. "I am the match manager", I cried, and I can't allow this match to go on. It should be stopped right now! This is not the way it's done. Hitting the referee is against the rules. It is also unfair. This referee has been trying to be as fair and objective as he can, and what does he get in return? Blows!"

Avner, Ora and Boaz stopped their activities and were looking at me, perplexed.

I said: "This match can be resumed only if the referee is out". I held Boaz's arm and said: "You sit here. You are not a referee any longer".

Avner asked: "Who will be the referee?"

I said: "No one. You don't need a referee. You can manage quite well on your own".

Then I took hold of "the microphone" and announced. "Ladies and gentlemen! You are now going to witness the first match in the history of boxing in which the contestants fight without a referee! They are going to fight to the bitter end! Today you are going to watch a knock out!"

Analysis

The play property *symbolic coding* helped the family members overtly express some of the features of their dysfunctional program which I wanted to expose, such as the violent power struggle between the parents, Boaz's unfortunate role in relation to it and the futility of his efforts.

The family members played a grotesquely exaggerated, symbolically coded version of their usual dysfunctional interactions. Since they were, simultaneously, the actors and the characters in the play, they must have become more sharply aware of the defects in these patterns than before. This was due to the automatic operation of the play property of basic duality.

I transmitted the therapeutic messages *covertly*. For example, I did not say: "You don't treat Boaz well" but "Hitting the referee is against the rules". This made it easier for the family members to accept the therapeutic messages.

Through "the boxing match" game the family members eased up the emotional tension associated with their dysfunctional program. The aggression, the anger, the frustration became overt. Purified of these emotional tensions, they became more open than before to the therapeutic suggestions that were supposed to lead to the required changes in their dysfunctional program.

I, exploiting the possibility of creating situations in make-believe play that are different from what exists in reality (*possible worlds*), extricated Boaz from his role in the dysfunctional triangle. I did this by canceling the role of the referee in the boxing match.

By placing myself in the roles of the announcer and the match manager, I succeeded in moving the family members to play in the way that suited my purposes.

Case 4: A Topsyturvy World

This case was mentioned briefly in the Introduction. Twelve-year-old Yudit became orphaned of her father when she was eight. She and her mother Shoshana became very close, looking to each other for warmth and emotional support. However, as Yudit approached adolescence, this excessive interdependence became somewhat burdensome for both of them. Each of them experienced a deeply felt need to disengage herself from the other and build her own life. But they found it difficult and did not know how to free themselves from one another. So each began to employ artificial, exaggerated and harmful means for keeping the other at a distance. For example, they would stop speaking with one another day in, day out, on some trivial pretext; one would leave the house when the other came in, and so forth. In the intake interview both of them asked to discuss the possibility that the daughter be sent to a boarding school. Both of them justified their wish to stay apart with the claim that they did not get along and made one another feel bad. It was obvious that they were not sufficiently aware of the strong mutual bond that lay behind their difficulties. I planned the following tactic for treating their problem.

A Tactic for Yudit and Shoshana

The dysfunctional program the therapist wants to change: the pattern of interrelations described briefly above can be reformulated as follows:

Yudit and Her Mother's Shared Goal

To create a distance between them, which would enable them to achieve some degree of autonomy without giving up their intimacy.

A presupposition shared by both mother and daughter

My mother/daughter is attached to me and is dependent on me. She does not want to and cannot disengage herself from me and become more autonomous.

Predictions shared by both mother and daughter

If I tell my mother/daughter that I want to free myself of the excessively close relationship between us, she will be deeply hurt. She will be unable to tolerate the rejection. She is likely to respond either by clinging to me or by becoming so angry that she might go away from me completely and then I am bound to lose her forever.

Output

(Again, shared by both mother and daughter) I should never express my wish to disengage myself from my mother/daughter in a direct manner. If I feel that my mother/daughter becomes too close to me, I should find some excuse for generating anger leading to a temporary rift between us, in accordance with my goal.

If my goal is not fully achieved by these means I should try to achieve it by creating a permanent external barrier between us, e.g. by sending the daughter to a boarding school.

The errors of information processing in this dysfunctional program on which the intervention will be focused, and the changes the therapist hopes to effect in them are:

Shoshana's and Yudit's presuppositions and predictions are not based on any serious attempts to find out what the other person really thinks and feels. Each of them denies her own internal conflict between her very strong attachment and dependency on the one hand and her desire to gain autonomy on the other hand. Each of them attributes the difficulty to the other.

Both Shoshana and Yudit fail to realize that they want the same thing. The drastic means they employ to advance their common goal are not necessary. They could reach their goal by negotiating a new way of conducting their relationship.

The changes the therapist wants to effect are:

Helping Yudit and Shoshana realize that they have the same goal; making them see that their presuppositions and predictions are wrong; assisting each of them to realize that she is torn between her dependency and her desire to gain autonomy; leading them to stop using the harmful means they have been using to achieve autonomy and encouraging them to negotiate a new kind of relationship.

The main therapeutically relevant properties of play applied and the manners by which they will be activated are:

The property of *arbitrariness of signifier* is based on the fact that in make-believe play there should not necessarily be any similarity between the signifier and its signified content. One of the main therapeutic uses of this property is *creating tension by revealing a contradiction between the signifier and the signified* (see Chapter 3). This property can be used in order to intensify, in both Yudit and Shoshana, the emotional experience of the conflict between the wish for autonomy and the wish to remain dependent. The intensification of the experience is likely to make each of them more aware of this conflict in herself as well as in the other. Hopefully this will give each of them a clearer vision and a better grasp of the emotional basis of their dysfunctional program. This is likely to make them more ready to re-examine their erroneous presupposition and predictions.

In the present tactic, this property of play will be activated in the following manner: within the play, the therapist will attempt to lead the mother and her daughter to physical proximity, which he will define as a signifier for physical distance and lack of intimacy. That is to say, the signifier (physical proximity) will serve, arbitrarily and paradoxically, as a make-believe play sign for a diametrically opposite signified content, namely distance. For example, in the context of a "topsyturvy world" game, the therapist can define smaller distance in the real world as "greater distance" in the make-believe world, and actual touching in the real world as "lack of any contact" in the make-believe world. The mother and daughter will be instructed to come closer and closer to one another until they actually hug one another. As they come closer the therapist will say: "Now you are getting farther and farther apart. You can hardly see one another. You become tiny distant dots." And when they hug he will say: "Now you've actually disappeared from each other's view. You cannot see or hear or feel one another any more".

Rationale

As stated above, the change the therapist hopes to effect by means of this use of the property of *arbitrariness of signifier* is to augment the mother's and daughter's awareness of their emotional ambivalence and its roots in their conflict between dependency and autonomy. The therapist assessment has been that at least in the particular case in hand this cannot be achieved by purely verbal means, since both Yudit and her mother have been captives of their own perceptions concerning their interrelations. He has also taken into consideration that psychological sophistication is not their forte. When intimate physical closeness between Yudit and her mother is created, but this closeness is arbitrarily defined as a signifier for remoteness, the therapeutic message is transmitted in the concrete language of play. The message gets through, since each of the two experiences simultaneously the two sides of her own ambivalence toward the other. The physical proximity, which is bound to be both pleasant and uncomfortable, is framed by the therapist as a signifier for distance. The two directly feel their proximity, experience it quite powerfully, but at the same time try to think about it as distance. A rift is formed between the direct sensual experience and the meaning assigned to it. This rift illustrates and magnifies their internal conflict. Therefore it is likely to sharpen the mother and daughter's awareness of the emotional basis of their dysfunctional program and make them more receptive to the other component of the therapeutic intervention.

The properties of *symbolic coding* and *covert communication*, which facilitate the expression and communication of complex or emotionally difficult messages (see Chapter 3), can be employed in order to help Yudit and her mother explicate and discuss their goal, their presuppositions and their predictions and examine them. The therapist's assessment is that it will be easier, both cognitively and emotionally, for Yudit and her mother to talk about these matters in the guise of make-believe play rather than in a direct manner.

The therapist will encourage Shoshana and Yudit to communicate, in make-believe play metaphors, their goal, their presuppositions and predictions, while they are in a state of maximal proximity signifying maximal distance. That is to say, they will talk about their dysfunctional program while they are directly experiencing their internal conflict. This is likely to make them particularly receptive and sensitive with respect to those aspects of their interrelations that are governed by the dysfunctional program.

The property of *possible worlds* can be activated in order to help Yudit and Shoshana stop using the harmful means they have been using to achieve autonomy. With the aid of this property they can be encouraged to negotiate a new kind of relationship, in which a better balance between intimacy and emotional closeness on the one hand, and personal autonomy on the other hand, is maintained. The therapist can use the state of maximal proximity–maximal distance in which the two discuss their relationships as a starting point for exploring, again totally within the frame of make-believe play, a new, healthier way of conducting the relationship. For instance, he can suggest that they look for locations and activities in the room which emphasize their autonomy but still enable them to maintain a sufficient degree of intimacy between them.

The therapist, in a light, playful manner, will suggest to the mother and daughter that they reconstruct, in a make-believe play, specific episodes where they deliberately kept one another at a distance. For instance, they will be asked to enact the situation in which one leaves the apartment when the other one comes in, the situation in which they are not on speaking terms, the situation in which Yudit is being sent to a boarding school, and so forth. At the point when the two are trying to find ways and means for reconstructing a given distancing situation, the therapist will intervene and, in a playful manner, will suggest situations where the distance the two want to achieve is signified by a considerable physical proximity.

Rationale

Since in these games the therapist wants to create, artificially, situations that are rather odd and absurd, he has to directly relate these situations to actual events in the daily life of the mother and daughter. Otherwise the two are apt to regard the intervention as a senseless indulgence in silly behavior, unrelated to the problem which brought them to therapy. The artificiality of these pre-planned play situations prevents the therapist from relying too much on play events which develop spontaneously in the course of the free play activity. He has to intervene in an active, directive manner.

When mother and daughter are in a state of maximal proximity, framed as a signifier for maximal distance (e.g. when the daughter is sitting on her mother's lap, which signifies "the area outside the apartment"), the therapist will, in a make-believe play role of a go-between, encourage them to have a conversation in which their goal, their presuppositions and their predictions are exposed and examined in a symbolic code. The communication will be indirect, that is, the pragmatic messages will be expressed metaphorically, through the semantic contents of the play.

Afterwards, the therapist will help Yudit and Shoshana to negotiate, again, through indirect communication and in a symbolic code, a change in their relationships, with a better balance between intimacy and autonomy. The new arrangement will be exercised in the possible worlds of make-believe play, again in a symbolic code.

Expected obstacles and ways to overcome them are:

Again, since the planned games are artificial and odd, the mother and daughter are likely to be slightly embarrassed and reluctant to perform the behavior they are expected to perform. The therapist can overcome this difficulty if he prepares the ground for the intervention by creating an atmosphere in which games are permissible and legitimate. For example, he can embed his interventions in a "topsyturvy world" game in which everything is possible and nothing is really as it appears to be.

Here is an episode, taken out of a session in which the therapist attempted to put this tactic into practice:

Episode: A Nice Warm Boarding School

After Shoshana and Yudit expressed their wish that the latter be sent to a boarding school, I proposed a make-believe game in which the mother stays at home and the daughter lives in a boarding school. I explained that this game will enable the two of them to visualize Yudit's absence from home and her life in the boarding school. This experience can help them reach a decision on whether to sent Yudit to a boarding school or not. Shoshana and Yudit agreed and began—admittedly with a great deal of hesitation and embarrassment—to plan the game. Shoshana raised the question: "Where is this boarding school going to be?" At this moment I pointed at her lap and said: "Here". Shoshana looked backwards, searching for the place I had in mind, but I told her: "You are looking in the wrong direction. I said 'here', on your lap. Your lap is going to be the boarding school in this game". Shoshana looked at me with an embarrassed, uncertain smile, and said, "Are you sure?" I said "yes" and then held Yudit's hand and told her: "Come with me to the boarding school". I led her slowly toward her mother and told her: "Sit here, on your Mummy's lap. Here is your make-believe boarding school".

Yudit sat in her mother's lap reluctantly and then I told Shoshana: "Embrace her. This is a closed boarding school". Then I gave Yudit and Shoshana a toy telephone and said to Shoshana: "Now you are alone at home and Yudit is in the boarding school. I am her instructor in boarding school and I know she wants to speak with you on the phone".

Then the mother and daughter were having a telephone conversation, with the daughter sitting on her mother's lap. Shoshana said: "How do you feel there in the boarding school, Yudit?"

"I'm OK", said Yudit. "I've made new friends that I like, and the teachers are nice and there are lots of things to do".

"Really?" said Shoshana, quite surprised. "I thought it would be very difficult for you to stay away from home".

"I was afraid you would be worried about me", said Yudit. "Aren't you a bit lonely, being alone at home?"

"You should not worry about me", said Shoshana. "I'm all right. I have so many things to do!"

At this point I intervened and said kindly:

"Please don't be angry with me for intervening, but do tell your mother that you miss her a little, or she'll think that you don't love her any more".

Yudit said: "Mummy, I hope you were not hurt by my saying that I enjoyed being here. I do miss you. And sometimes I do feel lonely, but I overcome it and get along".

Then I said, again in that kindly instructor's voice:

"You know, Yudit, next week you are going to stay home for a whole week. It's Pessach vacation".

"Really?" said Yudit, pleased.

"It's next week now", I declared and held Yudit's hand. I led her gently off her mother's lap and said: "You are on vacation now. You are home again with your mum". Yudit started to wander around the room aimlessly. I said: "Here I am, your instructor from the boarding school, remember? I can see that it is difficult for both of you to be under the same roof again, now that you have got used to being free from each other's company. But you know, you don't have to stay in the same room all the time. You can stay in different rooms and still feel close to one another, and, when you want to be together you can invite the other to visit you in your room".

I took two pieces of chalk, gave Yudit and Shoshana one each and said: "Here you are. Draw your separate rooms on the floor".

Shoshana and Yudit spent some time trying to decide where each of them wanted to have her own room drawn on the floor. Then each of them drew a square and stepped inside it, looking at the other.

Analysis

In accordance with the tactic, I reframed mother's lap, a most intimate location, as a signifier for the signified content "the boarding school". When Yudit sat on her mother's lap, embraced by her mother, both she and her mother were transferred into a self-contradictory, paradoxical state of mind, in which both of them experienced the intimacy and warmth as well as the slight discomfort of embracing and being embraced, and the imagined state of affairs in which the mother was alone at home and the daughter in boarding school. Presumably this state of mind reflected and amplified the mother's and daughter's internal conflict with respect to intimacy and dependency versus autonomy, and therefore increased their readiness to talk about matters related to this conflict in a meaningful way.

Profiting from this hypothesized readiness, I encouraged the mother and daughter to conduct a meaningful conversation about those aspects of their relationship which were governed by their dysfunctional program. In order to stimulate such a conversation I provided the two with toy telephones and assumed, through the make-believe role of the instructor, the function of a go-between.

Indeed, in the conversation that ensued, both of them expressed their wish to be more independent, re-examined their assumptions about the over-dependence of the other one and re-affirmed their love for one another. *The properties of play* that facilitated this were *possible worlds* (the idea of sending the daughter to a boarding school was "realized" in the make-believe game), *symbolic coding* and *covert communication*.

The property of *arbitrariness of signifier* was activated again when Yudit's homecoming was marked by getting off mother's lap. I gave the mother and the daughter pieces of chalk and asked them to draw separate rooms on the floor. The properties of play that were put into operation here were: *possible worlds* (the new balance was "materialized" in the make-believe world), *symbolic coding, covert communication* and again, *arbitrariness of signifier* (the squares on the floor, drawn by chalk, were signifiers for "separate rooms", but these rooms had no walls, and the mother and daughter could remain in direct contact with one another despite the fact that each of them was "enclosed within her own room").

Summary

The main components of the tactics employed in the cases presented in this chapter are summarized in Table 16.

Table 16 Main components of the tactics employed in the cases presented in this chapter.

Name of case	Therapeutic aims	Properties of play employed	Therapist's main moves
The Scriptwriter	Help father share his "secrets"; encourage son to admit his involvement in his parents' problems (recovering suppressed information).	Regulation of emotions, symbolic coding, owning and alienation (to facilitate expression of suppressed emotionally laden family problems).	Creating a playful atmosphere by participating in the family play as an actor; reinforcing the play properties by reflecting and emphasizing important points.
The Boy Who Begged to Differ	Help family to see that one does not have to conform to be a full member of family.	Possible worlds (to differ and participate at the same time); Basic duality (to show family how they provoke rejection).	Exaggerating dysfunctional pattern (The Foundling; The Happy Orchestra); Creating a compromise between family and individual activity (The Journey).

(*continued*)

Table 16   (cont.)

Name of case	Therapeutic aims	Properties of play employed	Therapist's main moves
The Referee	Help family become aware of their dysfunctional program of detouring; free son of his role in the triangle.	Basic duality (family play their dysfunctional program and observe themselves playing it at the same time); symbolic coding, covert communication (to facilitate self-observation); emotional regulation (to ease tension); possible worlds (to let family experience triangulation-free interactions).	Assuming various make-believe roles, therapist modifies family-initiated play situations so that they serve as metaphors of the triangulation program. Subsequently, therapist, in make-believe, extricates Boaz from the triangulation.
A topsyturvy world	Help mother and daughter realize that both of them are torn between dependency and desire for autonomy (exposing unavailable information); make them see that they misunderstood one another; encourage them to use constructive means for achieving autonomy.	Arbitrariness of signifier (creating a dissonance between body contact (an index of dependency) as a signifier, and distance (an index of autonomy) as a signified.	In a make-believe play role, the therapist encourages physical contact between mother and daughter, but defines the contact as a signifier for distance. While mother and daughter are in maximal proximity, the therapist encourages them to communicate their interpersonal thoughts on play metaphors.

PART 4

Carrying out the therapy

CHAPTER 11

The Relationship Between a Tactic and its Execution

As has been shown in Chapters 9 and 10, the strategic family play therapeutic interventions are rigorously planned ahead of time. The assessment leads to designing an overall strategy which is based on the assessment. Each particular intervention is planned as a tactic, which is subordinated to the overall strategy. The tactic is structured. It includes the main forecast elements of the intervention. However, as is the case in many areas of life, the planning and its execution do not directly correspond. In a chess game, in a football game, in military operations, the strategies and tactics are very rigorously planned ahead, but the execution is never parallel to the plan. The carrying out is done flexibly, with many changes and modifications of the original plan in accordance with the changing conditions in the field. The tactic should not be carried out rigidly, because it will fail. It should be carried out flexibly, in a manner that is sensitive to what is actually happening in the room at any given moment. When the therapist enters the play therapy room he should push the tactic to the back of his mind. His moves should be dictated by the moves made spontaneously by the family members, with the tactic, as it were, behind the scene.

A grave mistake the therapist can make is to attempt to impose or force his tactic upon the family. He should adjust his intervention to the family's spontaneous behavior, and not the other way round. He should subtly and gradually change the course of the family's spontaneous behavior by harnessing it to his own therapeutic goals, according to his own tactic.

The Steps in the Intervention

Strategic family play therapeutic interventions should be carried out according to the following steps:
Letting the faimly members engage in free, spontaneous play.
Observing their free play and attempting to interpret and understand it.

Planning some moves ahead of time, as in a chess game. Intervening by making a move that is subordinated to the tactic. Some of the moves anticipate the family members' moves, and prepare the ground for the therapist's future moves.

Beyond executing the tactic, the therapist must join each of the family members in his play as much as possible, reflect their feelings and communicate with them on various levels.

Let me explain and illustrate each of these steps:

Letting the Family Members Engage in Free, Spontaneous Play

Before the therapist invites the family to the session he prepares the room. He removes obstacles to the family members' free movement. He exposes toys and playthings which suit the tactic, that is, such that reflect the family members' preferred media of expression and communication, and are likely to stimulate the kind of play that would facilitate the execution of his tactic. When the family comes into the room the therapist suggests that they play freely, do what they want, children and adults alike. They are not restricted in their play, beyond limitations that are dictated by the therapeutic contract, which have to do with considerations of security, damage to property and decency. The therapist tells the family members that he is also willing to participate in their play, but not necessarily right from the beginning.

Observing Their Free Play and Attempting to Interpret and Understand It

In Chapters 4–8 a method of assessment based on a microscopic and a macroscopic semiotic analysis of spontaneous family play has been presented. It was emphasized that the assessment is not done once and for all before the treatment itself starts. The therapy itself is accompanied by a running assessment, in which the therapist re-examines the initial hypotheses and if necessary changes them. It was also stressed that no therapist is expected to actually transcribe, analyze or interpret his observations of family play in the manner proposed in the extended technical version of the method of microscopic and macroscopic analysis. Mastering this technique is an effective way of acquiring the skills vital for a therapist who wishes to specialize in strategic family play therapy. Once the transcription and interpretation techniques have been acquired, practiced and internalized, they can become imprinted in the therapist's mind as skills and habits which enable him to process and interpret the family's behavior very rapidly while it is actually taking place in front of him.

In the family play therapy session the family is engaged in its own free spontaneous play. The therapist is, at first, just a passive observer. He is equipped with his initial assessment of the family, his strategy and his tactic for the session. If he is well trained in the semiotic method of transcription and microscopic and macroscopic analysis, he can also record in his mind and analyze the family members' behavior as it unfolds moment by moment. This requires that the therapist takes very quickly the following steps at any given moment of the therapy session: (a) Watching all the family members and attempting to see and perceive what each of them says and does at any given moment. He should attempt to be aware of their verbal behavior (speech and other vocal signals), spatial (proxemic) behavior (location, body orientation, etc.), kinesic (body and facial postures and motions) and tactile (manipulative) behavior at all times. But he should also attempt to see the ensemble, the aggregate of all these at each moment. In this respect the family play therapist is like a soccer commentator, who has to be aware of the motions of each player on the pitch at each given moment, but also of their general display in relation to the development of the game. This is not at all easy, but a well-trained family play therapist can do it, as can a well-trained soccer commentator. (b) He should instantly divide the behavior of each family member into activity units and describe each activity unit on the raw-material level, that is, describe its vocal, kinesic, proxemic and manipulative characteristics. Then he should interpret it on the semantic and pragmatic levels, that is, hypothesize about its thematic and emotive meaning and about its communicative functions (purpose, presuppositions, prediction, etc.) (c) He should attempt to decide whether the combinations of activity units he observes reflect the dysfunctional program referred to in the tactic as the potential target of his strategic family play therapeutic intervention or not. In some cases he will be surprised to discover, in an instant macroscopic analysis, dysfunctional programs that have not been found in the pre-therapy assessment. Or he may be even more surprised to find that the behavior he observes contradicts his former hypotheses about the family's dysfunctional programs. This can indicate that either the family has changed since the pre-therapy assessment was made, or that the assessment was incorrect or at least restricted to just one subset of situations. The instantaneous macroscopic analysis and the comparison with the results of the pre-therapy assessment constitute a process of hypothesizing and checking the hypotheses with the data streaming in. The criteria by which certain hypotheses are preferred are simplicity, that is parsimony, completeness and consistency. The hypotheses that do not agree with in-streaming data and are inconsistent with them or are not parsimonious enough are discarded and other hypotheses are preferred.

Intervening by Making Moves that are Subordinated to the Tactic

When the therapist is clear about the meaning of the behavior he observes and its relevance to the dysfunctional program, he can intervene in order to carry out the tactic. The moves he can make are produced by his own creative imagination, although a rich repertory of types of moves has been accumulated by practitioners. These are classified, explained and illustrated in Chapter 12. The moves the therapist makes should however be subordinated to the following principles. (a) A move must never clash with the behavior of the family to whom the move is directed. That is, the move should not contradict the behavior, its emotive or thematic meaning or communicative functions. Here Milton Erikson's principle of "going with" rather than "going against" should apply (see Haley, 1973). The move should agree with its target behaviors and their meaning or naturally complement them. (b) The move should not look like a move. It should be integrated with the natural course of the activity, in a playful manner, so that the stitches are concealed. (c) The move should be subordinated to the tactic, that is, it should serve the goal of changing the dysfunctional program on which the tactic is focused, and in particular contribute to changing an error of information processing which maintains the dysfunctional program. It has to utilize the therapeutically relevant properties of make-believe play which have been decided on in ways described in the tactic. However, it can also use other therapeutically relevant properties of play in other ways, should the target behaviors of the intervention so require, and the alternative therapeutically relevant properties also serve the same goal of correcting errors of information processing that underlie the dysfunctional program. It should also take into account the predicted and unpredicted difficulties and obstacles that present themselves in the situation, and detour or overcome them.

Quite often, the crucial moves, that is, the moves that actually realize the tactic, cannot be carried out immediately and directly because of the conditions in the room. *Preparatory moves* should be made, to prepare the ground for the crucial moves. Here the moves are like those of a chess player, who plans his moves some steps in advance.

It should be emphasized that the role of the therapist in strategic family play therapy is not restricted to making the moves that carry out his tactics. After all, quite a lot is going on in the room while the therapist is making his tactics-relevant moves. For example, if the therapist's moves bring him in close contact with one family member, and this close contact is necessary for the tactic, the other family members are likely to feel left out. They may attempt to draw the therapist's attention or to disrupt his interaction with the particular family member. The therapist is expected to be aware of these attempts, and react by giving the others some kind of attention, even if this is not called for by the tactic. This is not easy, because the therapist's attention is directed chiefly to the relevant family member and to the execution of the tactic. However, in strategic family play therapy the therapist has to divide his attention and to act on a number of arenas at one and the same time. The therapist has to attempt to continuously get verbal and non-verbal feedback from all the family members concerning the impact of his move on their mood, actions, etc. and judge whether all goes well according to his plan. If there is a problem, he must attempt to solve it on the spot, even at the cost of retracting certain moves.

Common Errors

As the reader has no doubt realized by now, strategic family play therapy is a rather complex art, not at all easy to master and practise. Beginners find it quite difficult to carry out and tend to commit typical errors. Most of these errors can be eradicated with experience and some properly supervised practice (see Appendix 2). Here is a list of some of the most common errors, illustrated by examples:

Simplification

Often, trainees simplify the family play therapeutic activity and turn it into a kind of individual verbal therapy in disguise.

Sandy, a gifted therapist in the early stage of her training as a strategic family play therapist, conducted a family play therapy session with a family of Israeli immigrants from the US—Sheila, the mother, Andy, the father and their two sons, Bob (eight years old) and Al (five years old). Bob was referred to therapy because he developed fears following the death of his grandfather. The main purpose of the session was to help the family members express their feelings with respect to the loss of the grandfather and provide emotional support to each other. The dysfunctional program that was to be changed was the family's plan of helping each other by denying the existence of unpleasant feelings or difficulties. The planned tactic included the use of the properties of play *symbolic coding*, *covert communication* and *emotional regulation* in order to facilitate the expression of the emotions associated with mourning.

In the session, themes related to the death of the grandfather, disguised in a variety of metaphors, appeared almost continuously. Consider for instance the following episode:

Father is sitting on the carpet next to mother. He wears a hand puppet representing grandfather and she a hand puppet representing grandmother. The younger son Al is walking aimlessly around the room. The older son Bob is drawing on the blackboard with colored chalks.

Mother says: "Grandpa disappears under the carpet". She hides the hand puppet representing grandfather underneath the carpet. Al takes a toy gun and starts shooting at the bulge in the carpet where "grandfather" is hidden. Then he tramples the bulge quite hard with his foot. The father says: Al, stop behaving this way!

Bob fills in the upper part of the blackboard with brown chalk marks. His mother looks and says: "I can see you are drawing the ground above, instead of sky".

An obvious interpretation of this sequence is the following: the mother's act of covering grandfather's puppet with the carpet is a symbolic representation of his death. Al's response of shooting the bulge and stepping on it reflects his fear and anger concerning his grandfather's death. His father's reaction indicates his anxiety concerning his son's expression of anger, in accordance with the family program which blocks emotional expressions. Bob's drawing symbolizes the burial of grandfather (what is above is the earth instead of the sky).

This was an excellent point for Sandy, the therapist, to come in and carry out her tactic. But she failed to do so. She addressed Al, the younger son, and said "I am a journalist. I see a lot of shooting and fighting and I want to know what this is all about."

AL. I like shooting.
SANDY. I see. May I ask why?
AL. I don't know why.

This went on in this manner for a while.

Although Sandy attempted to assume a make-believe role and conduct the therapeutic communication within the framework of a make-believe game, in fact her intervention was a result of her failure in reading and interpreting the relevant information presented in the family play. It did not address itself to this information in a manner that issued from the tactic. She conducted a verbal communication with a single person, the little boy, attempting to elicit the motives for his behavior in the characteristic individual "insight therapy" style. Apparently, it was too difficult for Sandy at that early stage of her training to cope with the complex task of seeing and interpreting the observed behavior and carrying out the tactic creatively. Therefore she fell back on a familiar, much simpler behavioral set.

Failing to Make Preparatory and Auxiliary Moves

Common errors committed by inexperienced family play therapists include attempting to dash headlong into the main moves without making the necessary preparatory moves and neglecting the need to make auxiliary moves. These errors reduce the motivation of family members to cooperate or participate in the session in a meaningful way.

In a workshop for beginners in strategic family play therapy held in Holland the participants role-played simulations of therapeutic sessions. Each such simulation was followed by a discussion in which the participants shared their feelings and impressions and analyzed the intervention. This was an excellent opportunity for realizing how powerful the emotions aroused during the family play therapeutic experience can be in general. But what is particularly relevant in this juncture are the emotional reactions reported by participants who were not directly attended by the role play therapist or approached in a too direct, abrupt manner. Those who were not attended to described their feelings by expressions such as "I felt left out", "I needed some support and did not know where to get it", "I felt lonely", and the like. Those who were subjected to main moves not preceded by preparatory moves used expressions such as: "I felt assaulted", "It made me angry", "I could not make myself do it".

One of the role play sessions was related to the following case:

Pieter, an eight-year-old boy, contracted some chest disease when he was six months old. In the first two years of his life he spent long periods in a hospital. When he was home he had to be looked after incessantly by members of his family, particularly his mother. There was always an atmosphere of anxiety and concern surrounding him. He was treated like a special child, vulnerable and fragile, whose very life is at hazard.

In the third year of his life Pieter completely recovered from his illness, but the attitude of the people surrounding him remained extremely over-protective. It appeared that the common goal of all the family members, especially the mother, was to preserve the degree of protective intimacy with Pieter that had been maintained during the first two years of his life and ever since. In their plan they filtered out information indicating that Pieter was not ill any more, that he was developing normally and no longer needed any special treatment or protection.

The role play therapist Ina wanted to help the family members to stop ignoring the information they had been filtering out, and change their goal and their plan accordingly. The main properties of play she wanted to activate were possible worlds, owning and alienation, symbolic coding and covert communication. She hoped to enable Pieter to experience, within the framework of make-believe play, situations in which he would behave in a relatively mature, independent manner and take risks. She wanted to demonstrate this to the other family members and convince them that Pieter was perfectly capable of functioning like a normal eight-year-old boy.

In the simulated play therapeutic session the role play family members constructed a make-believe farm and populated it with various toy animals. The parents and Pieter's older sister played with farm animals. Pieter played with wild animals: a lion, a tiger and a crocodile.

Ina approached Pieter and said: "Hullo hunter! I am a hunter too. Come on, we are going to hunt rhinos in Africa".

Pieter turned his back on her. He built a fence of blocks around his animals. Ina said, "Come on, don't be afraid".

Pieter took a toy lion and made it pounce at Ina and tear her apart.

Ina, half laughing, said. "Ouch! The lion ate me up!" *At this point Pieter said,* "OK, let's go hunt". *He made his lion follow Ina in the direction of* "*Africa*".

When the two left the farm, the mother made her cow moo rather pathetically. The father made his donkey bray.

In the follow-up discussion, Sander, the workshop participant who played the role of Pieter, told how he felt when Ina approached him with the invitation to go hunting. The idea thrilled him, but frightened him as well. He felt that he was not ready yet to take such a big step toward independence. He could not tolerate the loneliness and the danger. He also felt sorry for his parents. He did not want to betray and neglect them. He felt he still needed their protection.

All this was translated in his mind into fear of the therapist. She became a frightening and threatening figure. That is why he had to turn his back on her and protect his animals by building a fence around them. When she insisted, his fear increased. Moreover, he was enraged because she did not understand him, put pressure on him and threw him into a conflict. That is why he attacked and rent her. However, her playful, joking reaction calmed him down. He suddenly felt that all that was just a make-believe game. At this point he was willing and ready to follow her lead.

Katrien, the role play mother, said that when Pieter had left with Ina she felt betrayed and lonely. She was worried about Pieter and felt very angry at the therapist who took him away. That is why she made her cow moo. Her role play husband, Pim, said that he could not tolerate the cow's heartbreaking mooing. He made his donkey bray to silence her.

Obviously, Ina's mistake was in plunging headlong into her main moves, without preparing the ground by preparatory moves, which would help the family members accept her and her intervention and tolerate the change. She also failed to accompany her main moves by auxiliary moves which would attend to the emotions aroused by her main moves in the other family members.

Therapist's Hyperactivity

In a family play therapy session, the therapist does not have to be active all the time. It is better for him to sit aside observing the family members' play, attempting to understand it, contemplating and planning his further moves. He should carefully choose the right moment to step in.

Usually, the family members do not miss the therapist's active involvement. They are busy playing.

Inexperienced therapists often feel uncomfortable if they are not actively involved in the family's play activity all the time. They work too hard, do too much. This, as a rule, is counterproductive, since no time is left for them to understand what they observe, and plan their intervention.

"Going Against" Instead of "Going With"

Beginners often fail to obtain the family members' cooperation with their moves, because they do not adapt their moves to what has already been happening in the spontaneous play activity of the family members.

In a family play therapeutic session, Dov, the father, Malka, the mother, and their older daughter Moran sat in a big box, pretending that it was the family car, and that they were on their way to visit granny, who was sick. Nine-year-old Tammy sat in a separate box. She said she wanted to ride in her own car.

Leah was the therapist. Her goal, dictated by her tactic, was to get Tammy into the family "car". She said: "Come on, Daddy, do invite Tammy to join you in the family car".

The father said: "Tammy, did you hear what she said? Come and get into the car with us".

Tammy ignored this invitation.

This move failed because it went against the natural course of the activity instead of going with it. More specifically, it ignored the purposes and predictions which, according to the diagnostic analysis, lay behind Tammy's decision to ride in her own separate make-believe car. Her prediction had been that should she join the family she would be downtrodden and suppressed in all kinds of ways. Her purpose was to avoid this.

This session was conducted under live supervision. The supervisor suggested that Leah make the following moves: she would play the part of a traffic policeman riding a motorcycle. In this role she will stop the family car for a checkup. The policeman will find that the car is in a bad state of repair and is not allowed to continue its travel. It will have to be towed. He will ask Tammy to put her car at the service of the family car and tow it.

This intervention succeeded. Tammy's car was tied to the family car with a rope. Tammy was "driving, towing the family car", with a wide, happy smile on her face.

This success can be accounted for as follows: the therapist joined the family play, assuming a role that was significant in the context of the spontaneous activity in the room. Her preparatory moves and main moves were in agreement with Tammy's goal of avoiding being downtrodden and did not contradict the family's goal of making her join them. Tammy was made to join the family without physically leaving her own "car" and going into the family "car". Furthermore, instead of being downtrodden she was given a role which put her in a superior position in relation to her family. All the steps in the intervention went *with* the family's activity and its pragmatic functions. No move went *against* these.

Moves That Take the Fun Out of the Play

In the case just described, the therapist, prior to being instructed by the supervisor, intervened in a manner that made her position as a therapist too obvious. Therefore she broke the illusion and took the magic out of the playful atmosphere. Instead of joining the family play in a make-believe role, she remained an outsider who gives instructions. The father reacted accordingly when he told Tammy: "Did you hear what she said? Come and get into the car with us".

Summary

The steps in a family play therapeutic intervention and the common errors discussed in this chapter are summarized in Table 17.

Table 17   Steps in family play therapeutic intervention and common errors.

Step	Nature of therapist's activities
Observation	Therapist observes family's free play and attempts to decipher its semantic and pragmatic meanings and functions
Planning	Therapist plans some moves ahead of time
Preparatory moves	Therapist makes play moves that prepare the ground for his main, tactic-governed moves
Main and auxiliary moves	Therapist makes main, tactic-governed moves and auxiliary moves whose purpose is to control or neutralize side effects of main moves

Common errors: simplification, failure to make preparatory and auxiliary moves, therapist's hyperactivity, "going against" instead of "going with", taking the fun out of the play.

A Case Illustration

The relation between the assessment, the strategy, the tactic and its execution will now be illustrated by the following case:

Sarah Romano, a stubby, sluggish thirty-five-year old woman, arrived at the welfare agency with her two children, nine-year-old Yaffa and eight-year-old Mosheh. Pinhas, the father, had left home about a year before, since he felt himself unable to go on shouldering all the housework and child care tasks that Sarah forced upon him. Pinhas was a rehabilitated criminal. Sarah was, in her childhood and adolescence, a parental child. She had to function as a housewife and a surrogate mother to her brothers and sisters and even to her sickly mother and father, who was an alcoholic. One of the motives for her marriage with Pinhas was her wish to unburden herself of this yoke and get herself a parent substitute.

The identified patient was eight-year-old Mosheh. He had behavior problems in school and at home. He was very restless, stubborn and domineering. Sarah asked for therapeutic help because she could not handle him.

The case was taken up by Reena, a student in a training course for social workers.

The initial assessment included an interview with Sarah and a free play observation with Sarah and her two children, which was analyzed microscopically and macroscopically. It was concluded with the formulation of the following dysfunctional program, which describes the interrelations between Sarah and her two children:

Sarah's Goals

To get from her children the affection and warmth she needed and was denied; to control them so that they do their duties, do not give her too much trouble, and do not make too heavy demands on her.

Sarah's Plan

If the children demand services beyond the minimal duties of preparing food or providing some clothes, I should remain passive and ignore the demand, until they give up and help themselves. From time to time I cry and pretend to be sick until the children bring me food and kiss and hug me. At night I let the children sleep in my bed.

Yaffa's Goal

Not to lose mother. Secure at least a minimal amount of warmth and care from her.

Yaffa's Plan

Presuppositions

If mother is too sick, helpless and unhappy to act according to my goal, I achieve my goal by serving her, giving her food, hug and kiss her until she reacts.

If Mosheh demands things or does not do his duties or behaves in a disruptive manner, this contradicts my goal, because it makes mother even more passive and helpless. Therefore, I should comply with his demands, until he is hushed up.

When mother feels better, I ask her to act according to my goal.

Mosheh's Goal

To be present for mother; not to be neglected.

Mosheh's Plan

Demand services from mother.

If mother does not react, this means that my goal has not been reached, that is, my presence is not felt, so I have to step up my demands and act disruptively.

If my sister reacts to my demands, I accept what she offers. Her reaction shows that my presence has been felt. I also predict that if I accept, my mother will feel that she does not have to make too much effort for me, so she will be freer to act according to my goal.

If my sister tells me to serve mother, I comply. When I serve her, my goal is partly fulfilled, that is, I am present for my mother, I am not fully neglected.

This program is dysfunctional for a number of reasons. First, the mother's goals are inconsistent with minimal parenting. Instead of giving her children the care, warmth and affection they need, she expects them to give her all that. She makes demands on them that are too much for their age and level of development, without granting them what they need to have the strength to fulfil all these duties.

The mother's plan fails to see other possible ways of getting what she wants from her children except by remaining passive, ignoring them, letting them sleep in her bed and playing the part of an unhappy, sick, helpless being. She also fails to realize that her children's behavior, especially her son's plan of being disruptive, is influenced by her own output.

Yaffa's plan is also dysfunctional. She does not realize that her habit of serving her mother and her brother reinforces her mother's plan. She fails to validate her presupposition that her mother is really too sick and helpless to act according to her goal.

Mosheh's plan is based on the wrong presupposition that his presence is not felt. His prediction that accepting what his sister offers him will serve his goal with his mother is also wrong.

The strategy decided on was the following:

The main objective of the therapy is to help all three family members to achieve their respective goals. On the face of it these goals seem to be mutually incompatible. Sarah wants to get affection from her children, putting in as little effort as possible. The children want to get from her what she does not want to, or is unable to, give. However, these goals are not as contradictory as they appear to be. If the children and the mother give affection and help to each other, using functional rather than dysfunctional plans, they can all get what they need. What should be changed is their dysfunctional plans, not their goals.

The main errors of information processing in the dysfunctional plans that should and can be changed are the following:

The mother has to understand that it is within her reach to get warmth and affection from her children, without using passivity, neglect and misery as means. She can be more active, caring and happy and still get what she needs. If she realizes this, she is likely to be able to mobilize the energy needed to maintain this achievement.

Yaffa should come to believe that her mother can give her the warmth and care that she needs and is potentially willing to do so. She could not comply with her brother's demands and serve as a mother substitute for him. She should transfer the responsibility to him.

Mosheh should be made to realize that his presence is felt anyway. He should be made to see how his own disruptive behavior reinforces his mother's, in contradiction to his own goal. He ought to learn to direct his demands to the right address—his mother rather than his sister.

In the first phase of the therapy the family will be encouraged to play out their dysfunctional program in a symbolic code. In the second phase the therapist will join with them to create a new make-believe possible world, in which the errors of information processing are corrected and the dysfunctional plans are made functional. In the third phase the new, sound family program will be transferred to the out-of-play reality in the play therapy room. The former dysfunctional program will be allowed to continue to exist *within* the make-believe play. This gradual, progressive induction of the change is necessitated by the nature of this family. A more direct approach would in all probability be met with unbending resistance, especially on the mother's side. It will be recalled that her dysfunctional plan is the product of a very problematic life history.

This overall strategy was broken down into tactics. Here is one of these, followed by an illustration of how it was carried out by moves according to the steps described above.

This tactic belongs to the second phase of the strategy, that is, the phase in which the dysfunctional plans are repaired *within* the make-believe play.

The Tactic

The main purposes are:

To make Yaffa realize that her mother can, and is willing to, give her and her brother the warmth and care that they need. To help her dare and ask her mother to care for her and give her love.

To lead her to stop serving as a substitute mother to her brother.

To achieve these purposes the following therapeutically relevant properties of play will be activated in the following ways:

Yaffa will be persuaded to ask her mother for expressions of love and care. Sarah will be required to comply in the possible, symbolically coded world of make-believe play. If Sarah fails to respond, the therapist will model symbolically coded compliance, perhaps with the aid of puppets. At the same time various techniques of emotional regulation will be used to reduce Sarah's difficulty in bringing herself to give her children what they need. This can be achieved, for instance, by introducing symbolic figures that satisfy the mother's need for throwing off her yoke and getting love and warmth.

The property of *basic duality* can be used to help Yaffa realize how inappropriate it is for her to parent her brother. The therapist can emphasize this point by saying things such as "You are pretending to be his mother".

These were the main elements of the tactic. Here is a description of a part of the session in which some of these moves were made by the therapist:

> Sarah is slumped on a low stool in the corner, motionless. Yaffa is "cooking food", glancing from time to time at her mother. Mosheh, a steering wheel in both his hands, is running toward Yaffa, shouting loudly: "Bee Beep! Bee Beep!" He knocks the utensils she is playing with off the table, as if by mistake, and continues running. Yaffa kneels down and collects the toy utensils, saying nothing. Then she approaches her mother, holding a dish, and tells her: "Here's some soup for you". Her mother pretends to drink the soup, without smiling or moving from her seat.

Reena, the therapist, decided that this interaction was an instance of the dysfunctional program described above. This decision was based on a quick intuitive application of the method of observation and analysis presented in Chapters 6–8. The process of analysis can be approximated as follows:

The first combination of activity units was Sarah's being slumped motionless in the stool in the corner. On the semantic level this seemed to express being passive, tired and lacking of energy. On the pragmatic level Reena thought that it had the purpose of signalling to her children that she was too weak and tired to do anything for them.

The next combination of activity units was Yaffa's "cooking food" and glancing from time to time at her mother. On the semantic level the theme of cooking food appeared to be related to an emotive of Yaffa: her feeling of responsibility for providing for the whole family. On the pragmatic level this seemed to be a message to her mother. This message was based on the presupposition that her mother was too weak and helpless to participate. Its presumed purpose was signalling to the mother that she would soon get some food from Yaffa.

The next combination of activity units was Mosheh's holding a steering wheel, running toward Yaffa, shouting "Bee Beep!" and knocking her toy utensils down, as if by mistake. This seemed to signify, semantically, bossiness, as if the whole place belonged to him, and a dangerous, destructive power. Probably this was Mosheh's way of defending himself against his emotive of feeling ignored. Apparently, in this way he also expressed his anger at his mother (perhaps also at his sister for taking mother's place). On the pragmatic level this behavior had, presumably, two purposes: making his presence felt by his mother and sister and disturbing his sister's preparation of food. He was acting on the presupposition that this was his mother's duty. He probably predicted that his mother would eventually come around and take over.

The next combination of activity units was Yaffa's saying nothing, kneeling and collecting the utensils. On the semantic level, this seemed to express her subdued anger. On the pragmatic level, this appeared to reflect her presupposition that her mother cannot handle the boy and also the prediction that starting a row will make it difficult for her mother.

The next combination of activity units was approaching her mother with a dish and telling her: "Here's some soup for you". On the pragmatic level this seemed to be based on the presupposition that her mother wanted attention. She wanted at least a symbolic expression of love. She needed soothing because she had been annoyed by Mosheh's behavior. The prediction was that mother would accept the offer and give Yaffa at least a minimal amount of warmth and attention.

The last combination of activity units was Sarah's pretending to drink the soup without smiling or moving. Semantically, this seemed to signify enjoying the food on a very elementary level. Pragmatically, the purpose was probably to accept the offer without giving anything in return.

Then Reena, the therapist, asked herself, again intuitively and instantaneously, what the macroscopic pattern behind these analyzed microscopic units was. Was it an instance of the dysfunctional program described in the initial assessment? Reena's answer was positive. The interpreted combinations of activity units added up to something that paralleled faithfully the descriptions of the family members' respective goals and plans.

There were a number of points at which Reena could break into the family's play activity. In each of these points she could participate in the game and attempt to use herself as an agent of change. She could for instance assume a role that would enable her to persuade Sarah to accept the soup offered to her by Yaffa in a different, more welcoming way. Later, she could join with Yaffa in preparing the food and might even feed Yaffa. If Sarah does not comply, Reena herself can model this by becoming "mother" in the game. At the same time, the mother could be offered food and rendered other services by Reena in various roles.

Another point of intervening can be using *basic duality* to emphasize, for the whole family, the dysfunction manifested in the fact that Mosheh was allowed to knock down Yaffa's play things without meeting with any protest or intervention on the side of Yaffa or Sarah. Reena decided to intervene in these two ways simultaneously. However she had to make some preparatory moves in order to be accepted and gain a position of influence. Like a chess player she should calculate some steps ahead of time.

Her first move was to make herself a part of Yaffa's game of preparing food. To achieve this she assumed the role of "granny". In this way she also placed herself in a position of authority. This choice was also influenced by her knowledge of the family situation, in which Pinhas' mother enjoyed considerable authority over Sarah and her children, and often intervened in the household affairs in the role of a helper.

At the very point where Sarah tasted the soup, Reena took a paper bag, put some objects in it, assumed grandmotherly mannerisms and voice, stepped in and said: "Here's granny coming. I brought some food for you from the market! What was that noise I heard when I came in, like utensils falling on the floor? Did anything break?"

REENA *(taking some objects from her bag and handing them over to Yaffa).* Here are carrots, here is rice.

YAFFA *(taking the objects from Reena and starting to "cook" them, referring to Reena's previous question).* The pots and pans fell down, but I picked them up.

REENA *(in her "granny's" voice).* That's interesting. You have magical kitchen utensils that can fall off the table by themselves, without anybody pushing them off.

YAFFA *(smiling).* No! Somebody pushed them.

REENA. And Mummy told you to pick them up?

YAFFA. No! Mummy did not say anything!

REENA. And you did not say anything either, you just picked them up.

In this conversation Reena's moves were already dictated by the tactic. What she said, and what she led Yaffa to saying, had the purpose of focusing on certain aspects of the dysfunctional program and emphasizing them. The property of *basic duality* was deliberately used here to underline the fact that Yaffa covered up for Mosheh and freed him from any responsibility. Likewise, this conversation emphasized the fact that Sarah did not protect Yaffa, nor demand anything from Mosheh.

Then came other moves that attempted to realize other aspects of the tactic. Reena said to Yaffa: "You are working too hard. I'll cook a meal for all of you. I'll do some cleaning and have a surprise ready for all of you". Reena took two stools and placed them flanking both sides of Sarah. Then she held the two children by the hand and led them toward the stools. Mosheh evaded her, but Reena let him do it. She helped Yaffa sit by her mother. Yaffa leaned on her mother. The latter laid her arm on her shoulder, patted her a little, and whispered: "Don't you want to ask her what's the surprise?" Mosheh took a toy guitar and yelled: "Quiet! I am going to give you a performance!"

Reena's moves here followed her tactic quite faithfully. When she told Yaffa "You are working too hard" she used the property of *covert communication* to tell Yaffa something about her error of information processing: too much irrelevant output. In offering to prepare food and do the chores she used the properties of *possible worlds* and *alienation* in order to relieve Yaffa of her usual burden. At the same time she gave Sarah what she wanted from Yaffa (*emotional regulation*) so that she could free Yaffa of her duties. By placing the stools and leading the children to them she put Yaffa in the same position as her mother. She created a connection of give and take between them by making them alike on the raw material level. Following all these moves Sarah was readier than before to give her children what they needed from her.

Sarah and Yaffa were watching Mosheh doing his pop music show. At the same time Reena, as grandmother, served them a light meal made of little building blocks and cleaned the apartment. She also patted Yaffa lightly on her shoulder, saying: "It's good to see how my daughter-in-law and my granddaughter enjoy each other's company". She cheered Mosheh for his excellent performance.

After the show it was time to give the family the surprise grandmother had prepared for them. It was a trip to the safari park. Since some of the animals were dangerous, the family members would have to protect one another. Grandmother would take care of mother because she was her mother. Mother would take care of Yaffa and the latter would take care of Mosheh.

These moves accorded with the tactic. Reena did not attempt to change the dysfunctional pattern of Yaffa taking care of Mosheh. However, this pattern was reflected to the family by *symbolic coding* and *basic duality*. On the other hand the property of *possible worlds* was mobilized to change the pattern of relationships between Sarah and Yaffa. To make it easier for both of them, Reena protected Sarah. By *emotional regulation* and *symbolization*, she gave her what she needed and in this way helped her make the required change in the dysfunctional program on the level of play.

Reena had planned to use the safari trip game as a way of expanding her original tactic. Seeing that the execution of his tactic went so well, she wanted now not just to *reflect* the dysfunctional pattern with Mosheh, but also to *change* it using *symbolization* and *possible worlds*.

The main change aimed at was that Mosheh should learn to demand and accept not from his sister but from his mother. Another desired change was that he come to realize that his presence was felt even if he did not make any special efforts. He should have also come to understand how his own disruptive behavior influenced his mother's. He had to learn how to behave in a way that encouraged his mother to react according to his goal.

On the imaginary safari drive Mosheh insisted on being the driver of the car improvised with chairs. Reena agreed, because this reflected Mosheh's dysfunctional plan. However, during the drive she said things such as: "Watch it! You almost hit a tree!", "You are going too fast, you almost hit a zebra!". Then she said: "I'm afraid our driver needs help. Driving in a safari requires a special skill, because you must have very good control of the car. Who can help our driver?" Yaffa said: "I'll help him".

Mosheh objected: "I don't need your help! I can drive very well!"

In this segment, *symbolic coding* and *possible worlds* were put into operation in order to encourage Mosheh to refuse help and services offered by his sister Yaffa, in accordance with the tactic.

At this point Reena decided to make another move in her chess game, with the dual purpose of preparing the ground for her next move and supporting Yaffa, who was beginning to lose her former role.

Reena told Yaffa: "You should not worry. If anything happens it is not your responsibility. Mummy and grandmother will take care of both of you". She got up, took a chair and hit it against Mosheh's chair, yelling: "You hit your car against a tree! Let's pretend you got hit and fainted". She held Mosheh in her arms and whispered to him: "Pretend to faint, it's going to be great fun". Then she said in an urgent manner: "Mummy, your son the driver hit a tree and now he's fainted. You hold him and I'll try to calm down your daughter, who is very frightened".

At this point Mosheh complied, he pretended to be fainting and abandoned himself in the arms of his mother. The latter was genuinely frightened and concerned. She attempted to wake him up. Yaffa was on the move to help her, but Reena said: "Mummy does not need help. She can handle this very well by herself. I see you yourself are frightened."

Reena, as granny, hugged Yaffa and brought an imaginary cup of water to Sarah.

These moves achieved what Reena wanted them to achieve. By *possible worlds* Mosheh abandoned himself in his mother's arms. This accorded with Reena's therapeutic aims. The emotional satisfaction Mosheh derived from letting his mother care for him was rewarding. At the same time Reena made some auxiliary moves: blocking Yaffa's attempt to get into her usual role, calming Sarah down and caring for both of them.

The safari game went on for a while. At a certain point Mosheh pretended to have a camera and take pictures. Reena said: "Now granny will take the picture of the three of you hugging and kissing". By taking a family photograph in this manner she took the family for a while to a possible world which was much more rewarding than the world they were so accustomed to.

CHAPTER 12

Some Types of Strategic Family Play Therapeutic Moves

As has been shown in Chapter 11, the moves taken by the therapist are his verbal and non-verbal therapeutic acts. The *main moves* are governed by the tactic. They are supposed to contribute, however minimal each of these contributions may be, to the achievement of changes toward the objectives decided on in the tactic. Other moves are *preparatory moves*. They prepare the ground for the main moves. A third type of moves are *auxiliary moves*. These accompany the main moves or the preparatory moves. They are neither governed by the tactic nor are they preparatory toward the tactic-governed moves. The auxiliary moves serve various purposes such as directing attention to family members that are not in the focus of the tactic-governed intervention, reflecting people's feelings, reducing anxiety provoked by the tactic-governed moves, securing cooperation and overcoming resistance, keeping an atmosphere of interest and excitement, etc.

As can be seen from the illustrations in Chapter 11, the therapist's intervention in the strategic family therapeutic process is basically a creative activity, in which the main tool is the therapist's own creative imagination and playfulness. However, cumulative experience in strategic family play therapy has compiled a large repertory of moves, which can by now be standardized, classified and more or less formally defined. These types of moves can be learned and used by strategic family play therapists.

Most of these types of moves were created by strategic family play therapists. Others were borrowed from children, whose spontaneous play behavior had been observed and analyzed. Children, we noticed, make all kinds of clever moves to achieve purposes similar to those of strategic family play therapists. Other types of moves were borrowed from various schools of therapy and adapted to the specific purposes of strategic family play therapy. Major sources were the hypnotic and strategic techniques developed by Milton Erikson and his followers. (See Bandler and Grinder, 1975; Haley, 1973; Watzlawick, Weakland and Fisch, 1974.)

The common object of all types of moves is to direct the natural course of the spontaneous family play in the direction desired by the therapist. The moves are calculated to make the participants do in their play what the therapist wants them to do, without giving them a feeling that they are being coerced and without taking the fun out of the activity. The moves should be such that they interweave naturally with the activity into an harmonic whole, with the stitches concealed.

Therapeutic Positions

The therapist can make his moves from various positions, alternatively or simultaneously. The major positions are those of an *audience*, a *director* or an *actor*. As an *audience* the therapist stays outside the family play, but still serves in the make-believe role of an onlooker. In this position he can make a great variety of verbal or non-verbal comments on the family's make-believe play, its raw-material, semantic or pragmatic features. He can interpret it by explicating what is implicit. He can reinforce various aspects by cheering, clapping or booing, mimicking the actor's behavior, or even leaving the room. As *director* (which includes also the positions of playwright, producer and other theatrical functions such as dresser, make-up person, prop-person, prompter, etc.) he can tell the participants what their behavior should be on the raw-material, seman- tic or pragmatic levels. He can disqualify certain ways of doing things and recommend other ways. He can influence the course of the family's make- believe play in every possible way. As an *actor* he becomes a full participant in the family play. From this position he can interact with the family members verbally and non-verbally. He can influence their actions and feelings by the very fact that he communicates his own feelings and ideas. In short, he enjoys all the means available to a person involved in a fully improvised theatrical performance. This is in fact an extremely rich repertory of means of therapeutic expression and communication.

Here are some examples:

In the family play therapeutic sessions presented in Chapter 11, the therapist assumed various positions, particularly those of director and actor. When she entered the scene as "granny" she was an actress, a full participant in the family play. But in her role of actress she also served as a director. She brought in new contents (the safari trip, the accident, etc.), arranged objects in the room (inter- vention on the raw-material level) and changed the scene in various ways. While playing the part of grandmother, she also served here and there as an audience, for instance when she cheered Mosheh for his excellent performance.

We see then that the positions are not exclusive. A participant can be an actor but while an actor he can also serve as a director or as an audience.

In each of these positions the therapist can perform moves of various types.

In general, the moves in each of these positions can serve the following functions: becoming a participant (joining), and influencing the course of the people's play or non-play behavior, in accordance with the tactic or other therapeutic considerations.

Types of Moves

Here some of the main types of moves are discussed and illustrated.

Mimicking

The therapist simply mimics, or imitates, the play behavior of a family member.

This type of move can serve as a means of joining. If the mimicking is done subtly, the person whose behavior is being imitated can feel akin to the therapist; close to him. He is, therefore, more likely to be receptive of the therapist's attempt to approach and join. Mimicking serves this function in the hypnotic and therapeutic techniques developed by Milton Erickson and his followers (cf. Bandler and Grinder, 1975).

This type of move can also be used as a means of influencing the course of the person's behavior in accordance with the tactic. It can serve the function of mirroring or reflecting. The therapist becomes a living mirror. This can help the family member see himself from outside and as a result have more control over his own behavior. In this respect mirroring is similar to the use of the play property of *basic duality* (see Chapter 3). However, the basic duality of the play is an abstract, purely reflective entity in the mind of the player, whereas mirroring is a raw-material, behavioral entity performed by the therapist as a move.

Mimicking can also influence the course of the play behavior by serving as a kind of comment on this behavior. If the mimicking is done in a grotesque, exaggerated or otherwise emphatic way, it can create in the player various emotional reactions relating to his own behavior and to the therapist, which can lead him to change this behavior.

While mimicking, the therapist can be in an audience, a director or an actor position.

Example

Mimicking as a means of joining: within a family play therapy session a seven-year-old boy was "hunting lions in the jungle" with a stick. The therapist took another stick and said: "I am also hunting lions in the jungle", and started imitating the child's gestures and sounds. The boy welcomed this and immediately formed a warm contact with the therapist. In this move the therapist served as an actor. The mimicking fulfilled the function of joining the boy's game.

In the session described in Chapter 11 Reena cheered Mosheh for his excellent pop music performance. She served as an actress and as an audience at the same time. When she cheered Mosheh she subtly mimicked his playing movements and body motions. This served a double purpose: to reinforce Mosheh's positive way of getting attention, but also to show him, by mimicking, that she was with him and acknowledged his presence and existence. This move was designed to make Mosheh feel (in accordance with the tactic) that his presence was felt anyway. Another purpose was to join Mosheh, to become his playmate.

Mimicking as a means of change according to the tactic

Eight-year-old Neri used to throw tantrums. He believed that his mother Orna hated him. His trantrums were triggered by events that "proved" this belief. When he started behaving violently Orna would grab him aggressively and spank him. This would "confirm" his preconception and reinforce the tantrum.

The therapist, Hedva, wanted to help Orna change her manner of handling Neri's tantrums. When the pattern described above actually occurred in the room Hedva picked a doll representing a boy. She grabbed it and handled it in the same way as Orna, mimicking the latter's behavior. Orna saw that and almost automatically changed her manner of handling Neri and made it milder. She was influenced by the reflection of her own aggressiveness in Hedva's playful mimicking. She was taken aback by it. This caused her to change her behavior.

Pacing

This type of move was also borrowed from Milton Erickson and his followers and adapted to family play therapy. (See Bandler and Grinder, 1975; Haley, 1973.) Essentially, it consists of a combination of mimicking and modelling. The therapist starts by mimicking the play behavior of a family member (in the role of an audience or an actor). When he succeeds in joining the family member and a good contact is established, he slightly and gradually modifies his own play, until the family member starts following his model and imitating his play behavior. At this point the therapist becomes a director who leads the course of the family member's play in the desired direction.

Example

A part of Salim's plan for avoiding a close relationship with his father Ali was to take whatever Ali offered him and put it aside. The therapist Khaleel made the following moves: he sat by Salim, mimicking his posture, facial expressions and movements. Whenever Salim put aside an object (a toy, a musical instrument, etc.) given to him by Ali, Khaleel picked up the object, examined it and put it aside in the same way as Salim. After a while, when Khaleel noted that Salim was fully aware of his actions and involved in them, he changed his behavior. He did not put aside the object when he had picked it up, but played with it a little. Soon Salim followed his lead and played with the objects offered by his father. This was a prelude to leading Salim to accept his father's approaches.

Focusing

In this type of move the therapist emphasizes a particular aspect of the play behavior in order to turn the family members' attention to it, stress its importance or help interpret it. Focusing can be done by the therapist when he is in the role of an audience, a director or an actor. It can be carried out by various means such as accompanying a certain play activity with sound effects, using various lighting effects and making verbal or non-verbal comments.

Example

The purpose of the session was to help Rahamin and Rivka, the parents of Erez, to exercise appropriate control over, and set proper limits on, Erez. A part of Rahamin's plan was to become an uninvolved bystander. In the context of a game, Erez began behaving in an extremely disruptive manner. Rivka tried to set limits and Rahamin was undecided and did not take a stand. The therapist Orly drew up a table, sat by Rahamin in a non-committal manner and started to whistle the tune of a popular Israeli song whose opening words are "I am sitting on the fence, neither here nor there".
    Focusing is also one way of reinforcing.

Explicating

In this type of move the therapist explicates, makes explicit, hidden aspects of the participants' play behavior, such as purposes, presuppositions, emotive meanings, etc. The explication can be done verbally or non-verbally, in the therapist's position as an actor, a director or an audience.

Examples

A family symbolized one of its dysfunctional programs by a make-believe game of "bank-robbery" in which the father Herzel was "the bank manager", the mother Mazal "the robber who shot the manager and wounded him", and the daughter Maya "a customer, who was a witness to the robbery, chased the robber, fought with him, wounded him, recovered the money and brought it back to the manager". At the end of this scene, the therapist Sari assumed the role of a TV reporter. She interviewed the bank manager, the witness and even the robber who was handcuffed. She questioned them about their feelings, their motives for acting as they did, their objects and their presuppositions.

Another example: the family were asked to prepare a script for a TV show (which should hopefully reflect their dysfunctional programs). Galila, the therapist, was the director. As a director she discussed the script and the roles with the participants. This enabled her to explicate their hidden thoughts and feelings.

Explication can be also non-verbal. The therapist acts as an alter ego of the players, partly mimicking them but partly reflecting the covert aspects of their behavior. For example, if a person is sad but pretends to be happy, the therapist plays the alter ego, but in a sad voice. The non-verbal behavior reflects emotive meaning. Thematic meaning is explicated by objects or pictures which convey the thematic meaning, the presupposition, etc. Shahar took a rubber snake and pretended to bite his mother. Miriam, the therapist, picked a doll representing a boy and said: "Let's pretend this is the snake". (Here *arbitrariness of signifier* is also used.) Leedor attacked her mother hoping to draw affection. Miriam picked up a doll representing the mother and caressed it, explicating Leedor's covert messages.

The Double

The therapist, or a doll used by the therapist, can serve as the double of a family member. This move is particularly helpful when the family member resists letting the therapist join his play or influence its course.

Example

The case entitled "The Invisible Guest", the prologue of this book, includes a scene in which I played *the double* for David. I lay on the carpet by his side and imitated his play of a screaming baby, but I also spoke out his mind.

Providing Stimuli

The therapist can provoke a game of a certain kind or change the course of a play by providing behavioral (verbal or non-verbal) or other stimuli (sounds, toys, etc.) which are likely to provoke the kind of play he is interested in.

Examples

In the case, The Boxing Match, described in Chapter 10, the boxing gloves, placed in a conspicuous place, served as stimuli for the ensuing boxing scene.

In one of her cases, Galila's therapeutic purpose was to help a mother named Eerit to actively participate in her children's game. Her son and daughter Hen and Yaffit played a make-believe game in which they were popular singers performing on the stage. Eerit got hold of a camera and pretended to photograph them. Galila gave her a microphone. Galila started to take pictures of the three of them with another camera. These were non-verbal stimuli, encouraging Eerit to actively join the children's game.

Illusion of Alternatives

This type of move too is taken from Milton Erickson's hypnotic and therapeutic techniques (see Haley, 1973). It can be used to assist the therapist join the play or influence its course. It can be performed from the position of an actor or a director. Here the therapist suggests to a family member two alternatives, one better and one worse from the latter's viewpoint. The therapist of course wants the family member to agree to the possibility that looks better from his (the therapist's) viewpoint. The illusion here is that the family member does not realize that he can decide not to choose any of the two possibilities, or choose some third possibility.

Example

Ayala, the therapist, wanted a girl named Meery to assume an aggressive make-believe role. Ayala knew that Meery did not like to appear aggressive, but her therapeutic purpose was to help Meery express her angry and aggressive side. She asked Meery: "Do you want to be a tiger or a scorpion?" Naturally, Meery chose to play the part of a tiger, because being a scorpion seems to her less attractive. However, she failed to realize that she has a third possibility: to be neither a tiger nor a scorpion.

An Obedient Actor

This move is a way of becoming a part of the play (joining). The therapist asks for a family member's permission to participate in the game. He lets the member decide which role he will have in the game. Having taken a part in the game in a certain role, he is already an equal partner. He can influence the course of the game in this role or assume a different role.

Example

Leah, the therapist, asked a seven-year-old girl named Michal: "Can I play in this game too?"

MICHAL: "Yes".
LEAH: "What shall I be in this game?"
MICHAL: "A mouse".

Leah agreed to play this unpleasant part, but then she turned herself into a "mighty mouse".

Willynilly

In this type of move the therapist somehow takes the family member by surprise and casts him or her in a certain role or makes him or her do something in the play almost unawares. I learned this technique from children. The therapist commits a certain make-believe play act which involves a family member, and that family member is cast in a role or described as involved in some action in the game.

Examples

Ayala wanted Meery to express her covert aggressive side (see above). She said: "I am a gazelle. I am afraid of the lion. Please lion, don't devour me!" Meery had to "become" a lion whether she liked it or not. She started to act according to the role assigned to her by Ayala, that is, attack "the gazelle".

Summary

The main types of therapeutic positions and moves are summarized in Table 18.

Table 18   Types of therapeutic positions and moves

Therapist's positions: audience, director, actor

Type of moves	Description	Therapeutic functions
Mimicking	Imitating family members' play behavior.	Joining; Chanelling behavior to tactic-governed routes; Reflecting; Commenting.
Focusing	Stressing aspects of play behavior, by sound and lighting effects or verbal and non-verbal comments.	Turning attention to important features; Interpreting.
Explicating	Making hidden entities explicit, by verbalizing them or acting them out non-verbally.	Emphasizing important features; Interpreting.
The double	The therapist, directly or through a doll, represents a family member.	Speaking for a family member who refuses to participate in the family's play activity.
Providing stimuli	The therapist provides behavioral or material stimuli which are to provoke the kind of play he is interested in.	Encouraging certain kinds of activities or changing the course of an activity.
Illusion of alternatives	The therapist suggests two alternative play ideas. The more attractive alternative is the one he wants the family member to choose.	Enabling the therapist to join the family play or influence its course.
Obedient actor	The therapist asks family members for permission to join their play and lets them decide on his role in it. Once inside, he is free to make his own choices.	Enabling the therapist to become an equal member of the family play group.
Willynilly	The therapist performs a play act which engages a family member in a complementary play act.	Engage family members in play or influence their play in accordance with the therapist's aims.

PART 5

The therapeutic process and its general structure

CHAPTER 13

Generalization and Transfer from the Session to the Family's Reality

So far we have dealt with the family play therapeutic process just on the within-session range. In the following chapters the therapeutic process will be discussed from the viewpoint of its between-sessions and global characteristics. Therapeutic influences that run across sessions and characterize phases in the general therapeutic process or its global properties will be discussed and illustrated.

This chapter is devoted to the question of the generalization and transfer from the make-believe family play therapeutic experience in the therapy room to the family's psychological and practical reality at home and out of the therapy room in general.

A query often raised by people who get themselves familiarized with strategic family play therapy is whether this generalization and transfer occurs, and if so, how. Suppose, for instance, that a cold, rejecting mother is led to express warmth and affection toward her son in the context of a make-believe game. She plays the role of a bird and her son the role of a fledgeling. Does this guarantee that she really changes and continues giving warmth and affection to her son at home?

In fact, this query has a number of aspects:

How is the therapeutic experience translated from the fantasy world of play to the harsh world of reality?

Can such a transfer occur without the mediation of verbal, explicative, interpretive discussion?

Although to the best of my knowledge no direct research evidence confirming the process of generalization and transfer exists, the hypothesis that such a process actually takes place is based on my own and my students' clinical experience and on various kinds of indirect research evidence that will be reviewed presently.

My main hypotheses with respect to this question are:

Generalization and transfer from the purely make-believe play experience to the family's psychosocial reality do take place quite often. There is no need for this process to be accompanied by a explicative, organizing verbal discussions.

This hypothesis is based mainly on the supposition that the experience the family members go through acts on the emotional as well as on the cognitive level. The errors of information processing on which the dysfunctional programs are based are tackled on the cognitive-emotional plane. Let us view these processes of change in detail. I shall endeavor to make explicit how they are carried over to the out-of-the-session family reality. These explanations will be backed with research evidence.

The Mechanisms of Generalization and Transfer

The main change effect of strategic family play therapy comes from the selective use of therapeutically relevant properties of play. Therefore, we have to go back to the discussion of these properties in Chapter 3. What is characteristic of the therapeutic use of all these properties is that all of them create a cognitive change which is accompanied by an emotional experience.

The main cognitive change achieved by the property of *owning* and *alienation* is the fact that it enables the player to *own* convictions about himself or others of which he has been alienated, or the other way round, to become alienated from convictions about himself and others which he formerly owned. Since errors of information processing are in fact distortions of one's conception of oneself and others, this property can contribute to correcting errors of information processing that take part in dysfunctional plans.

The emotional impact of owning and alienation comes from two sources: first, the owning and alienation result from the very fact that the player is engaged in make-believe play. It is an automatic involuntary experience that accompanies the very fact that the player does what he does as make-believe play. The emotional defenses that bar this cognitive change are bypassed, or have no time to operate. On the other hand, the owning and alienation are simultaneous, so that if one owns certain convictions he does not have to give up his former alienation and if he alienates himself from certain convictions he does not have to stop owning them. This eases the emotional difficulty of accepting the change.

The property of *basic duality* also creates a cognitive change, since it makes the player aware of the errors of information processing of which he was unaware. Again, since this awareness does not require a special conscious thinking effort, but is an automatic result of the very fact that the player is engaged in make-believe play, it bypasses the defenses and takes them by surprise. Since at the same time *alienation* operates, it softens the emotional impact and makes it easier to accept the new awareness.

The property of *arbitrariness of signifier* works on the same principle. It can be used to create a tension or a contradiction between a signifier and a signified. In this way it introduces a rift or a cognitive dissonance between a certain conviction about oneself or others and another way of looking at things. This dissonance is created automatically, by the very fact that the player is playing in a certain way. The player becomes aware of it indirectly, through the choice of signifier. It takes him by surprise and catches his defenses unprepared.

The same property can also be used to soften the emotional significance of the signified. Therefore it makes it easier to accept the meaning of the signified.

Covert communication also makes the interpersonal messages easier to understand or accept. This property also bypasses the defenses which contribute to the erection of faulty information processing.

Symbolic coding has the same effect. It bypasses emotional difficulties related to a direct approach to the central theme of one's emotives. So it contributes to cognitive change while bypassing the emotional resistance.

Regulation of emotions also serves to decrease the emotional tension related to themes associated with one's emotives. It prepares the emotional ground which makes one receptive to the reparation of his dysfunctional plans.

Possible worlds enables one to experience unrealized possibilities, without fear of the reality of these possibilities. This is due to the soothing effect of the properties of *alienation* and *symbolic coding*. This can create a cognitive change with an emotional impact. Possibilities that seemed intolerable and were therefore blocked in the emotional world of the player become realized. They are accompanied by a pleasant, rewarding, playful experience. Therefore change is created both on the cognitive and on the emotional level.

To sum up, the therapeutically relevant properties of play work as change agents because they create a sudden cognitive change indirectly and automatically. They take the defenses by surprise and bypass them, without involving a conscious process of thinking, which could leave time for the defenses to be erected again. At the same time the impact of the sudden cognitive-emotional change is softened by the very fact that it is done in a playful atmosphere.

Proponents of the systemic approach to family therapy are likely to be surprised that the process of change is described above in terms of individual psychology (cognitive-emotional) rather than in terms of interpersonal systems. Admittedly, the information-processing theory of family dysfunction on which these intervention methods are based attempts to explicate the family-systemic concepts in terms that are related to individual intra-psychic psychology. The family programs are stored in an individual person's mind, although they refer to interpersonal relations. The dysfunctional information-processing programs and the errors of information-processing in them are entities which belong to the individual person's cognitive-affective system. The distortions in information processing in these programs are influenced by one's emotives, intra-psychic conflicts and defenses. They are maintained by strong emotional factors rather than by cognitive operations or by some mysterious "system".

Therefore the change of the system must start on the level of the individual. If a cognitive-affective change occurs in the individual this can prepare the ground for the errors of information processing, which are maintained by cognitive-affective structures, to be corrected.

How is the cognitive-emotive change transferred from the level of make-believe play to the level of reality? To answer this question one should consider again the meaning of the properties of play. *Owning* and *alienation* are two inherent properties of make-believe play. Whenever there is owning there is also alienation and vice versa. This is implied, as explained in Chapter 3, by the very fact that in make-believe the claims of *realification* and *identication* and the claim of playfulness, which denies the former, are made at one and the same time. Therefore, whenever one plays a make-believe game, one makes at least one claim about out-of-play reality, although this claim is denied at the same time. A boy believes his father hates him but emotionally denies this belief. He is led to *play as if* he believes his father hates him. That is, his denied belief is placed *within* a make-believe game. Then, inevitably, the following take place: the property of *alienation* (represented by the mental claim of playfulness) lets him continue denying his belief, be alienated from it. However, at the same time the mental claim of *realification* makes him *own* this belief, treat it momentarily as something which belongs to his own *reality*. One sees then that the transfer from the *as if* to reality is done automatically. It is a function of the very fact that the boy's denied belief has been placed within a make-believe game. The emotional impact of this experience of reality is likely to carry over to the out-of-the-playroom context.

The *basic duality* of make-believe play, by the very definition of this property takes the play away from the level of make-believe to the level of reality. For example, if the child who denies that he believes his father hates him acts in the framework of the game as if he does believe so, the property of basic duality makes him see, from the standpoint of reality, his own play behavior. So the cognitive-emotional experience of observing himself believing that his father hates him is a reality experience. The emotional impact of this experience guarantees that it will be transferred to the out-of-play context.

The property of *arbitrariness of signifier* can be used to soften the emotional impact of the signified. It can also be utilized to create emotional tension, resulting from a contradiction between the signifier and the signified (see Chapter 3). Examples: the mother's embrace signifies emotional distance; a toy snake signifies a bagel given by a father to his son.

The transfer to the out-of-play reality comes in these cases from the fact that the signifier *symbolizes* the signified. Since the signified is *realified* it becomes a part of the player's out-of-play reality by the property of *owning*. When real

closeness signifies realified distance, both the distance and the imaginary closeness belong to the player's reality.

A similar kind of transfer is achieved by the property of *symbolic coding*,
which facilitates the expression and communication of complex or emotionally
difficult themes associated with one's emotives. Take for instance the example
in which the fear of absence of parental authority is symbolically coded as "no
ruler in the ocean" (see p. 64). Here the transfer from the inside-the-play to the
out-of-play reality is based on the idea that the meaning of the symbols is
understood by their users, at least subconsciously. That is, the symbol is related
by a chain of associations to the central theme of the emotive. For example, the
player knows that "the absence of a king in the ocean" in his make-believe
game symbolizes the absence of parental authority in his conception of his real-
life family.

The play property of *covert communication* also bridges the child's make-
believe play and his reality. When the player uses the thematic (signified)
content of the play to communicate messages (presuppositions, purposes) on
the pragmatic level, he immediately expresses himself both on the in-play and
on the out-of-play levels. Returning to the above example, when the child says
"There is no king in the ocean" he expresses an imaginary, make-believe content, but he also invites his real-life parents to become more authoritative.

The property of *regulation of emotions* is not related to the out-of-play
situation so directly. Its purpose is to balance the level of arousal around certain
emotives. When it is balanced, the other properties of play mentioned above
can operate better.

The property of *possible worlds* realizes unrealized possibilities. This realization is done with the mental claims of realification and identication in mind.
Therefore, the play simulation of potential situation is sometimes hardly dis-
tinguishable from real-life situations. For example, if a mother who never hugs
her son does this in make-believe play, she *really* hugs him. The hug is self-
reinforcing, because it is accompanied by a positive emotional experience.

Another question raised above was why the generalization and transfer from
the play situation to the family reality should not be mediated by a verbal
interpretation of the meaning of the play experience. The answers to this are,
first, that this is not required, because, as shown above, the transfer occurs
automatically, by the very properties of play. However, the main reason why
verbal mediation should not be used is not just that it is redundant but also that
it *reduces* the effectiveness of the play therapeutic experience and intervention.
As claimed above, the properties of play work as change agents because they
create a sudden cognitive change indirectly and automatically. They take the
defenses by surprise and bypass them. They do not give time for a conscious
process of thinking to develop and for defenses to be erected again. At the same
time the impact of the cognitive-emotional change is softened by the very fact
that it is done in a playful atmosphere.

It would seem, then, from this analysis, that an attempt to verbally analyze and discuss the meaning of the play experience with the family must reduce the effectiveness of the therapy. Such a verbal discussion will undermine the very advantage of not using a conscious process of thinking and relying on a sudden partly conscious cognitive-emotional experience.

Research Evidence

So far the discussion has been purely theoretical. Let me now bring some empirical research evidence for these hypotheses about the processes of transfer and generalization from the in-the-play experience to the out-of-play situation. As has been stated above most of the evidence supports these hypotheses indirectly:

Process and Outcome Research in Strategic Therapy

Madanes (1982) reports an immediate disappearance of symptoms and other problems presented to the therapy, following strategic therapeutic interventions in which the therapist gives the family members directives to pretend to enact the problematic behavior or the dysfunctional interaction pattern. Madanes explains this result as follows:

> With the directive to pretend, a metaphor no longer represents reality. It becomes a representation of a "pretend" reality or a meta- phorical reality and is therefore a different order of a metaphor: a metaphor of another metaphor. Reality has disappeared. The first order of metaphor can no longer be distinguished from this second order metaphor and therefore can no longer express reality or be used in an attempt to change it . . . When a sequence of interaction is labeled "this is pretend" it is difficult for the participants in the sequence to go back to the framework of "this is real". This diffi- culty can be used by the therapist to confuse and to eliminate the reality of a symptom and to change the system of interaction on which this reality is based (p. 93f).

This factor of discrediting the dysfunctional programs is found in the method of strategic family play therapy presented in this book too. It is com- mon to most of the strategic family therapeutic methods which make use of paradoxical techniques. It partly accounts for their "magical" power, that is for their relatively high rate of success in producing fast changes in the family's reality. This success has been amply documented in case reports and in process and outcome research relating to strategic and paradoxical therapeutic techniques. See for instance Beach and O'Leary, 1985; Bodin, 1981; Cross, 1982; Fish, Weakland and Segal, 1984; Green, Fortune and Vosler, 1988; Gurman and Kniskern, 1981; Hazelring, Cooper and Borduin, 1987; Hill, 1987; Lebow, 1981; Rabkin, 1977; Todd and Stanton, 1983; Weeks and L'Abate, 1979; Wells and Dezen, 1978.

Emotional and Affective Experiences as Facilitators of Change

In the discussion above the role of the immediate emotional experience accompanying the play acts in producing the cognitive and behavioral changes whose repercussions spread beyond the therapy room was emphasized. This view has been directly and indirectly supported by numerous theoretical and empirical research studies. All these affirm the central role of the emotions and affective states as motivational factors directing people's cognitive processes and behavior. See for instance Atkinson, 1958; Bativa and Khomskaya, 1984; Blaney, 1986; Bock, 1986; Bower, 1984; Frijda, Kupiers and Schure, 1981; Greenberg and Safran, 1987; Izard, 1978; Izard and Tomkins, 1966; Lang, 1979; Mastumodo, 1986; McKenn, 1986; Rachman, 1980; Singer, 1970, 1973; Suler, 1985; Tomkins and Izard, 1965; Tucker and Newman, 1981; Zachary, 1982; Zajonc, 1980 (but see Lazarus' critique, 1982).

Spontaneous Changes Following Make-believe Play

It has been argued above that the family's make-believe play leads to changes in cognition and ideation and in interpersonal behavior that stretch beyond the play therapy room itself. This is supported by a whole body of observational and experimental research showing that children's make-believe play leads to positive developmental changes in ego functioning and emotional balance, cognitive capacity, social cognition and social behavior. Play has been found to contribute to cognitive and linguistic abilities (Blohm and Yawkley, 1976; Curry and Arnaud, 1974; Leiberman, 1965, 1977; Somers and Yawkley, 1984), problem solving, self concept (Gomez and Yawkley, 1983), impulse control (Freyberg, 1973; Saltz, Dixon and Johnson, 1977), and interpersonal perspective taking (Burns and Brainerd, 1979).

The Outcomes of Expressive Therapy

The above hypotheses concerning the generalization and transfer of the play therapeutic experience find support from case reports and outcome research relating to psychotherapy based on expressive, largely non-verbal methods or on means of expression and commumciation which emphasize direct emotional experience rather than rational thinking or guided behavior. See for instance Beck, 1970; Emunah and Johnson, 1983; Johnson, 1984; Landgarten, 1981; McNiff, 1987; Michel, 1976; Robbins, 1980; Rubin, 1985; Singer, 1974; Singer and Pope, 1978; Tessa, 1984; Witztum, Dasberg and Bleich, 1986.

Particularly relevant at this juncture are studies centering around the process of outcome of play therapy and emotional-experiential family therapy, e.g. Bishop, 1986; Courtney and Schattner, 1981; Goldman, 1986; Greenberg and Johnson, 1986; Mann and Janis, 1986; Mills and Crowly, 1986; Schaefer, 1985.

Another class of relevant studies are observations and experiments which show that changes in cognition and behavior occur as results of purely mental, imaginal activities conducted in the framework of directed therapeutic or educational activities or occurring spontaneously. Our therapeutically relevant play property *possible worlds* includes such an activity, in which some future or potential state of affairs is mentally (but also behaviorally) represented. Subcategories of studies falling within this overall class deal with vicarious processes and modeling (e.g. Bandura, 1965 a, b, 1971), biofeedback (White and Tursky, 1986), hypnosis (Hilgard, 1986) and guided imagery (Kaufmann, 1985; Leuner, 1978; Morrison and Cometa, 1980).

Finally, it has been argued above that change in strategic family play therapy occurs as a result of tipping the internal balance, or homeostasis in the family system. This view finds direct and indirect support in many research studies which deal with developmental changes (e.g. Boadman and Hagen, 1985; Case *et al.*, 1988), changes in individual therapy (e.g. Brenner, 1982; Foa and Kozak, 1985; Goldfried, 1980; Greenberg and Pinsof, 1986; Jones, 1982; Luborsky *et al.*, 1971; Rice and Greenberg, 1984; Smith and Glass, 1977; Wolpe, 1958; Zegarnik, 1982) and changes in family therapy (e.g. Hill, 1987; Pinsof, 1981; Postner *et al.*, 1971; Rice and Greenberg, 1984).

Failures in Generalization and Transfer

The process of generalization and transfer sometimes misfires. Here are some types of situations in which this can happen:

Literal Interpretation of the Play Therapeutic Interventions

Nine-year-old Gal felt rejected by his parents. His anger at them was not expressed directly. It was chanelled into a bizarre behavior such as shouting for no apparent reason or exposing his teeth.

In a family play therapeutic session the therapist Ruttie used *owning* and *basic duality* to bring Gal's anger to the family's consciousness. She encouraged the use of direct expressions of anger, such as hurling objects at the parents. For this purpose she mobilized the property of *arbitrariness of signifier.* She defined light objects such as pieces of paper as signifying heavy objects. Ruttie also served as an interpreter. She pointed out that these expressions of anger occurred when the parents made Gal feel an outsider.

Following this session the parents asked for a session without Gal. There they declared their wish to discontinue the therapy. They explained this by their being unable to cope with Ruttie's instruction to let their boy attack them. Following the session—they said—he began throwing metal toy cars at them and kicking them. They interpreted the therapist's tolerance of such make-believe actions in the play sessions as an instruction that they should tolerate such real acts of aggression on the part of the boy at home.

In this case a process of transfer and generalization did take place, but in a wrong way. The parents failed to draw the distinction between the signifier (light objects) and the signified (heavy objects). They owned the child's aggression without alienating themselves from it. They did not distinguish between the symbolizing and the symbolized. They took the therapist's intervention too literally. That is to say, they failed to draw a clear distinction between the level of make-believe and the level of reality. More specifically, they failed to take into account the mental claim of playfulness and the feeling accompanying it.

How can this failure be accounted for? There can be various reasons for it, including some insensitivity on the side of the therapist. One possible reason is a cognitive limitation. Some people are relatively limited in their ability to understand subtle, sophisticated forms of communication such as irony, double meaning or make-believe. Another reason can be a limiting conception of the therapist's role. The therapist is conceived of as an authoritative person who gives instructions. Being engaged in children's make-believe games is not compatible with this conception, so this behavior is interpreted as an unusual way of telling people what to do. A third possible reason is a powerful defensive resistance on the part of the family members, especially the parents, which erects a barrier against the complex, emotionally laden meanings and messages transmitted through the make-believe play.

No Transfer or Generalization

In some cases no transfer and generalization seem to take place at all. At first the family enjoys playing but then they start complaining that although they enjoy playing the play seems to have no relevance to their life. It is no more than playing amusing, childish games.

In many cases this phenomenon can be explained in roughly the same way as the literal interpretation of the make-believe play discussed above. It can be due to some failure in the act of make-believe. The family members, especially the adults, just go through the motions of playing and "doing silly things", but they do not really play a make-believe game at all, since they do not make the mental claims of realification, identication and playfulness. This may be due to some limitation or inhibition. Or it may be due to the fact that the therapeutic make-believe experience runs against very heavy defenses mobilized by the family members, which neutralizes the effect of taking the defenses by surprise so characteristic of make-believe techniques. It is as if the defenses are very alert and ready for any kind of surprise. Or, it can result from stiff resistance on the side of the family.

How can such a literal interpretation of the family play therapeutic experi-ence and the general failure of transfer and generalization be prevented or repaired? Of course it is always possible to verbally explain to the family members how they should take the play experience, but we would like to avoid this.

With people whose difficulty in this respect is due to a cognitive limitation or to a misconception of the therapist's role, a clear distinction can be made between what is inside the play experience and what is outside it. The difference between the role of the therapist inside the play and his role outside the play should be explicated too. For example, if the boy in the play goes on to apply real aggres-sion, the therapist should stop playing and say in a stern voice: "Now I am not playing. I am my real self, and I am not going to allow this here".

The distinction between play and non-play can be emphasized by all kinds of means, some of which have been learned from children: giving the players special make-believe names in the game; using special play gestures and a special manner of speech; using expressions such as "pretend" and "play as if", employing special sound effects indicating playfulness, etc.

Other techniques can be used to instill the make-believe play attitude in the family members' mind: the introduction into the play can be done in a more formal way than usual. The therapist suggests that the family stage a theatrical show or make a TV feature. Roles are allocated. Masks, fancy dresses, lighting and sound effects are employed. As the director of the show, the therapist imprints the mental claims of realification, identication and playfulness in the family members' minds by saying things such as: "You are not Mrs Miller now. You are Red Riding Hood"; "This is not my room now. This is the house in the forest".

Failure of the Softening Effect of the Make-believe

It sometimes happens that the softening and ameliorating effect of the thera-peutic properties of make-believe play does not work. The play therapeutic experience breeds very powerful emotions in the participants that cannot be reduced by the fact that they have arisen in the context of a playful make-believe experience. For example, the child's wish to live with his father in a single parent family was expressed for the first time by a symbolic play in which the boy made a boy doll leave the home and go to the house of an old man through the roof. After that the family members had a fit of anxiety and left the therapy.

It seems then that the therapeutically relevant properties of make-believe play are in some cases too weak against powerful emotions, rigid defenses or stiff resistance for generalization and transfer to take effect. In such cases these properties of play should be reinforced or fortified. This can be achieved by the following, among other, methods:

Maintaining a Cheerful, Playful Atmosphere

Anxiety can be reduced, resistance loosened and rigid defenses relaxed if the therapist conducts the session in a pleasant, cheerful, playful atmosphere. One of the main advantages of family play therapy is that it can be fun. The therapist's responsibility is to preserve this advantage by being light and playful in his style of verbal and non-verbal expression.

Eran, an eight-year-old boy, became fearful of the pictures of his beloved grandfather after he died. He said he believed in ghosts, and was afraid that the ghost of his grandfather would come out of his picture and attack him. A part of the tactic used by Sari, the therapist, was to activate the property of *owning and alienation* and revive a make-believe play replica of the grandfather's ghost. Sari would play the role of the ghost. She would encourage Eran to start a dialogue with the ghost and make peace with it.

Sari performed this tactic in a very playful manner. She played the ghost in a rather funny way. It was a cute ghost Eran could accept. The cheerful, funny way in which Sari conducted the session and in particular the ghost act reduced Eran's anxiety and resistance and therefore helped him fully assume the make-believe play attitude. This paved the way for the process of transfer and generalization to take effect.

Providing Support by Auxiliary Moves

The therapist can reinforce the action of the therapeutically relevant properties of play by being supportive and serving as a good container for the family members' emotions. If the therapist concentrates on his main moves and does not attend to all the family members and their emotional needs by auxiliary moves (see Chapter 11) resistance can be built up which will reduce the power of the therapeutically relevant properties of play.

Introducing the Resistance into the Make-believe Play

The family members' resistance which neutralizes the therapeutically relevant properties of play and causes a failure of transfer and generalization can be weakened by making it a part of the make-believe play itself.

The dysfunctional program of Eran's family included blocking any kind of unpleasant input and output. Only nice and pleasant feelings were admitted.

In one of the sessions the family told me about a serious road accident they witnessed on their way to the clinic. When asked they denied any emotional reactions such as fear or sadness. I decided to stage a make-believe game in which the road accident would be replicated. I hoped the family members would profit from the properties of owning and alienation and covert communication and would overcome their reluctance to express unpleasant emotions. I did not have a chance to stage this game, because the children did, quite spontaneously. I put myself in the role of the driver of one of the cars involved in the accident. In this role I expressed feelings of pain, anger, sadness and fear, attempting to serve as a model for the family. The parents followed suit and verbalized some feelings of this kind, but then they laughed and told me: "On the way here we decided, as a joke, to pretend to express some unpleasant emotions, because we knew you expected this of us. Although we must admit we find all these games rather childish".

At this point I turned these expressions into a part of the make-believe game. I said: "I see that some of the people who are watching this accident pretend not to be feeling anything. They pretend that they just pretend to be afraid and sad when they see this accident".

The parents responded with a bewildered, uneasy smile. It was obvious that this latter move somehow touched them. This was probably due to the operation of the property of *basic duality*. The parents could not escape observing themselves denying their own emotions.

Emphasizing the Make-believe Aspects versus the Reality Aspects of the Play

The therapeutically relevant properties of play have two opposite aspects, a make-believe aspect and a reality aspect. In the property of *owning and alienation* the owning is the reality aspect and the alienation is the make-believe aspect, or the other way round. For example, if a girl plays as if she is a boy, the alienation is the reality aspect and the owning is the make-believe aspect. But if a girl plays as if she is a girl the alienation is the make-believe aspect and the owning is the reality aspect.

In the property of *basic duality* the player as self-observer is the reality aspect and the player as observed by himself is the make-believe aspect.

In the property of arbitrariness of signifier, a similarity between the signifier and the signified is a reality aspect and a dissimilarity between the two is a make-believe aspect. For example, if a doll representing a baby is used as a signifier for the signified "baby" the reality aspect is emphasized. But if the same doll is used as a signifier for the signified "a lion" the make-believe aspect is emphasized.

In the property of *symbolic coding* a direct representation of the main theme of an emotive emphasizes the reality aspect, whereas a symbolically coded representation emphasizes the make-believe aspect. For example, if the main theme of a child's emotive is loss of a parent, a make-believe game in which a parent is lost emphasizes the reality aspect, whereas a make-believe game in which a ball is lost emphasizes the make-believe aspect.

In the property of *covert communication*, an indirect communication through the semantic content of the game emphasizes the make-believe aspect, whereas a direct communication through explicit pragmatic messages emphasizes the reality aspect. For instance, in a make-believe game a little boy staged a scene in which a little bear was kidnapped by a gorilla. This conveyed an implicit message to the parents to come to his rescue. The communication is covert and what is stressed is the make-believe aspect. However, had the boy said: "Mummy, Daddy, come and rescue me!" this would be a direct message and the reality aspect would be more obvious.

In the property of *regulation of emotions*, themes that are directly related to the intense emotions that find expression in the game (that is, themes belonging to a "higher row" in a table such as represented in Chapter 2 are closer to the reality aspect, whereas themes which belong to a lower, more defensive row are closer to the make-believe aspect. For example, a theme such as drowning is closer to the reality aspect, whereas a theme such as "a red-cross submarine" which prevents people from drowning is closer to the make-believe aspect (see p. 40).

In the property of *possible worlds* a make-believe situation that is compatible with the family's reality and its programs is closer to the reality aspect, whereas a make-believe situation that is incompatible with the family reality and programs is closer to the make-believe aspect. For example, in a second-marriage family, a game in which better relations between the ex-husband's new family and the ex-wife's new family is achieved would in some cases be closer to the reality aspect than a game in which the original families are restored.

Now, the following rule can be adopted: if the therapeutically relevant properties of play have proved too weak to contain the overflow of emotions, so that the softening and ameliorating effect of these properties is lost and the process of internalization, transfer and generalization misfires, the properties of play should be reinforced by strengthening their make-believe aspect. However, if the properties of play have been found to be too weak to bypass rigid defenses or unbending resistance, the properties of play should be reinforced by strengthening their reality aspect. The make-believe aspect has a soothing, relaxing effect. The reality aspect encourages exposure and confrontation.

Avraham, a thirty-five-year-old father of three, fell sick with cancer. The illness was never openly discussed with the children, but the atmosphere was thick with unrelieved tension.

In a family play therapeutic session I attempted to bring up the theme of Avraham's illness in a make-believe game and help the family give vent to their emotions. I said: "I am the doctor and your father is coming to me for a medical examination". Avraham complied, but the other family members looked literally petrified and could not cooperate. I realized that they were overwhelemd with emotions. I understood that the reality aspect in the game that I was trying to develop was over-emphasized. Then I decided to continue with games in which the reality aspect is toned down and the make-believe aspect is reinforced. This was achieved in the following, among other, ways:

Stressing the make-believe aspect by *symbolic coding*: instead of playing about "doctor and patient", I led the family to play a game where household appliances went out of order and had to be taken to a repairman.

Stressing the make-believe aspect by *emotional regulation* and *possible worlds*: in the above-mentioned game, I emphasized the theme of restored health. For example, objects that went out of order were repaired so effectively, that "they will never go out of order again".

Techniques emphasizing the reality aspect of the therapeutically relevant properties of play in order to overcome resistance and massive defenses were employed by the therapist with the family that denied any emotions in response to the road accident they had witnessed:

Stressing the reality aspect by *owning* and *basic duality*: I led the family to play make-believe games in which they, undisguised, found themselves in emotionally laden situations such as accidents, failures in school or work or illness. I assumed a make-believe role in which I could comment about their behavior. In my comments I described the fact that they were denying their emotional involvement. My descriptions were expressed in such a way as to make the family's habit of denying their own emotions look excessively obvious and quite funny.

Stressing the reality aspect by using *covert communication*: In these games I put words into their mouths, as if representing the missing dialogue in a silent film. I would say things like: "I am afraid but I am not going to admit it openly", "I am sad but I have to do my best to conceal it", and so forth.

Summary

Table 19 summarizes the mechanisms of change and its generalization and transfer which can be triggered by the therapeutically relevant properties of play.

Table 20 is a summary of the types of failure of generalization and transfer discussed above, and the methods for avoiding such failures suggested. Table 21 lists the reality and make-believe aspects of the therapeutically relevant properties of make-believe play.

Table 19   Mechanisms of change and its generalization and transfer, induced by properties of play.

Play property	Change mechanism	Generalization and transfer mechanism
Owning and alienation	Easing emotional difficulty of becoming aware of distortions in one's conception of oneself or others.	Make-believe necessarily implies belief (i.e. statements of fact about out-of-play reality).
Basic duality	Making family members aware of errors of information processing of which they were not aware, by means of an immediate emotional experience which bypasses their defenses.	The player as an emotionally involved observing ego automatically translates the play reality into his own out-of-play reality.
Arbitrariness of signifier	Shaking convictions about oneself or others by creating an emotional experience of a dissonance; making it easier to be in touch with unpleasant information by introducing a pleasant signifier for an unpleasant signified.	Signified becomes real because it is realified. Signifier is real because it is taken from the immediate concrete vicinity. Thus, signifier and signified belong both to make-believe and to out-of-play reality.
Covert communication	Making interpersonal messages easier to accept; bypassing defenses.	Make-believe themes serve as indirect vehicles for exchanging messages in the real out-of-play social world.
Symbolic coding	Making both semantic contents and pragmatic messages easier to digest.	The symbol is related by a chain of associations to the central theme of one's emotive, which is closer to one's out-of-play reality than the play symbol.

continued

Table 19   (*continued*).

Play property	Change mechanism	Generalization and transfer mechanism
Regulation of emotions	Decreasing emotional tension, therefore preparing emotional ground for repairing errors of information processing.	Reduced emotional tension makes one more receptive to reality-based corrective information.
Possible worlds	Emotionally rewarding experience of formerly unrealized possibilities.	Play experiences include real elements.

Table 20   Types of failures of generalization and transfer, and methods for avoiding them.

Class of failures	Type of failure	Corrective measures
Cognitive-emotive experience too weak	Literal interpretation of play intervention. No transfer and generalization.	Stressing the distinction between play and reality. Emphasizing reality aspects.
Cognitive-emotive experience too powerful	Failure of softening effect of make-believe.	Maintaining a playful atmosphere. Supporting by auxiliary moves. Introducing resistance into the make-believe play. Emphasizing make-believe aspects.

Table 21   Make-believe and reality aspects of therapeutically relevant properties of play.

Property	Make-believe aspects	Reality aspects
Owning and alienation	Owning, but also alienation.	Alienation, but also owning.
Basic duality	Player as observed.	Player as observer.
Symbolic coding	Symbolic representation of central theme of emotive.	Symbolized main theme of emotive.
Covert communication	Covert messages through make-believe themes.	Direct messages.
Regulation of emotions	Themes associated with highest level of emotional arousal.	Themes associated with lower, defensive levels of emotional arousal.
Possible worlds	Themes incompatible with the family's potential reality.	Themes compatible with the family's potential reality.

CHAPTER 14

Changes Between Sessions

How Does Change Take Place in Strategic Family Play Therapy?

In previous chapters the question was taken up of how change in dysfunctional family programs occurs as a result of the deliberate application of therapeutically relevant properties of play and their transfer and generalization beyond the play situation. Since the presenting problem is maintained by the dysfunctional programs, the change in the dysfunctional programs is expected to solve the presenting problems.

The questions taken up in this chapter are:

How do the changes achieved by individual play therapeutic interventions add up session after session, so that the long range goals of the whole therapy are achieved?

How can the process of change and its outcome be assessed?

The changes in the dysfunctional programs are not all achieved at once. The therapeutic interventions are designed to produce small changes. These add up within and across sessions. Some changes give rise spontaneously to further changes.

Here are some examples:

The Gold Family

This family was discussed in Chapter 3. A short reminder:

The family consisted of forty-year-old electronics engineer, Yakov Gold, his wife Dinah and their twelve-year-old son Shaul. Shaul was brought to therapy by his mother, because of his habit of locking himself up in his room. In the safety of his room—it will be remembered—he used to spend his time writing obsessively "TV series" in tiny, tight, barely readable and largely meaningless scrawl. When asked why he was writing in this manner his answer was: "to save paper".

Yakov, the father, formerly a well known soccer player, was a spendthrift and a gambler who showered useless though expensive gifts on his wife, thus compensating for what he took to be her rejection of his love, and for the fact that he had lost his former status. His irresponsible wasting of money got him entangled in heavy debts and there were rumours of his having embezzled some sporting club money. Dinah was making desperate efforts to cover his debts. This put her under great physical and mental strain, but also strengthened her position in relation to her husband.

The overall therapeutic strategy adopted was directed to the following objectives:

Exposing the dysfunctional programs. Helping the son achieve his goal by direct, active means. Attempting to convince the mother that her husband is capable of shouldering the responsibility for his own problems. She should transfer this responsibility back over to him.

It was predicted that if these two goals are achieved, an attempt to make the husband realize that his wife's love is independent of his being successful would become redundant. The changes specified above are likely to spontaneously lead the husband to be more responsible and consequently regain his wife's love and admiration.

In Chapter 10, a tactic for one of the first sessions was proposed. Its actual execution was illustrated by the episode of a police invasion into the office of Jack Reilly, an FBI agent. The main purpose of the tactic, and, accordingly, the episode, was to expose the problems that were denied by father and son.

Let us see now how the process of gradual and cumulative change applies in this case:

I observed that in the "police invasion" episode some progress was made toward one of the aims set in the overall strategy, namely revealing Shaul's goal and plan to his parents and helping him achieve his goal by direct, active means. Profiting from the properties of *owning and alienation, symbolization* and *possible worlds*, Shaul, in the role of Robert Crosby, braced himself and declared openly: "I am going to wash my hands of this whole affair". When he took refuge in the cupboard and his parents wanted to come in too he held the cupboard's door fast, to keep it closed, and said: "Take your hands off! There's room for just one person here!" And when his mother said: "You are abandoning your father and mother!", he said: "That's an exact description".

In the next session I wanted to reinforce this achievement, and included this aim in my tactic. However, I did not have to work too hard, since the process which started in the first session had been taking its own course and accelerated itself. Shaul's corrected plan was maintained in the second session, gained strength and even generated further changes, quite spontaneously. Some of these undirected changes appear in the following episode, taken out of the second session:

The scene is the district attorney's office. Senator Crosby and his wife Jane are brought in handcuffed. Their son Robert stands in the corner, leaning against the wall.

DA *(addressing Senator Crosby and his wife)*. You know what the charges against you are. I have to warn you that everything you say can serve as evidence against you. Have you anything to say to defend yourselves, or at least explain yourselves?

JANE *(referring to Senator Crosby)*. He got me into this damn affair!

SENATOR CROSBY. She is not involved.

JANE. What do you mean I am not involved?

SENATOR CROSBY. Sir, I am asking you to let my wife go home. She has nothing to do with this affair. I am willing to account for everything, but please don't get her into it.

THE DA. I like this bit. What do you think about it, Robert?

ROBERT. I don't think anything. I learned not to think when I am not asked to.

As in the first episode, Yakov Gold was Senator Crosby, his wife Dinah was Jane and their twelve-year-old son Shaul was Robert. I, the therapist, was the District Attorney and my office was his office.

In this episode too Shaul, under the cover of symbolization and covert communication, made his own plan of being uninvolved in the conflict between his parents explicit by saying: "I don't think anything. I learned not to think when I am not asked to". This was in line with his play behavior in the first session. However, something else, very important, happened in this episode, namely, the father, again under the cover of *alienation*, symbolization and *covert communication* wanted his wife to be released from her responsibility for his own misdeeds and demonstrated his willingness to shoulder this responsibility. This was in accordance with one of the aims stated in the overall strategy.

How can the fact that these changes occurred spontaneously in the second session be explained? It is reasonable to surmise that they would not have happened if the ground had not been prepared for them in the first session. In particular it does not seem plausible that Yakov, the father, whose emotional investment in his dysfunctional plan was, as claimed above, quite massive, would have suddenly given up his unbending resistance so easily, unless we are led to believe that the first session had made a considerable impact on him.

One can go on and speculate, or, rather, propose a hypothetical analysis of the process that led from what happened in the first session to the changes that manifested themselves in the second session:

The crucial elements in the episode described in Chapter 10 were: (a) The family's financial difficulties and their source in Yakov Gold's misdemeanor were openly discussed (of course, within the make-believe play), with Yakov himself participating. (b) The possibility of suffering a heavy penalty was brought to the open, through the police raid scene. (c) Shaul's plan of avoiding being involved in the family troubles was exposed. Shaul, for the first time, actively resisted his parents' expectations of him to take part in their problems and help them.

In information-processing terms, these elements retrieved the relevant information that was filtered out. The properties of *basic duality, owning* and *possible worlds* helped the family process this retrieved information both cognitively and emotionally. Consequently Yakov Gold could not go on denying the problems and his responsibility for them. His shame and fear of the final consequences mounted considerably. Shaul became more aware of his fear and anger concerning his parents and their problems. These thoughts and feelings prepared the ground for the changes in the second session. Yakov's willingness to admit his responsibility and ask that his wife be released, manifested in his dialogue with "the DA", was motivated by the fear and shame that arose in him in the first session. Likewise, Shaul's cynical statement "I don't think anything. I learned not to think when I am not asked to" continues his increased awareness of his fear and anger with respect to his parents, which was gained in the first session.

Although I have long been aware of the fact that what happens in the family's make-believe play in the therapeutic session is often generalized and transferred to the family's real everyday life, and have tried to analyze and explain this process (see Chapter 13), I am still intrigued and amazed when I see this actually happen again and again. That is how I felt when Yakov Gold told me that he had decided to make a great effort to solve his obsessive spending and had even taken an additional job to make this possible. Consequently, the atmosphere in the family improved considerably. All this happened a short time after the onset of the therapy, after the fourth session. And then came another unexpected turn in this drama. The fifth session included the following episode:

A courtroom. The accused in the dock is Senator Crosby. His wife Jane and his son Robert sit on the witnesses stand. I, of course, played the part of the judge.

THE JUDGE *(to Crosby)*. Do you plead guilty?

CROSBY. I do.

THE JUDGE. That's interesting. Does anyone have anything to say?

ROBERT. I do.

THE JUDGE. Go ahead.

ROBERT *(pointing at Jane)*. She made him do it!

JANE *(jumping)*. Me?

THE JUDGE. Order in the courtroom! You go on.

ROBERT. She made him do it. She kept getting on his nerves until he did it!

In this session the therapeutic process took its own course, deviating quite considerably from the overall strategy. Robert gave up his neutrality and joined his father. He defended his father and protected him from the accusations directed at him and from his self accusation. He blamed his mother for his father's misdeeds, revealing his belief that she was the one who drove him there by her aggressiveness.

Again, one can attempt to reconstruct the process that led from the family play therapeutic experiences in the previous sessions to the developments in this last session. This process seems to have stemmed both from the family make-believe games in the play therapy room and from the above-mentioned developments in the family's real life outside the therapy. In the episode taken out of the second session above Shaul was a witness to a scene in which his mother accused his father ("*He* got me into this damn affair") and his father reacted in a chivalrous fashion: he asked that his wife should be exempted and expressed his willingness to take upon himself the accusations directed at both of them. This was a far cry from the pattern he had been witnessing before, in which his mother spoke harshly to his father and his father reacted by a flat denial or by being apologetic. Now, in the analysis of the family's dysfunctional program the son's goal was defined as keeping his parents together, preventing the widening of the rift between them. His plan was based on the prediction that if he supported one side this would widen the rift between them and therefore run against his goal. However, when he saw his father accept the verdict and take the blame, he could conclude that his prediction was not valid any longer. The relationship between his parents, initially governed by a conflict, became one of cooperation. One presumes that the properties of *symbolization* and *owning and alienation* helped Shaul own this realization and turn it into an emotionally significant experience. Apparently this realization enabled him to change his plan and support his father against his mother without fearing that this would seriously jeopardize the relationship between his parents, and therefore run against his goal. This changed plan of his was, presumably, reinforced by his anger at his mother's aggressiveness. He could now identify with what looked like his father's courage and chivalry. Since the change was generalized and transferred to the family's out-of-therapy reality and the atmosphere at home was improved considerably, Shaul could allow himself to introduce this drastic change into his plan, at least within the make-believe play.

Although this change in Shaul was contrary to the overall strategy, I thought there was a good side to it. His newly acquired identification with his father suited his age and gender and was good for his development. His expression of anger at his mother had a freeing, cathartic effect. However, it indicated that he was still overly involved in the relationship between his parents. In some of the sessions that followed I attempted to show him that he could achieve a good relationship with each of his parents without getting entangled in their conflicts.

Home, Sweet Home

Here is another case.

Eight-year-old Barak was referred to therapy because he was caught helping himself to various objects taken out of children's satchels in school.

Barek lived with his mother Zehava and his nine-year-old sister Nizan in a single room apartment in a low socioeconomic area of Tel Aviv. His father had left home two years earlier with Barak's two older brothers. He lived with another woman.

This family was admitted to family play therapy in the framework of a practicum in a training program for social workers. Following an interview with Zehava and a family play observation, the trainee-therapist Ruttie formulated the following dysfunctional program:

Mother's Goal

To keep her children close to her and form together with them a solid, united family that cannot break up.

Mother's Plan

Presupposition

My husband left me and took my two older sons with him because I did not try hard enough to keep the family united round me.

Prediction

There is still danger that my husband will "steal" my other children.

Output

I should watch over the children constantly.
I should not let them quarrel, and insist that they play nicely together.
I should forbid and prevent any contact between my children and my husband.
He, my older children who live with him, his new home and new wife should under no circumstances be mentioned or discussed in my home.

Daughter's Goal

To keep mother close to herself.

Daughter's Plan

Prediction

If I am "a bad girl" and do things Mother does not like, such as quarrel with my brother or talk about my father and older brothers, my mother can become so upset that she might decide to give me up and send me away to live with my father.

Output

I should never mention or openly discuss my father or my older brothers when my mother can hear me.

If my brother provokes me, I should give in and avoid an open conflict with him. To avoid conflicts with him I should keep myself to myself and minimize contacts with him.

I should obey my mother and try not to do things she does not approve of.

Son's Goals

To be relatively free and independent of his mother's and sister's control and as close as possible to his father and older brothers.

Son's Plan

Presupposition

My mother and sister want to dominate me totally. They want to prevent me from having any contact whatsoever with my father and older brothers.

Prediction

If I do anything my mother does not approve of, and in particular mention my father, my older brothers and their home, she will become very upset and angry and my sister will not dare contradict her.

Output

I should avoid my mother's and sister's company as much as possible. In this way I can escape their control without confronting them. By being not so close to them I can feel somewhat closer to my father and brothers.

If my mother prods me to play with my sister I ignore her, pretending not to hear.

I misbehave only in school, where my mother cannot watch over me.

Prediction

If my mother hears bad reports about me from school, she is likely to decide that she cannot handle me and ask my father for help.

Barak's main symptom, "stealing" in school, is an expression of the last part of his plan. It also has a metaphorical, symbolic meaning. He cannot get what he needs, his father and brothers, directly, so he has to "steal" it.

The main anomalous information-processing operations Ruttie identified in this dysfunctional program were:

The mother's presupposition that her husband left because she did not try hard enough to keep the family united around her. It includes the prediction that he is likely to "steal" the other children. This presupposition and prediction have not been properly supported or validated. Her policy of forbidding any mention of her husband and his family prevents her from finding out whether this presupposition and prediction are correct. She fails to consider other, less extreme and less harmful means for achieving her goal of keeping her children close to her. She does not consider the disadvantages of her output.

Nizan's prediction that her mother might decide to yield her over to her father fails to take into account that her mother's main goal is to keep her children close to her.

Her decision to minimize contact with her brother does not take into account her mother's wish that she be close to her brother.

She fails to consider other, less harmful means for achieving her goal of keeping her mother close to her.

Barak's prediction, that his problematic behavior in school can lead his mother to ask his father for help, does not take into account his mother's goal and plan and is not validated. He does not consider other, less harmful means for achieving his goal.

Ruttie's strategy was designed to correct these errors.

Here is the tactic for one of the first sessions:

The Changes Wanted

In the overall strategy, the planned changes were ordered in sequence: priority was given to changes that were not expected to be met with unbending resistance on the side of the mother. This session will concentrate on attempting to contribute to the achievement of the following changes: helping the mother to understand that her goal, keeping her children close to her and forming together with them a solid, united family can be reached by constructive means. Possible means are: developing an open, supportive relationship and sharing with them enjoyable activities; helping the children to understand that their mother wants them to be close to each other; encouraging them to stop avoiding each other and participate in joint activities.

The Properties of Play Activated and the Ways in Which They Would Be Put into Operation

The very fact that the mother and children will play together may constitute a step toward these goals. Beyond that, the property of *possible worlds* will be activated to create an atmosphere of cooperation and mutual support within the make-believe play. The property of *arbitrariness of signifier* can be used to overcome the children's expected resistance to giving up their seclusion and mutual avoidance.

The behavioral ("raw-material") manifestations of avoidance (e.g. physical distance, lack of contact) will be framed as signifiers for closeness and intimacy. The property of *owning and alienation* will be activated to have the mother assume the role of a positive parental figure who encourages openness and mutual support. With the aid of the properties of *covert communication* and *symbolization* the mother can be helped to transmit her messages to the children.

The therapist will assume a make-believe role which will place her in a position of authority. She will appoint the mother to be her assistant. The therapist will instruct her how to take a positive supportive role. Later the therapist will direct the mother to replace her in her position as leader. The therapist herself will step aside and serve in an "advisory" capacity.

Here is an episode in which this tactic was put into practice:

Barak sits on the floor in one corner of the room, playing with a toy house. He tries to get little toy animals into it through the window.

Zehava stands over him, watching him. Nizan stands by her, holding her arm.

ZEHAVA *(addressing Ruttie, the therapist)*. He always plays little children's games.

RUTTIE. So do I, sometimes. I think it's fun.

ZEHAVA *(addressing Jane)*. You should do something too.

NIZAN. I'm going to draw.

Nizan gets sheets of paper and chalks. She sits at the table and starts drawing trees.

ZEHAVA. What are you drawing?

NIZAN. A forest.

The two children are absorbed in their activities. Zehava looks lost and somewhat depressed.

ZEHAVA. Barak! Why don't you sit at the table? You'll be more comfortable there!

Barak ignores her. She takes a seat by the table watching Nizan anxiously.

RUTTIE *(the therapist, declares)*. I am the superintendent of the forest authority. Zehava, you are my chief assistant. *Ruttie draws a chair and places it by Zehava's chair. She turns to Zehava.* I see you have been waiting for me in the jeep. That's nice. OK, we can start our daily tour round the forest to see if everything is all right. I'll drive this time. *She gets a toy steering wheel, sits on the chair, turns the wheel and makes "engine" noises with her lips. Then she imitates the screeching brakes. She addresses Zehava.* You see? They keep planting trees. Let's drive to the house. *She turns her wheel and makes engine sounds.*

RUTTIE *(pointing at Barak's house)*. You see that house over there, underneath that big tree? That's the zoo house in the forest. We've just finished building it. It's a special shelter for the animals of the forest. OK, now you drive, I'm tired.

Analysis

What had happened in the room before Ruttie intervened reflects some of the main aspects of the dysfunctional program described above. Zehava, the mother, was keeping a constant anxious watch over the children. When Nizan sat at the table Zehava attempted to get Barak closer to herself and her daughter by suggesting that he sit at the table. When she failed in her attempt to get everybody together she became upset, she kept watching Nizan.

Ruttie took this behavior to be a manifestation of the mother's dysfunctional plan which included output such as "I should watch over the children constantly . . . I should insist that the children play together".

Nizan clung to her mother, but when Zehava told her to play she did not join her brother but occupied herself in some "nice" activity of her own, drawing. This was interpreted by Ruttie as reflecting parts of Nizan's plan—"I should obey my mother and try not to do things she does not approve of . . . To avoid conflicts with my brother I should keep myself to myself and minimize contacts with him".

Barak played alone. He put toy animals into a toy house. Ruttie speculated that this game symbolized his wish to go into his father's home. When his mother invited him to sit at the table he ignored her.

Ruttie understood this behavior as reflecting parts of his dysfunctional plan "I should avoid my mother's and sister's company as much as possible. In this way I can escape their control without confronting them. By being not so close to them I can feel closer to my father and brothers. If my mother urges me to play with my sister, I ignore her, pretending not to hear".

Ruttie's intervention was in accordance with her pre-planned tactic. She assumed the make-believe role of the superintendent of the forest authority, and appointed Zehava her assistant. Later she asked Zehava to drive the make-believe jeep, as a first step toward turning the position of authority over to Zehava.

The main purpose of the intervention was to get the family to play together and enjoy it, and at the same time demonstrate to Zehava that this can be achieved without begging or using ineffective coercive means. Ruttie's main move was framing the "forest" in Nizan's drawing as a make-believe forest, which accommodated not only Nizan but also Barak with his zoo house, Ruttie herself as the "superintendent" and Zehava as her "assistant". The properties of play activated by this move were *play-framing* (Nizan's drawing activity was framed as make-believe play), and *arbitrariness of signifier* (the four separate room spaces occupied by each of the participants were arbitrarily defined as signifiers for a single joint location: the forest. This turned separate activities into a single joint activity around the different aspects of the single theme of forest life).

With the aid of this move Ruttie managed to stage a rich and interesting joint family activity in which Zehava took a leading part, without in fact asking the children to do anything different from what they had been doing anyway. More specifically, she achieved her objective without pressing them to give up that part of their plan which required each of them to avoid the others' company.

Here is another episode from the same session:

Nizan leaves her drawing and approaches Barak. She kneels by his side, she observes him putting toy animals into his dolls' house and taking them out again.

Zehava, who has meanwhile been appointed "the superintendent of the forest authority" by Ruttie, sits on a chair watching them. Ruttie, who has "retired from her position as a superintendent but remained in an advisory capacity", sits by her side on another chair.

RUTTIE. I see your staff members cooperate and help one another, more than they used to in my day. I see this one finished planting trees and now she helps this one get animals into their zoo-house. I guess you encourage this sort of cooperation, don't you?

ZEHAVA. Of course I do.

RUTTIE. I envy you. You direct this forest very skillfully.

Zehava picks up a toy cow and hands it over to Nizan, saying. You forgot this one.

Analysis

In this episode, which came shortly after the former, some changes in the desired direction took place spontaneously. Nizan, on her own initiative, approached Barak and actively participated in his game. Later on Zehava, the mother, left her controlling position and joined their game too. These changes fitted some of the goals specified in the tactic, namely: helping the mother understand that her goal of keeping her children close to her and forming together with them a solid, united family can be reached by constructive means; helping the children understand that their mother wants them to be close to each other and participate in joint activities.

One might suppose that these changes resulted almost directly from Ruttie's intervention in the former episode. The effect of the intervention can perhaps be explained as follows: Nizan's keeping a distance from Barak was motivated by her wish to avoid conflicts with him. Barak's avoiding his mother's and sister's company was reflected in his desire to escape being controlled by them. Zehava's inability to participate in the children's activities in a supportive and enjoyable way was caused by her feeling that she should always be on the alert, controlling and supervising the children. (See the dysfunctional program on pp. 219–221).

Ruttie's intervention bypassed these motivations. As a result of this intervention Nizan could feel that she might play with Barak without falling into the danger of quarreling with him. Barak could be reassured, realizing that playing together does not necessarily mean being controlled. Zehava could recognize that her goal of having a united family does not necessarily require of her to be always on the alert. Therefore, each of the family members felt more at ease with the others and could change his or her behavior toward a more genuine cooperation.

How did Ruttie's intervention accomplish this? As explained above, she activated the properties of play-framing, arbitrariness of signifier and possible worlds in such a way that each of the family members could go on doing what he or she had been doing, in accordance with his or her dysfunctional plan, and yet all of them were made to feel that they participated in a joint interesting play activity which gave them a great deal of fun. One could do his or her own thing and yet feel that he or she is a part of a united family. This mitigated their dysfunctional plans.

In the latter episode this achievement was reinforced by Ruttie in the following ways: she handed the role of "the superintendent" (a parental role) over to Zehava. She gave Zehava the credit for the children's willingness to play together. By complimenting Zehava for having encouraged the children's cooperation she covertly communicated to her the suggestion that she can and should do it. This reinforcement and show of faith helped Zehava give up her rigid controlling position and join the children's game. The toy cow she introduced into the game may have very well been a symbolic embodiment of herself. In the next session Ruttie planned to reinforce the achievements of the latter session. Here is an episode from this session:

Nizan and Barak sit on two adjacent chairs at the table. Zehava sits opposite them. On the table there are two dolls' houses. Nizan and Barak move toy animals from one toy house to the other.

RUTTIE *(still in the role of the consultant to the Superintendent of the Forest Authority)*. Since my last visit here, the animals got another house. I see they like moving from one house to another and back.

ZEHAVA. They kept nagging me, saying they needed an extra house. I don't know why. Is one not enough?

RUTTIE. I don't know. It's a difficult question. Anyway, they seem to enjoy it, shuttling between their two houses.

Analysis

In this episode the achievements of the former session were preserved. The children went on playing together with their mother. However, as we see, in this session a new element appeared—again, quite spontaneously: the children added a new "zoo house" to their game, and were making toy animals move from one of the houses to the other one and back. Ruttie interpreted this as a fairly transparent symbolically disguised expression of their wish to belong not just to their mother's home but to their father's home as well. Using *symbolic coding* and *covert communication* Ruttie focused on this wish and emphasized it. Zehava, the mother, took the message and expressed, again through covert communication, her dissatisfaction with the children's wish. Ruttie attempted, without contradicting the mother outright, to hint that she approves of this wish.

This change was not included in Ruttie's tactic for this session. She thought it was too early for the problem of the father and his family to be exposed. She assessed that the family members, in particular the mother, were not yet ready to bring this into the open. She expected strong resistance on the part of the mother. However, since this issue was raised on the family's own initiative, Ruttie decided to follow it through. She relied on the properties of *symbolization, covert communication* and *owning and alienation* as softening agents, which could facilitate the interaction around this issue.

How can the spontaneous introduction of the theme of the father into the make-believe play be explained? This was certainly a significant change in the family's dysfunctional program. The mother's plan includes the clause: "I should forbid and prevent any contact between my children and my husband. He, my older children who live with him, his new home and new wife should under no circumstances be ever mentioned or discussed in my home". Nizan's plan includes this clause: "I should never mention or openly discuss my father or my older brothers when my mother can hear me". Barak's plan also avoids referring to his father, his older brothers or their home in any direct manner. One can hypothesize that the change in Nizan's and Barak's plans was due to the following factors: as a result of the intervention in the former session Zehava became less rigid in her watch over and control of the children. She participated in their play in a supportive and cooperative parental role. The children stopped avoiding one another's company and came together. Therefore they felt like a united, more powerful front in relation to the mother. Presumably these changes reduced the emotional impact of Nizan's prediction "If I am a 'bad girl' and do things mother does not like, she can become so upset that she might decide to give me away". They also diminished the intensity of the emotions supporting Barak's presupposition "My mother and sister want to dominate me totally", as well as of his prediction: "If I do anything my mother does not approve of, she will become very upset and angry, and my sister will not dare contradict her". This reduced emotional impact enabled them to change their plans and express, albeit in a symbolic disguise, their wish to be with their father.

In the next session Ruttie planned to continue these changes and reinforce them, as they accorded with her overall strategy. However, things did not turn out the way she planned. The family showed up dressed in their best clothes. Their behavior in the session was markedly different from their behavior in former sessions. They appeared to be quite cheerful and relaxed. The children left the room frequently to drink some water. Barak hid one of the dolls' houses underneath a mattress. Nizan arranged the toy animals in a row on the window-sill, facing the yard. Barak made his mother and sister sit on chairs and said: "I am a bus driver, we are going to have a pleasant trip". Following this session, the family left the therapy and never showed up again, nor answered Ruttie's telephone calls. They disappeared into thin air.

The family's departure was interpreted by the team as a statement of their unwillingness to change those aspects of their dysfunctional program that banned any mention of the father, his older sons, and their home. The dysfunctional program was breached in the former session and this should not have happened. The therapy was dangerous. It should be stopped.

The family's behavior in the room was interpreted as a symbolically coded expression of their resistance and decision to leave. The communciations were covert. The atmosphere in the room was that of a farewell celebration.

Presumably this cheerful, festive atmosphere reflected also the family's attempt to counterbalance the depressive mood caused by the emergence of the father's theme in the former session. The general direction of the family was outwards: the toy animals facing the yard, the bus trip and the frequent leaving to go to the bathroom. The theme of the father's home (represented by the dolls' house) was hidden underneath the mattress.

Summary—Tracing the Process of Change

What can one learn from these examples?

One cannot always fully control the process of change in strategic family play therapy or predict its course. Changes that have occcurred as a result of a carefully planned intervention can lead in a spontaneous, unpremeditated way to other changes, not necessarily expected or desirable. The therapist has to get the feedback which would enable him to continuously supervise the process of change, control it and correct uncalled-for deviations. The main source of this feedback is a careful observation of the family's behavior in the therapy room, in particular their make-believe play behavior. This behavior can be registered and interpreted by the method of observation and interpretation specified in detail in Chapters 6–8.

As manifested in the above cases, change can take place in the following manners:

The skilled use of therapeutically relevant properties of play by the therapist undermines the emotional defenses that have maintained and supported certain errors of information processing in a family member's dysfunctional plan (see Chapter 9). The same emotional defenses lie at the basis of other information-processing operations, which have not constituted the original target of the intervention. Therefore, the undermining of these emotional defenses automatically brings about changes in these latter information-processing operations.

This is the process that accounts for some of the spontaneous changes that took place in Nizan and Barak in the last case. For example, Nizan's avoidance of her brother was motivated by the same emotional defense as her avoidance of games symbolizing her relationship with her father, namely, the fear of annoying her mother. Once this fear had been reduced and she could feel at ease playing with her brother, she automatically felt more comfortable expressing—in a symbolic disguise, of course—her wish to be closer to her father.

Another way in which spontaneous change can occur is the following: when a family member changes his or her dysfunctional plan, the other family members are free to adjust and change those aspects of their own dysfuncational plans which have been associated with the former. For example, when Shaul Gold witnessed his father change his attitude toward his mother from belligerency to submissiveness, he could give up his neutrality, identify with his father and attack his mother.

CHAPTER 15

Termination

The Family Plays its Own Finale Notes

Often, when the time is ripe, the family's play in the sessions begins to display signals suggesting the approaching farewell.

A classification of termination signals often encountered in family play therapy is displayed in Table 22.

Table 22 Types of termination signals.

Level of semiotic analysis	Signals
Raw material	*Spatial*: Keeping at a distance; Leaving the room; Facing outdoors; Hiding. *Motional*: Closing up. *Tactile*: Avoiding contact; Aggressive touch. *Vocal*: Being unusually quiet or unusually noisy.
Semantic (thematic and emotive meaning)	Avoiding painful themes previously brought up; Introducing themes related to parting; Expressing anger at therapist or avoiding any expression of anger; Being unusually sad or unusually cheerful.
Pragmatic (interpersonal messages)	Messages expressing distancing; Messages expressing anger at therapist; Messages expressing over-appreciation of therapist.

Examples:

In the case entitled Home, Sweet Home, described at length in Chapter 14, Zehava and her two children, Barak and Nizan, expressed their wish to say goodbye by means of a whole series of play and non-play signals. These can be sorted, according to Table 22, into the following types:

Raw material. The children left the room frequently to drink some water.

Barak hid one of the dolls' houses underneath a mattress. Nizan arranged the toy animals in a row on the window sill, facing the yard (distancing and hiding).

Semantic. The family came to the session dressed in their best clothes. They appeared to be quite cheerful and relaxed. Barak made his mother and sister sit on chairs and said "I am a bus driver. We are going to have a pleasant trip" (avoiding painful themes, behavior unusually cheerful, introducing themes related to parting).

Let us turn to the case of Yoram and his two adoptive parents Gad and Neta (see Chapters 7–10). After a year of family play therapy Sari, the therapist, was convinced that the goals of therapy, as prescribed by the strategy, had been reached and that the time was ripe for termination.

Anxiety related to fear of rejection between Yoram and his adoptive parents was reduced to a negligible degree. The family system, including Yoram, seemed to be functioning as an integrated unit, with individual differences acknowledged and accepted. However, when Sari brought up the possibility of termination to the parents they expressed their worry that without the support provided by therapy the problems would return. The family's behavior in the play therapy sessions expressed this concern, but also their growing readiness to continue on their own.

One of the play themes introduced by Yoram and played over and over again by the family in the last sessions was "Train journey". Yoram would make a toy train run very fast and noisily around his parents and Sari and call out loud: "We are all going to Jerusalem to visit granny!" Then he would whistle sharply and stop the train. He would instruct Gad, Neta and Sari to each put his or her own little doll into one of the cars. With the dolls inside, he would make the train go away frenziedly. On the way he would take Sari's doll out and throw it aside.

This game includes termination signals which, according to Table 22, belong to the following kinds:

Raw material. Dolls inside train car; train is pulling out and leaving; taking therapist's doll out and throwing it aside (distancing, hiding, avoiding contact); moving fast and noisily; calling out loud (being unusually energetic and noisy).

Semantic. Train leaving to visit granny; excluding therapist's doll and throwing it away (parting themes, ambivalence and anger toward therapist).

Playing One's Way Out of Therapy

Terminating therapy and parting is not an easy experience. It can be softened a little by transferring it to the sphere of make-believe.

Table 23 displays some types of therapeutic intervention suitable for the termination phase, with the therapeutically relevant properties of playing that can facilitate these interventions (see Chapter 3), and some examples follow.

Table 23   Termination-relevant play therapeutic interventions with facilitating play properties.

Purpose of intervention	Principles of intervention	Facilitating play properties
Encouraging termination	Suggesting termination without making the family feel rejected.	Covert communication; symbolic coding.
Allowing expression of resistance to terminate	Transferring the resistance to the sphere of make-believe.	"Play"-framing; owning and alienation; symbolic coding.
Discouraging termination	Exposing the motives for the wish to terminate prematurely. Suggesting continuing without arousing insurmountable resistance.	Owning and alienation; basic duality; covert communication.
Allaying anger at therapist	Giving vent to anger within make-believe play.	Regulation of emotions.
Encouraging make-believe play regression	Returning to phenomena characteristic of earlier phases of the therapy in make-believe play.	Possible worlds.
Summarizing the therapy in make-believe	Telling the story of the therapy in make-believe play.	Play-framing; symbolic coding.
Make-believe continuation of the therapy	Facilitating termination and encouraging internalization of the therapy by "continuing" it in make-believe play	Possible worlds.

Encouraging Termination

Let us return to the case entitled The Invisible Guest, presented as a prologue to this book. Saying goodbye to David and Sivan was a delicate task, requiring tact and consideration. Both of them had gone through a painful experience of being deserted and ignored. During therapy I served, symbolically, as a substitute father figure for David and as a supportive male companion for Sivan. Neither of them was absolutely confident that their newly acquired mutual understanding was solid enough to withstand life's pressures without the support provided by therapy. In bringing the therapy to its close I made use of some of the principles listed in Table 23.

In the last stage of therapy David and I were playing "an adventure plane flight around the world". Sivan was excluded from the flight. She was restricted to the control tower. I had to be the pilot who rescued both of us from all kinds of dangers. In one of the sessions, when we returned to base, I said: Now she (referring to Sivan) is going to be the pilot and I am going to replace her in the control tower. David objected. I tried to make him agree to this suggestion by telling him that Sivan had graduated with distinction from a training course for "rescuing pilots". She was perfectly capable of taking my place at the rescuing pilot seat. Anyway, I would keep watch over both of them from the control tower for a while, until I was certain that the new automatic computerized control system worked smoothly and gave no trouble.

In this intervention I employed the play properties covert communication and symbolic coding to reduce the emotional impact of the message that David and Sivan were ready to cope on their own and therapy was about to be terminated.

Allowing Expression of Resistance to Terminate and Giving Vent to Anger at Therapist

As expected, David refused to accept my suggestion to exchange roles with Sivan. I persisted in my determination to step aside and prepare mother and son for my leave-taking. But, instead of arguing with David, I assumed an authoritative manner of speech and told him: I am the chief commander of this mission. I heard that one of our pilots, Shlomo, plans to desert. He should be punished. Handcuff him and detain him in custody! This command was obeyed by David willingly, even enthusiastically.

The following therapeutic properties of play were employed in this intervention: *Possible worlds*—I played both the part of the deserting pilot and the part of the commander who ordered David to remand the deserting pilot in custody.

This flexibility of roles enabled me to represent both my side of the story and David's.

Symbolic coding—David's reluctance to let me go and his anger were coded symbolically by the act of handcuffing and detaining me.

Emotional regulation—David was allowed to take out his anger on me.

Discouraging termination

In the introduction to this book strategic family play therapy was illustrated by the case of nine-year-old Ron, who was considered by everybody to be a failure in school. His under-achievement was analyzed as the result of his "having made himself silly". This was his way out of his identification conflict. He could identify neither with his father's submissive, dependent side, nor with his pedantic and intellectual facade, because these two facets of his father's personality were both rejected by his mother. On the other hand he was reluctant to join his mother in her rejection of his father. The treatment plan included the step of negotiating, in the "as if" world of make-believe, the possibility of releasing the children from their involvement in the conflict between the parents (see pp. 15–21).

In the first session in which this idea was implemented I re-introduced the puppets chosen by the family in the assessment session, namely Rami "cow", Edna "lion", Ron "devil", Ben "donkey". I directed the family to play a game in which the devil and the donkey became human, whereas the cow and the lion remained a cow and a lion.

In the next session Edna suddenly declared: "We discussed this at home and decided that Ron can manage without therapy now". Ron was all too ready to agree. "I am better at school now", he said.

I understood this declaration as a sign of anxiety, aroused by the possibility that the conflict between Edna and Rami would be fully exposed. I ignored what Edna and Ron said and continued playing. I wore a glove puppet representing a fox and spoke in a foxy manner: "I am a cunning fox. I dig out things animals in the forest try to hide and keep secret from other animals. I incite little animals to rise against their parents and go their own way, which is *my* way. Beware of me! Run for your life or get me out of the way!"

In this intervention I employed the play-properties *covert communication*, *symbolization* and *owning and alienation* to reflect to the family its resistance and expose what I believed to be its motives. I also prescribed to the family its own anger, fear and wish to discontinue the therapeutic contact with me, activating the play properties *possible worlds* and *emotional regulation*.

Encouraging Make-believe Play Regression

Therapists are familiar with the fact that with the approaching termination clients are inclined to regress to patterns of behavior characteristic of earlier stages of the therapy. To make this easier for the family, the therapist may induce them to regress in the "as if" world of make-believe. I used this technique with David and Sivan in the case entitled The Invisible Guest. In the last sessions I suggested that we played games of the kinds that we had been playing at various stages of the therapy: tying each other up with a rope, the telescope game, show contests, etc. In this way both make-believe play regression and the technique termed *summarizing the therapy in make-believe* (see Table 23 were implemented.

Make-believe Continuation of the Therapy

In the last session with David and Sivan, I played with them as if all three of us were in their home two years later, playing together and enjoying ourselves. The properties of *basic duality* and *possible worlds* were activated in this play to help David and Sivan take me home with them in a spiritual sense.

Epilogue

A number of times I had the opportunity to participate in some kind of reunion with families who had undergone family play therapy a few years earlier. These encounters were intriguing and instructive. It was interesting to meet the family again, see how they had changed and hear about their feelings in retrospect. Let me tell you about two such meetings.

The family play therapy with Shaul ("Robert Crosby"), Yakov ("Senator Crosby") and Dinah Gold ("Jane Crosby") was discussed and illustrated in Chapters 10 and 14. Shaul was fourteen at the termination of the therapy. Four years later he called me and asked me for an appointment. He was about to be drafted to the Israeli army. He was eager to join a prestigious military intelligence unit and wanted me to present a psychological evaluation.

The Shaul that I remembered was a strange-looking adolescent. He was limp and lanky. His face wore a permanent grin. The young man that entered my office looked different. He looked energetic and self-confident. His attitude was warm and friendly.

He recollected our family play therapy sessions. This—he said— was for him an extremely important experience that changed his life. It took him a long time to realize that our crime-and-the-law games were in fact metaphors of the family situation. Prior to this realization he had believed this was just exciting play. However, for sheer play these activities had an inexplicable emotional impact on him. In some of the sessions he was petrified with fear. In others he felt angry, depressed or cheerful, and he could not tell why. He felt that he was changing, that his father and mother were changing. He sensed that these changes were somehow related to the adventures of the Crosby family, but he could not tell how.

A few days later his mother Dinah called and asked for an interview. When she stepped in, I saw a woman who looked more serene but sadder than four years before. She used the opportunity of her son's earlier visit to thank me for what I had done for her and her family and to speak her mind. She said her husband Yakov wanted to come too but was too embarrassed to show up. She said he had been fully aware of the metaphorical meaning of our make-believe play sessions. These had a deep impact on him. He had changed. He had completely given up his habit of obsessive spending. He had become more cooperative and supportive both materially and spiritually. However, both Yakov and herself had become pensive and moody.

Shaul had grown very close to his father. He had begun to take after him in many respects. Dinah thought this was good for both of them, but she could not help feeling abandoned by her son.

Another interesting and moving reunion involved Avner, Ora and Boaz Green, the family whose play therapy is discussed and illustrated in Chapter 10 under the title "The Referee". Three years after termination Ora called. She said they had problems with their younger son Aviv, who had been two at the termination of the therapy. I invited the whole family for an interview. I was struck by the changes in their outward appearance. During the three years that had passed they had moved to an orthodox Jewish neighbourhood. This showed in their attire and body language. Ora, whom I remembered as a lively, outgoing, dominant woman, sat submissively in the corner of the room. She spoke in a soft voice. She said she had vivid recollections of our play sessions. The "boxing match" play had a particularly strong impact on her. She said she had been stunned and overwhelmed by the intensity of the aggression that had come out of her. Following each of the sessions in which this game had been played, at home, she felt self-pity and was sorry for her husband and her son.

During the interview Avner and Boaz were also markedly sober and earnest. Boaz asked me to have a look at the videotapes in which the play sessions were recorded. I took out the tapes and let them watch their own previous selves playing. They watched silently. Only from time to time they made remarks such as: "See how I changed", or "You looked younger then". But after the show Avner took his turn to speak about his own emotional experiences. He said that the play session had made him think that he had failed to live up to his own religious beliefs. He had made up his mind to become a better person, to set a good example to his children and give them solid religious values.

This meeting made me think that the family left therapy with a heavy sense of guilt. Play therapy was resumed with the purpose of helping them accept themselves and see their own strengths and good sides.

These encounters made me ponder again about play. How light and heavy play can be!

A Bird's-eye View of the Strategic Family Play Therapeutic Process

Assessment

Table A.1   Analysis of family play data.

Data gathering methods	Data analysis methods	Results of data analysis
Observing and recording the family's free play. Staging, observing and recording puppet shows created and directed by family members.	Microscopic semiotic analysis of recorded data: isolating activity units and interpreting each unit on the raw-material, semantic and pragmatic levels.	Semiotically interpreted text of family's play.
The results of the microscopic analysis serve as input to macroanalysis.	Macroscopic analysis of microscopically analyzed data.	Dysfunctional family programs: goals, plans and errors of information processing.
Dysfunctional family programs are input to further analysis.	Explaining presenting problems by dysfunctional programs.	Family information-processing explanations of presenting problems.

Planning

Table A.2   Components of strategies and tactics.

Entities to be changed	Change targets: priorities and sequence	Properties of play to be activated	Types of moves to be employed	Prognosis
Errors of information processing in dysfunctional programs.	Correcting errors of information processing. Focus should be on changes that will start a chain reaction of other desirable changes, but resistance should be detoured and dangerous results foreseen.	"Play"-framing, owning and alienation, basic duality, arbitrariness of signifier, symbolic coding, covert communication, emotional regulation, possible worlds.	Mimicking, pacing, focusing, explicating, the double, providing stimuli, illusion of alternatives, obedient actor, willynilly.	Assessing strengths, motivation, and resistance.

Therapy

Table A.3   The structure of a strategic family play therapeutic session.

Observing family's free play.

Identifying manifestations of errors of information processing in dysfunctional programs.

Deciding on a tactic-governed intervention.

Making moves for joining the family's play and preparing the ground for main moves.

Making main and auxiliary moves.

Evaluating results of moves and making corrective moves and additional moves as necessary.

Evaluation

Table A.4   Evaluating long-term between-session changes.

Observing the family's play in the session.

Identifying manifestations of planned, strategy and tactics-governed and unplanned, spontaneous, between-session changes in dysfunctional programs.

If spontaneous changes are not in desired directions, change strategy and tactics as necessary.

Termination

Table A.5   Uses of make-believe play in the termination stage.

Termination signals:
Distancing.
Hiding.
Closing up.
Avoidance.
Anger toward therapist.
Themes related to parting.

Play therapeutic interventions at the termination stage:
Encouraging termination.
Discouraging termination.
Allowing expression of resistance to terminate.
Allaying anger at therapist.
Encouraging make-believe play regression.
Summarizing the therapy in make-believe.
Make-believe continuation of the therapy.

Training in Strategic Family Play Therapy

Acquiring expertise in strategic family play therapy requires a good deal of supervised practice.

An international non-profit association named Liberi (Latin for "children") was founded recently. Its purpose is to promote strategic family play therapy, as a part of a more comprehensive integrative system called "multi-dimensional child and family therapy". Its functions include training, research and development, and provision of public and private therapeutic and consultation services.

Liberi's constitution specifies the conditions for being recognized by this association as Trainee in Strategic Family Play Therapy, Expert in Strategic Family Play Therapy and Authorized Instructor of Strategic Family Play Therapy.

Authorized Instructors of Strategic Family Play Therapy are authorized by Liberi to offer training courses, live supervision and workshops in strategic family play therapy both in Israel and abroad.

APPENDIX 3

Research in Strategic Family Play Therapy

A research project, evaluating the process and outcome of strategic family play therapy as a whole and specific assessment and intervention techniques included in it, has recently been initiated by the Child and Youth Service of the Israeli Ministry of Labour and Social Welfare. What is assessed in this project is the application of this form of therapy to multi-problem families referred to welfare agencies. Therapy is conducted by social workers who participate in a four-year training program in multi-dimensional child and family therapy.

Many ideas included in this book can be subjected to empirical research. Table A.6 proposes a classified list of some of these ideas.

Table A.6 Researchable hypotheses relevant to strategic family play therapy, with recommended research methods.

Area	Hypotheses	Recommended methods
Dysfunctional family programs and errors of information processing.	Programs and errors predict play and non-play behavior.	Longitudinal naturalistic observations. Clinical experiments.
	Programs explain symptoms.	Correlational analysis of types of programs and types of symptoms.
Emotives and play as emotional regulation mechanisms.	Cognitive processes are regulated by level of arousal of emotives.	Experimental research.
	Play signifiers and signified are restricted by emotives and level of arousal.	Combined experimental and observational research.

continued

Table A.6   (*continued*).

Area	Hypotheses	Recommended methods
Social aspects of make-believe play.	Play signifiers and signified are restricted by the players' mutual social interests.	Correlational and observational research.
Therapeutically relevant properties of play and play-therapeutic moves.	Cognitive-emotional experience induced by selective and skillful activation of these properties brings about immediate and long-term changes in dysfunctional family information processing.	Clinical experiments coupled with longitudinal observations.
	Interventions conducted exclusively within the sphere of make-believe play are automatically transferred and generalized to the family's out-of-play reality.	Observations, questionnaires and correlational analysis.
Scope of the method.	Strategic family play therapy is effective across a great variety of problems and types of population.	Comparative process and outcome research.

References

Abercrombie, D. (1964) *Elements of general phonetics.* Edinburgh: Edinburgh University Press.

Andolfi, M. (1979) *Family therapy: An interactional approach.* New York: Plenum.

Amen, E.W. and Renison, N. (1954) A study of the relationship between play patterns and anxiety in young children. *Genetic Psychology Monographs,* 50, 3–41.

Ariel, S. (1975) *Interpersonal communication in children's play.* Tivon, Israel: Study Center for Children's Activities.

Ariel, S. (1983) Experimental studies of the interpretation of children's play. Unpublished manuscript. Jerusalem: The Hebrew University.

Ariel, S. (1984) Locutions and illocutions in make-believe play. *Journal of Pragmatics,* 8, 221–240.

Ariel, S. (1985) Touchnotation; a notational system for transcribing tactile behavior. Unpublished manuscript. Jerusalem: The Hebrew University.

Ariel, S. (1987) An information-processing theory of family dysfunction. *Psychotherapy,* 24 (3S), 477–495.

Ariel, S. (1992) Semiotic analysis of children's play: A method for investigating social development. *Merrill-Palmer Quarterly,* January.

Ariel, S., Carel, C.A. and Tyano, S. (1984) Uses of children's make-believe play in family therapy: Theory and clinical examples. *Journal of Marital and Family Therapy,* 11 (1), 47–60.

Atkinson, J.W. (ed.) (1958) *Motives in fantasy, action and society.* Princeton, NJ: Van Nostrand-Reinhold.

Austin, J.L. (1962) *How to do things with words.* Cambridge, Mass: Harvard University Press.

Avocena, S.L. (1984) [The children: What is said in games is obscured by words in family therapy] (Spanish). *Psicopatologia,* 4 (3), 269–271.

Axline, V.M. (1969) *Play therapy.* New York: Ballantine.

Bandler, R. and Grinder, J. (1975) *The structure of magic.* Palo Alto, Cal.: Science and Behavior.

Bandura, A. (1965a) *Behavioral modification through modeling procedures.* In Krasner, L. and Ullman, L.P. (eds) *Research in behavior modification.* New York: Holt, pp. 310–340.

Bandura, A. (1965b) Vicarious processes: A case of no-trial learning. In Berkowitz, L. (ed.) *Advances in experimental social psychology,* Vol. 2. New York: Academic Press, pp. 1–55.

Bandura, A. (1971) *Psychological modeling.* New York: Aldine-Atherton.

Bateson, G. (1972) *Steps to an ecology of mind.* New York: Ballantine.

Bateson, G. (1979) *Mind and nature: a necessary unity.* New York: Dutton.

Bateson, G., Jackson, D., Haley, J. and Weakland, J. (1956). Toward a theory of schizophrenia. *Behavioral Science,* 1, 251–264.

Bativa, N.Y. and Khomskaya, Y.D. (1984) [Neuropsychological analysis of the influence of emotionality on reproducing of verbal material] (Russian). *Voprosy Psikhologii,* 3, 132–139.

Beach, S.R. and O'Leary, D. (1985) Current status of outcome research in marital therapy. In L'Abate, L. (ed.) *Handbook of family psychology and therapy,* Vol. 2. Homewood, Ill.: Dorsey Press.

Beaugrande, R.A. (1980). The pragmatics of discourse planning. *Journal of Pragmatics,* 4, 15–42.

Beck, A. (1970) Role of fantasies in psychotherapy and psychopathology. *Mental Disease,* 150, 3–17.

Bettlheim, B. (1955) *Symbolic wounds: Puberty rites and the envious male.* London: Thames and Hudson.

Bishop, J. (1986) Change lives in the poetry of its meaning. *Canadian Journal of Counselling,* 20 (1), 21–32.

Blaney, P.H. (1986) Affect and memory: a review. *Psychological Bulletin,* 99, 229–246.

Blohm, P.J. and Yawkley, T.D. (1976) Language experience approach and child's play. Unpublished manuscript. Wisconsin: University of Wisconsin.

Boadman, S. and Hagen, J.W. (eds) (1985) *History and research in child development.* Monographs of the Society for Research in Child Development, Serial no. 210.

Bock, M. (1986) The influence of emotional meaning on the recall of words processed for form or self-reference. *Psychological Research,* 48 (2), 107–112.

Bodin, A. (1981) The interactional view: Family therapy approaches of the Mental Research Institute. In Gurman, A.S. and Kniskern, D.P. (eds), *Handbook of family therapy.* New York: Brunner/Mazel, pp. 267–309.

Bower, G.H. (1984) [Emotions in cognition] (Spanish). *Revista Mexicana de Sociologia,* 1 (2), 110–118.

Brenner, C. (1982). *The mind in conflict.* New York: International University Press.

Bruce, B.C. and Newman, D. (1978) Interacting plans. *Cognitive Science,* 2, 195–233.

Brunner, J.S., Jolly, A. and Sylva, K. (1976). *Play: Its role in development and evolution,* Harmondsworth, Middlesex: Penguin Books.

Buhler, K. (1930) *The mental development of the child.* New York: Harcourt.

Burns, C.M. and Brainerd, C.J. (1979) Effects of constructive and dramatic play in perspective taking in very young children. *Developmental Psychology,* 15 (5), 512–523.

Carnap, R. (1950) *Logical foundations of probability.* London: Routledge and Kegan Paul.

Case, R., Hayward, S., Lewis, M. and Hurst, P. (1988) Toward a neo-Piagetian theory of cognitive and emotional development. *Developmental Review,* 8, 1–51.

Courtney, R. and Schattner, G. (eds) (1981) *Drama in Therapy.* New York: Drama Book Specialists.

Crabb, G. (1916) *English synonyms.* London: Routledge & Sons.

Elliott, R. (1984) A discovery oriented approach to significant change in psychotherapy. In Rice, L. and Greenberg, S. (eds), *Patterns of change.* New York: Guilford.

Cromwell, D.E., Olson, D.H. and Fournier, D.G. (1976) Tools and techniques for diagnosis and evaluation in marital and family therapy. *Family Process,* 15, 1–49.

Cronen, V.E., Johnson, K.M. and Lannamann, J.W. (1982) Paradox, double binds and reflexive loops: An alternative theoretical perspective. *Family Process,* 21, 91–112.

Cross, D.G. (1982) Overview of outcome research in family therapy: Methodological considerations. *Australian Journal of Family Therapy*, **3**, 149–54.

Curry, N. and Arnaud, S. (1974) Cognitive implications in children's spontaneous role play. *Theory into Practice*, **13** (6), 173–277.

Doane, J.A., Goldstein, M.J., Milkowitz, D.J. and Falloon, I.R.H. (1986) The impact of individual and family treatment on the affective climate of families of schizophrenics. *British Journal of Psychiatry*, **148**, 179–187.

Ekman, P. and Friesen, W.V. (1978) *The facial action coding system*. Palo Alto, Cal.: Consulting Psychologists Press.

Ellis, H.C., Thomas, R.L. and Rodruigez, I.A. (1984) Emotional mood states and memory. *Journal of Experimental Psychology, Learning, Memory and Cognition*, **10**, 470–482.

Emunah, R. and Johnson, D.R. (1983) The impact of theoretical performance on the self-image of psychiatric patients. *The Arts in Psychotherapy*, **10**, 233–239.

Erikson, E.H. (1940) Studies in the interpretation of play. *Genetic Psychology Monographs*, **22**, 557–671.

Erikson, E.H. (1965) *Childhood and society*. New York: Norton.

Eshkol, N. (1971) *The hand book*. Tel Aviv: Movement Notation Society.

Eshkol, N. (1980) *50 lessons by Dr M. Feldenkrais*. Tel Aviv: Movement Notation Society.

Eshkol, N. and Wachman, A. (1958) *Movement notation*. London: Weidenfeld and Nicolson.

Exner, J. (1986) *The Rorschach: a comprehensive system*. New York: Wiley.

Fein, G. (1989) Mind, meaning and affect: Proposals for a theory of pretence. *Developmental Review*, **9**, 345–363.

Fine, R. (1973) *The development of Freud's thought*. New York: Jason Aronson.

Fisch, R., Weakland, J.H. and Segal, L. (1984) *The tactics of change*. San Francisco, Cal.: Jossey-Bass.

Foa, E.B. and Kozak, M.J. (1985) Emotional processing of fear: Exposure to corrective information. *Psychological Bulletin*, **99**, 20–35.

Foulkes, D. (1978) *A grammar of dreams*. New York: Basic Books.

Framo, J.L. (1970) Symptoms from a family transactional viewpoint. In Ackerman, V.W. (ed.) *Family theory in transition*. Boston, Mass.: Little Brown.

Freud, A. (1937) *The ego and the mechanisms of defense*. London: Hogarth.

Freud, S. (1922) *Beyond the pleasure principle*. London: International Universities Press.

Freud, S. (1917) *Introductory lectures on psychoanalysis*. Standard Edition of the Complete Psychological Works of Sigmund Freud. London: Hogarth Press.

Freyberg, J.T. (1973) Increasing the imaginative play of urban disadvantaged kindergarten children through systematic training. In Singer, J.L. (ed.), *The child's world of make-believe*, pp. 129–154. New York: Academic Press.

Frijda, N.H., Kupiers, P. and Schure, E. (1989) Relations among emotion, appraisal and emotional action readiness. *Journal of Personality and Social Psychology*, **57**, 212–228.

Garvey, C. (1976) Some properties of social play. In Bruner, J.S., Jolly, A. and Sylva, K. (eds) (1976) *Play: Its Role in Development and Evolution*, pp. 570–583. Harmondsworth, Middlesex: Penguin Books.

Garvey, C. and Kramer, T.L. (1989) The language of social pretend play. *Developmental Review*, **9**, 364–382.

Gazdar, G. (1979) *Pragmatics, implicature, presupposition and logical form*. New York: Academic Press.

Gilmore, J.B. (1966) *Play: A special behavior*. In Haber, N.R. (ed.), *Current research in motivation*. New York: Holt, pp. 343–355.

Goffman, E. (1969) *Strategic interaction*. Philadelphia, Penn.: Pennsylvania University Press.

Goldfarb, W. (1945). Psychological privation in infancy and subsequent adjustment. *American Journal of Orthopsychiatry*, 15, 247–255.

Goldfried, M.R. (1980) Toward the delineation of therapeutic change principles. *American Psychologist*, 35, 991–999.

Goldman, A. (1986) The differential effects of emotionally focused marital therapy. Unpublished doctoral dissertation. Vancouver, BC: University of British Columbia.

Gomez, R. and Yawkley, T.D. (1983) An investigation of the effects of imaginative play and self concept on pretend play and self concept enactment. Montreal: Paper read at the Annual Conference of the American Educational Research Association.

Grayson, J.B., Foa, E.B. and Steketee, G.S. (1982) Habituation during exposure treatment: distraction versus attention-focusing. *Behaviour Research and Therapy*, 20, 323–328.

Green, R.G., Fortune, A.E. and Vosler, R. (1988) Evaluating family therapy: Divergent methods, divergent findings. *Journal of Marital and Family Therapy*, 14 (3), 277–286.

Greenberg, L.S. and Johnson, S.M. (1986) Affect in marital therapy. *Journal of Marital and Family Therapy*, 12 (1), 1–10.

Greenberg, L.S. and Pinsof, W.M. (eds) (1986) *The psychotherapeutic process: A research handbook*. New York: Guilford.

Greenberg, L. and Safran, J. (1987) *Affect, cognition and the process of change*. New York: Guilford Press.

Gurman, A.S. and Kniskern, D.P. (1981) Family therapy outcome research: Knows and unknows. In Gurman, A.S. and Knisern, D.P. (eds), *Handbook of family therapy*. New York: Brunner/Mazel.

Hahnloser, R. (1974) A comparison of cognitive restructuring and progressive relaxation in test anxiety reduction. Unpublished doctoral dissertation. University of Oregon.

Haley, J. (1963) *Strategies in psychotherapy*. New York: Grune and Stratton.

Haley, J. (1976) *Problem solving therapy*. San Francisco, Cal.: Jossey-Bass.

Haley, J. (1973) *Uncommon therapy: The psychiatric techniques of Milton H. Erickson*. New York: Norton.

Hall, E. (1983) Patterns of meaning in guided fantasy. *Journal of Mental Imagery*, 7 (1), 35–50.

Hathaway, S.R. and McKinley, J.C. (1943) *MMPI manual*. New York: Psychological Corporation.

Hazelrigg, M.D., Cooper, H.M. and Borduin, C.M. (1987) Evaluating the effectiveness of family therapies: An integrative review and analysis. *Psychological Bulletin*, 101, 428–442.

Hickson, M.L. and Stacks, D.W. (1985) *Non-verbal communication: Studies and applications*. Dubuque, Iowa: Brown.

Hilgard, E.R. (1986) *Divided consciousness*. Expanded edition. New York: Wiley.

Hill, K.A. (1987) Meta-analysis of paradoxical interventions. *Psychotherapy*, 24 (2), 266–270.

Hintikka, K.J. (1975) *The intentions of intentionality and other models for modalities*. Dordrecht: D. Reidel.

Honeck, R.P. and Hoffman, R.R. (eds) (1986) *Cognition and figurative language*. Hillsdale, NJ: Lawrence Erlbaum Associates.

International Phonetics Alphabet (IPA) (1964). London: The International Phonetic Association.

Ionesco, E. (1980) *Four plays*. New York: Grove Press.

Izard, C.E. (1978) *Human emotions*. New York: Plenum.

Izard, C.E. and Tomkins, S.S. (1966) Affect and behavior: Anxiety as a negative affect. In Spielberger, C. (ed.) *Anxiety and behavior*. New York: Academic Press.

Jackson, D.D. (1965) Family rules: The marital quid pro quo. *Archives of General Psychiatry*, **12**, 589–594.

Johnson, D.R. (1984) The creative arts therapies as an independent profession. *The Arts in Psychotherapy*, **11**, 209–212.

Johnson, S.M. and Greenberg, L. (1985) Emotionally focused couples therapy. An outcome study. *Journal of Marital and Family Therapy*, **11**, 313–317.

Jones, M. (1982) *The process of change*. Boston, Mass.: Routledge and Kegan Paul.

Kaufmann, G. (1985) A theory of symbolic representation in problem solving. *Journal of Mental Imagery*, **9** (2), 51–70.

Keenan, E.C. (1971) Two kinds of presupposition in a natural language. In Fillmore, C.J. and Langendoen, D.T. (eds), *Studies in linguistic semantics*. New York: Holt, Rinehart and Winston, pp. 45–52.

Keith, D.V. and Whitaker, C.A. (1981) Play therapy: A paradigm for work with families. *Journal of Marital and Family Therapy*, **3**, 243–251.

Klein, M. (1960) *The psychoanalysis of children*. New York: Grove Press.

Klinger, E. (1971) *Structure and functions of fantasy*. New York: Wiley.

Klinger, E. (1978) Modes of normal conscious flow. In Pope, K.S. and Singer, J.L. (eds), *The stream of consciousness*, pp. 225–258. New York: Plenum.

Klinger, E., Barta, S.G. and Maxeiner, M.E. (1980) Motivational correlates of thought content frequency and commitment. *Journal of Personality and Social Psychology*, **39**, 1222–1237.

Kobak, R. and Waters, D.B. (1984) Family therapy as a rite of passage: play's the thing. *Family Process*, **23**, 89–100.

Landgarten, H.B. (1981) *Clinical art therapy*. New York: Brunner/Mazel.

Lang, P.J. (1979) A bio-informational theory of emotional imagery. *Psychopathology*, **16**, 495–512.

Lazarus, R.S. (1982) Thoughts on the relations between emotion and cognition. *American Psychologist*, **37**, 1019–1024.

Leiberman, J.N. (1965) Playfulness and divergent thinking: an investigation of their relationship at the kindergarten level. *Journal of Genetic Psychology*, **107** (88), 219–224.

Leiberman, J.N. (1977) *Playfulness: Its relation to imagination and creativity*. New York: Academic Press.

Lebow, J. (1981) Issues in the assessment of outcome in family therapy. *Family Process*, **20**, 167–188.

Leuner, H. (1984) *Guided affective imagery: mental imagery in short term psychotherapy*. New York: Thieme Stratton.

Luborsky, L., Chandler, M., Auerbach, A.H., Cohen, J. and Bachrach, H. (1971) Factors influencing the outcome of psychotherapy: A review of quantitative research. *Psychological Bulletin*, **75**, 145–185.

Madanes, C. (1982) *Strategic family therapy*. San Francisco, Cal.: Jossey-Bass.

Mann, L. and Janis, I. (1986) A follow up study on the long term effects of emotional role playing. *Journal of Personality and Social Psychology*, **8** (4), 339–342.

Marshall, W.L. (1988) Behavioral indices of habituation and sensitization during exposure of phobic stimuli. *Behavior Research in Therapy*, **26** (1), 67–77.

Marshall, W.L., Gauthier, V. and Gordon, A. (1979) Current status of flooding therapy. In Hersen, M., Eisler, R.M. and Miller, E.M. (eds), *Progress in behavior modification*. New York: Academic Press, pp. 205–270.

Mastumodo, D. (1986) Preschoolers' moral actions and emotions in Prisoner's Dilemma. *Developmental Psychology*, **22** (5), 663–670.

McKenn, F.P. (1986) Effects of unattended emotional stimuli on color-naming performance. *Current Psychological Research and Reviews*, **5** (1), 3–9.

McNiff, S.A. (1987) Research and scholarship in the creative art therapies. *The Arts in Psychotherpy*, **14**, 285–292.

Michel, D. (1976) *Music therapy*. Springfield, Ill.: Charles C. Thomas.

Mills, J.C. and Crowley, R.J. (1986) *Therapeutic metaphors for children and the child within*. New York: Brunner/Mazel.

Minuchin, S. (1974) *Families and family therapy*. Cambridge, Mass.: Harvard University Press.

Minuchin, S., Baker, S. and Rosman, B. (1978) *Psychosomatic families*. Cambridge, Mass.: Harvard University Press.

Morrison, J.K. and Cometa, M.S. (1980) A cognitive reconstructive approach to the psychotherapeutic use of imagery. *Journal of Mental Imagery*, **4**, 35–42.

Murray, H.A. (1943) *Thematic Apperception Test*. Cambridge, Mass.: Harvard University Press.

O'Connor, J.J. (1984) The resurrection of a magical reality: treatment of functional migraine in a child. *Family Process*, **23**, 501–509.

O'Connor, J.J. and Hoorwitz, A.N. (1984) The bogeyman cometh: a strategic approach to difficult adolescents. *Family Process*, **23**, 237–249.

Olson, D.H., Russell, C.S. and Sprenkle, D.H. (1983) Circumplex model of marital and family systems: VI—Theoretical update. *Family Process*, **22**, 69–83.

Papp, P. (1982) Staging reciprocal metaphors in a couples group. *Family Process*, **21**, 453–467.

Paterson, T. (1980) The family rule concept in the theory of family therapy. *Australian Journal of Family Therapy*, **1** (3) 129–137.

Peller, L. (1959) Libidinal phases, ego development and play. In *Psychodynamic study of the child*, Vol. 9. New York: International Universities Press.

Perrig, W.J. and Perrig-Ciello, P. (1985) [Mood congruity effect in learning: Effect of mood state or simplicity of task character?] (German) *Psychologie-Schweiterische Zeitschrift für Psychologie und ihre Anwendungen*, **44**, 17–30.

Piaget, J. (1962) *Play, dreams and imitation in childhood*. New York: Norton.

Pillener, D.R., Rhinehart, E.D. and White, S. (1986) Memories of life transitions. The first year in college. *Human Learning: Journal of Practical Research and Applications*, **5** (2), 109–123.

Pinsof, W.M. (1981) Family therapy process research. In Gurman, A.S. and Kniskern (eds), *Handbook of family therapy*. New York: Brunner/Mazel.

Postner, R.S., Guttman, H.S., Sigal, J.J., Epstein, N.B. and Rakoff, V.M. (1971) Process and outcome in conjoint family therapy. *Family Process*, **10**, 451–472.

Rabkin, R. (1977) *Strategic psychotherapy*. New York: Basic Books.

Rachman, S. (1980) Emotional processing. *Behaviour Research and Therapy*, **18**, 51–60.

Ralph, (1985) Play in young children: Problems of definition, categorization and measurement. *Early Child Development and Care. Special Issue: Children's Play*, **19** (1–2), 25–41.

Rice, L.N. and Greenberg, L.S. (1984). *Patterns of change*. New York: Guilford.

Richie, A. and Watanabe, M. (Transl.) (1963) *Six Kabuki Plays*. Tokyo: Hokuseido Press.

Robbins, A. (1980) *Expressive therapy: A creative arts approach to depth oriented treatment*. New York: Human Sciences Press.

Rubin, J.A. (1985) Imagery in art therapy: The source, the setting and the significance. *Journal of Mental Imagery*, 9 (4), 71–82.

Sacerdoti, G.D. (1977) *A structure for plans and behavior*. New York: Elsevier.

Saltz, E., Dixon, D. and Johnson, D. (1977) Training disadvantaged preschoolers on various fantasy activities: effects on cognitive functioning and impulse control. *Child Development*, **48** (26), 367–380.

Satir, V. (1971) Symptomatology: a family production. In Hoveller, J.H. (ed.) *Theory and practice in family psychiatry*. New York: Brunner/Mazel.

Saussure, F. de (1972) *Cours de linguistique generale*. [1916] Edition Critique. Paris: Payot.

Schaefer, C.E. (1985) Play therapy. Early Child Development and Care. Special Issue: *Children's Play*, 19 (1–2), 95–108.

Searle, J.R. (1969) *Speech acts*. Cambridge: Cambridge University Press.

Sears, D.S. (1951) Doll-play aggression in normal young children. *Psychological Monographs*, **65**, 6.

Seltzer, M.R. and Wencke, J. (1983) Material, myth and magic: a cultural approach to family therapy. *Family Process*, **22**, 3–14.

Selvini-Palazzoli, M., Boscolo, L., Cecchin, G. and Prata, G. (1973) *Paradox and counterparadox*. New York: Jason Aronson.

Shahar, A. and Marks, I.M. (1980) Habituation during exposure treatment of compulsive rituals. *Behavior Therapy*, **11**, 397–401.

Shazer de, S. (1982) *Patterns of brief family therapy*. New York: Guilford.

Singer, J.L. (1970) Drives, affects and daydreams: the adaptive role of spontaneous imagery on stimulus independent mentation. In Antrobus, J.S. (ed.), *Cognition and Affect*. Boston, Mass.: Little Brown.

Singer, J.L. (1973) *The child's world of make-believe*. New York: Academic Press.

Singer, J.L. (1974) Daydreams and the stream of thought. *American Scientist*, 2, 417–425.

Singer, J.L. and Pope, K.S. (1978) *The power of human imagination*. New York: Plenum Press.

Singh, S. and Singh, K.S. (1976). *Phonetics*. Baltimore, Md.: University Park Press.

Smilansky, S. (1968) *The effects of sociodramatic play on disadvantaged pre-school children*. New York: Wiley.

Smith, M.L. and Glass, G.V. (1977) Meta analysis of psychotherapy outcome studies. *American Psychologist*, **32**, 752–760.

Somers, J.V. and Yawkley, T.D. (1984) Imaginary play companions: Contributions to creative and intellectual abilities in young children. *Journal of Creative Behavior*, 18, 77–89.

Soper, P. and L'Abate, L. (1977) Paradox as a therapeutic technique. *International Journal of Family Counseling*, 5, 10–21.

Staats, A.W. and Lohr, J.M. (1979) Images, language, emotions and personality: Social behaviorism theory. *Journal of Mental Imagery*, 3, 85–106.

Stanton, M. (1981) An integral structural/strategic approach to family therapy. *Journal of Marital and Family Therapy*, 7 (4), 427–439.

Suler, J.R. (1985) Imagery ability and the experience of affect by free associative imagery. *Journal of Mental Imagery*, 9 (1), 101–110.

Sutton-Smith, B. (1984) *The masks of play*. New York: Leisure Press.

Tessa, D. (ed.) (1984) *Art as therapy*. London: Methuen.

Todd, T.C. and Stanton, M. (1983) Research in marital and family therapy. In Wolman, B.B. and Stricker, G. (eds), *Handbook of marital and family therapy*. New York: Plenum Press.

Tomkins, S.S. and Izard, C. (eds) (1985) *Affect, cognition and personality*. New York: Springer.

Tucker, D.M. and Newman, J.P. (1981) Verbal vs. imaginal cognitive strategies in the prohibition of emotional arousal. *Cognitive Therapy and Research*, 5, 191–202.

Twain, M. (1973) *The adventures of Tom Sawyer*. New York: Dell Publishing.

Verschueren, J. (1978) Reflections of presupposition failure. *Journal of Pragmatics*, 2, 107–151

Watson, J.P., Gaird, R. and Marks, I.M. (1972) Physiological habituation to continuous phobic stimulation. *Behavior Research and Therapy*, 10, 269–278.

Watzlawick, P. (1978) A review of the double-bind theory. In Jackson, D.D. (ed.), *Communication, family and marriage*. Palto Alto: Science and Behavior Books.

Watzlawick, P., Weakland, J. and Fisch, R. (1974) *Change: Principles of problem formation and problem resolution*. New York: W.W. Norton.

Weeks, G. and L'Abate, L. (1979) A compilation of paradoxical methods. *American Journal of Family Therapy*, 7, 61–76.

Wells, R.A. and Dezen, A.E. (1978) Results of family therapy revisited. *Family Process*, 17, 251–274.

White, L. and Tursky, B. (eds) (1986) *Clinical biofeedback: efficacy and mechanisms*. New York: Guilford.

Witztum, E., Dasberg, H. and Bleich, A. (1986) Use of a metaphor in the treatment of combat-induced posttraumatic stress disorders. *American Journal of Psychotherapy*, 40 (3), 457–465.

Wolpe, J. (1958) *Psychotherapy by reciprocal inhibition*. Stanford, Cal.: Stanford University Press.

Yawkley, T.D. (1986) Creative dialogue through sociodramatic play and its uses. *Journal of Creative Behavior*, 20 (1), 52–60.

Zachary, R.A. (1982) Imagery and ongoing thought. *Journal of Mental Imagery*, 6, 93–108.

Zajonc, R.B. (1980) Feeling and thinking: Preferences or inferences? *American Psychologist*, 35, 151–175.

Zegarnik, B.V. (1982) [Methods of changing personality changes] (Spanish text). *Boletin de Psicologia (Cuba)*, 5 (3), 5–27.

Index

Index compiled by Caroline Sheard